EPOCHS IN THE LIFE OF PAUL

EPOCHS IN THE LIFE
OF PAUL

A STUDY OF DEVELOPMENT
IN PAUL'S CAREER

A. T. ROBERTSON, A.M., D.D.

BROADMAN PRESS
NASHVILLE, TENNESSEE

Paperback edition issued by
Baker Book House
with the permission of the
copyright owner,
Charles Scribner's Sons

Third printing, December 1976

Complete Set
4214-51
ISBN: 0-8054-1351-0
This volume
4213-48
ISBN: 0-8054-1348-0

TO THE MEMORY OF

JOHN D. ROBERTSON

BROTHER BELOVED AND

SERVANT OF CHRIST

PREFACE

THE generous reception accorded "Epochs in the Life
of Jesus" on both sides of the water has emboldened
me, in response to many requests, to publish a companion volume on Paul. Here also detailed critical
discussions will be subordinated to the positive interpretation of the story. The books are legion where
one can find in English and German all sides of nearly
every point of criticism in the lives of both Jesus and
Paul. Critical discussion is invaluable, but that is not
the service attempted here. After all, criticism is only
a means to an end. The aim of the present work is
rather to give as the result of criticism a constructive
picture of Paul and his work as set forth in the Acts
and Paul's own Epistles.

I have faced the manifold problems of criticism
which meet one at every turn in such a study, and
have formed my own judgment where the evidence
justified such a conclusion. I am still a learner about
Paul and still in the dark on many points. But enough
is known (reasonably clear, I think, to one who is open
to historical evidence) to enable one to project a vivid
and true outline of the life of Paul. The main outline
is all that is here attempted. Questions of geography
and general history are touched upon only incidentally.

Paul wrought so widely and wrote so much that it is well-nigh impossible to compass it all from every point of view in one volume of moderate size. The great events in Paul's career are just the ones which it is most important to seize upon and which are often missed. If one does this well, he will have less trouble in filling in the details. Sometimes one cannot see the wood for the trees.

The task is complicated further by the fact that Paul has so many sides. He cannot be understood unless all sides of his life are brought up adequately and together. His own environment, his intellectual and spiritual development, his relation to Jesus, his outward activities, his literary remains, must all be kept in mind. The Epistles furnish rich personal material and illustrate the growth of Paul's theology. The formal exposition of the Epistles and of his theology is not attempted. The interest is centred in Paul himself. But the orderly and progressive study of his life in its main points helps one to solve the riddle of Paul, as some scholars make him.

Paul is so masterful as to be beyond praise. Some, indeed, go to the point of making him the real author of modern Christianity and the perverter of the original Christianity of Jesus. How far short that view falls of the truth the present volume will endeavor to show.

Nearly twenty years ago I first read Dr. James Stalker's "Life of St. Paul." This powerful little book has left a deep mark upon my conception of Paul.

In common with the whole world I am debtor to Sir W. M. Ramsay, Litt. D., of Aberdeen, for fresh light on Paul. It is a pleasure to acknowledge this obligation here. I cannot make detailed acknowledgment of my debt to the many books on Paul. The bibliography will show the way for those who wish to go further in this great subject. In the nature of the case the specific references to the literature must be few. Conybeare and Howson's "Life and Epistles of St. Paul" is still the classic on the subject.

For twenty-one years now I have been a teacher of Paul's life and Epistles. Each year this chief Apostle fascinates me more and more. He richly deserves the power that he still holds over modern men in spite of antique modes of thought. His mighty heart grappled with the new fresh problems of Christianity as it first fought its way into the hearts and lives of men in the Roman world. Because his trained and gifted intellect met the issues of his day as a missionary statesman, a philosophical theologian, an intensely practical preacher, he is an unfailing source of light and leading for men of force to-day.

I shall not undertake to justify my use of the Acts and all of Paul's thirteen Epistles as reliable sources of information. I am fully aware of the fact that some critics credit none of these books with real historical value. Critics vary all the way from the absurd position of Van Manen to the acceptance of them all. I have satisfied myself that even the Pastoral Epistles are justly credited to the Pauline authorship. If one waited till all critics agreed about all points of dispute in Paul's career before he wrote his own convictions, the pen would drop never to be taken up again. But it is only just to say that the tendency on the whole is steadily to increased confidence in Luke as an historian and to acceptance of all of Paul's Epistles as genuine. I do not claim that this volume represents all modern scholarship. It is my own interpretation of Paul after prolonged study of what others have had to say. I have come back to Luke and Paul to hear what they have to tell about the young Jew who turned about face and turned the world to Christ.

I wish to acknowledge the kindness of Rev. P. V. Bomar, of Marion, Ala., for help in the making of the indexes.

A. T. ROBERTSON.

LOUISVILLE, KY.

TABLE OF CONTENTS

EPOCHS IN THE LIFE OF PAUL

CHAPTER I

SAUL THE PHARISAIC STUDENT

"And I advanced in the Jews' religion beyond many of mine own age among my countrymen." (Gal. 1 : 14).

1. *A Word of Appreciation.*—Saul of Tarsus was a man of such vehemence and power that he was head in whatever circle he moved, whether as Saul the persecuting Pharisee, or Paul the laboring missionary. If he was chief of sinners, he became chief of saints. If he was the man of action whirling over the Roman Empire, he was doing it with constructive statesmanship with no less a purpose than to bring the Roman Empire to the feet of Christ. He was the very type of missionary statesman[1] demanded to-day in China, Japan, India, Africa, Turkey. It is a curious turn of the wheel of history that the very scenes of Paul's struggles and triumphs for Christ are now the hardest spots on earth to reach with the message of the Cross. We need a new Paul for the new situation.

Paul was no less a man of thought than a man of

[1] Cf. Lock, "St. Paul the Master Builder," pp. 38–67; Sir W. M. Ramsay, "Pauline and Other Studies," pp. 49–100.

action. He loved his books and missed them when without them (II Tim. 4 : 13). He was the busiest of men, but he kept up his habits of study to the shame of every city pastor (for Paul was a preacher in the great cities of the world) who lets his books go unused even at the call of pastoral work. He solved the problem for himself as every minister must do. I agree with Sir W. M. Ramsay[1] that Paul was a real philosopher, perhaps not in the technical sense of the term, though he knew how to hold his own with the Epicurean and the Stoic philosophers (Acts 17 : 18 ff.). But he possessed a higher and nobler world view than those opportunists in philosophy. Paul knew how to think and had such passion of soul and keenness of intellect that he still challenges the respect of the greatest minds of the modern world. He knew the technical terms of the Jewish rabbi and the Greek philosopher (Gnostic and Agnostic), but he was able to drop mere abstract verbiage and deal with the heart of things in words that burn into the very conscience of men. Certainly Paul had a real philosophy of history[2] and a definite programme for the redemption of the empire as well as the salvation of individuals.

But it is as the exponent of Christ that Paul commands chief attention. This matter will call for fuller treatment further on, but a word is needed here. He claimed a place on a level with the very chiefest Apostles (II Cor. 12 : 11), when that place was denied him

[1] "Cities of St. Paul," p. 4   [2] *Ibid.*, p. 10 f.

by the Judaizers. Indeed, he is the real primate among the Apostles (not Peter), though not one of the Twelve. He rebuked Peter, not Peter Paul. So powerful is Paul's conception of Christ that it has dominated Christian theology. It is a pertinent inquiry whether Paul accurately grasped the truth about Jesus when he probably did not know him face to face in the flesh, for in II Cor. 5 : 16 he does not imply ("even though we have known Christ after the flesh, yet now know we him no more") that he had ever seen Jesus before his death. He had even looked upon Christ from the Jewish or fleshly standpoint. The inquiry about Paul is greatly important, for, if Paul went astray, he has led the world after him. Augustine and Calvin, Pelagius and Arminius, Origen and Clement, all drink from the fountain of Paul's theology. We are indeed recovering the Johannine view of Christ, the Petrine and the Jacobean, but after all they do not radically differ from Paul's conception, though each gives an interesting personal touch. In simple truth, it is idle to hope to get back to Christ except through the medium of the first interpreters of Jesus who told their wonderful story. Paul's story is not the first in order of time, but it is first in order of apologetic interest, and apologetics is still worth the while of every intelligent Christian. We strike *terra firma* in Paul, begging Van Manen's pardon. Taking one's stand by Paul, one can work his way more securely through the mazes of Johannine and Synoptic criticism to the truth as it is in Jesus. He will at last come to see that Paul and the Gospels give us the same Christ with just the differences in detail that one had a right to expect.

Passing by Jesus himself, Paul stands forever the foremost representative of Christ, the ablest exponent of Christianity, its most constructive genius, its dominant spirit from the merely human side, its most fearless champion, its most illustrious and influential missionary, preacher, teacher, and its most distinguished martyr. He heard things in the third heaven not lawful to utter (II Cor. 12 : 4), but he felt himself a poor earthen vessel after all (II Cor. 4 : 7). He sought to commend himself in the sight of God to every man's conscience, for he had seen the light of the gospel of the glory of Christ and was the servant of all for Jesus' sake (II Cor. 4 : 3 ff.).

We have a clear picture of Paul in the Acts. It is a legend that Luke was a painter and left a portrait of Paul. He was obviously a master in word painting, though we have no painting in oil. We may pass by as worthless the legend that Paul was a hunchback, though his personal appearance probably was not remarkably prepossessing, since his enemies ridiculed him on that score (II Cor. 10 : 10). There is an advantage in a commanding personality provided undue expectations are not excited which cannot be fulfilled. Paul in action was impressive enough as when he, "filled with the Holy Spirit, fastened his eyes on" Elymas the sorcerer (Acts 13:9) and exclaimed "Thou son of the devil, thou enemy of all righteousness, wilt thou not cease to pervert the right ways of the Lord?" But his Judaizing adversaries belittled his speech as of no account (II Cor. 10 : 10) because, forsooth, he reasoned in possibly a conversational manner. Some, indeed, much preferred the more ornate oratory of Apollos, who "powerfully confuted the Jews"at Corinth (Acts 18 : 28). But he did have an infirmity "a stake in the flesh, a messenger of Satan" (II Cor. 12 : 7), which kept him humble and reminded him again of the earthen vessel which carried the gospel treasure. If weak eyes was this infirmity, he had loving friends who would have plucked out their own if it would have done him any good (Gal. 4 : 15). But one cannot doubt that all human frailties were forgotten when Paul poured out his very soul in passionate speech and stirred men to heroic endeavor. He could change his tone and strike the deeper note of pathos himself (Gal. 4 : 20), for he was a man of the strongest emotion. He could challenge men to duty by his very tears (Acts 20 : 19) as well as by his independent self-reliance.

One could not well plunge into the life of Paul without this much of panegyric, certainly not one who has felt that "charm of Paul" of which Ramsay[1] so winningly writes. The richness of his nature will appear in ample fulness as we proceed. If he could go up to the third heaven and bring down unutterable glories,

[1] "Pauline and Other Studies," pp. 27–45.

he could spend a day and a night in the deep (II Cor. 11 : 25). He knew human and inhuman nature. He had loyal friends, but he felt to the quick the treachery of false brethren, the ostracism of his own race, the jealousy of some preachers of the Gospel (Phil. 1 : 15) far more than he did the open hostility of a Roman emperor like Nero.

2. *Saul's Ancestry.*—Saul loved his people with intense patriotism. Few things gave him keener anguish of heart than the refusal of his Jewish brethren, his kinsmen according to the flesh, to take Jesus as the Messiah of promise (Rom. 9 : 2 f.). He was almost ready to be cut off from Christ himself if that would win them. He had once boasted, as other Jews did, of descent from Abraham (II Cor. 11 : 22). He had felt the proud scorn of the Gentiles which animated the strict Jews. Indeed, he was a Hebrew of the Hebrews and set much store by the stock of Israel. His blood went back to the tribe of Benjamin (Phil. 3 : 5) whose glory was another Saul, the first king of the Hebrew people. He probably once took a keen interest in the "endless genealogies" (I Tim. 1 : 4) and family trees of the Jews of his time. He knew what pride of race was, the heritage of a long and noble ancestry that reached far back into the distant centuries. The Jew had enough in his history to give him some right to be proud. His was the chosen people "whose is the adoption, and the glory, and the covenants, and the giving of the law, and the service of God, and the

promises; whose are the fathers" (Rom. 9 : 4 f.). It mattered little with a story like that if the hated Roman yoke was upon the neck of the Jews. The day of the Roman would pass as had that of the Seleucid kings, the Ptolemies, Alexander the Great, the Persian, the Babylonian, the Assyrian, the Hittite, the Egyptian. Kingdoms came and went, but the Jew remained, proud, isolated, defiant, conscious that he was to fulfil a strange Messianic mission in the world. True, the Messianic hope was trailing now in the dust of a deliverer from Rome who would establish a Jewish empire in Jerusalem, yet it was to come with great eschatological features. But to make the whole world Jewish was honor enough for the human race. All this and more ran in the blood of Saul's ancestors.

3. *His Family.*—One can draw a closer picture yet of the home in Tarsus into which Saul was born, though many details are sadly wanting. We do not know what was the name of either his father or mother. And yet the picture is not wholly blank. We know that his father was a strict Jew, for his son was "instructed according to the strict manner of the law of our fathers" (Acts 22 : 3). He was not merely a Pharisee himself but the son of a Pharisee (Acts 23:6). Hence we know that, though his father lived in Tarsus when Saul was born (22 : 3), he was not a Hellenizer. His father was indeed a Hellenist and lived in one of the great Greek cities of the world, but he was loyal to the traditions of Palestine and was at heart a real Jew,

though actually one of the Dispersion. One other detail is certainly known about Saul's father. He was a Roman citizen. The time came when Paul would take great pleasure in saying: "But I am a Roman born" (Acts 22 : 28). Whether his father was also Roman born or was made a Roman citizen for some deed of valor or for money, as was true of Claudius Lysias (Acts 22 : 28), is not known, or at least was not known till recently. Ramsay[1] has shown that there had been a body of Jews settled in Tarsus since 171 B.C. It was only possible for individual Jews to become Roman citizens in a Greek city like Tarsus by being enrolled in "a Tribe set apart for them, in which they could control the religious rites and identify them with the service of the synagogue.'[2] If this is true, and Ramsay proves it, Saul's father was enrolled in this City Tribe of Jewish citizens in Tarsus for his high standing in the Jewish community, unless indeed his grandfather had been a citizen also. We do not know how long the family had been in Tarsus. At any rate Saul's father was a man of position in the Jewish community and was able to send his son later to Jerusalem to school. He may have been a man of some wealth. The fact that he was a tent-maker and taught his trade to his son does not prove anything, since Jews generally knew a trade and taught it to their sons. This custom stood Paul

[1] "Cities of St. Paul," pp. 169 ff.
[2] *Ibid.*, p. 176.

in good stead later. There is every reason to think that Saul was proud of his father.

The mother shrinks still further into the background except that we know she must have been a woman of force to have reared such a son. We catch a faint glimpse of her also when Paul says: "I thank God, whom I serve from my forefathers" (II Tim. 1 : 3). She is in that pious line. That is the noblest heritage of all. In the mention of Timothy's mother, Eunice, and grandmother, Lois (1:5), it is not difficult to catch the reflection of Saul's own fireside. When Paul reminds Timothy of whom he had learned the Holy Scriptures even from a babe (3 : 14 f.) he was echoing his own experience in the home in Tarsus. This Jewish matron must not be overlooked when we study the influences that moulded Saul. She made the home where he grew and whose stamp he always bore.

When we ask for the other members of that family group we can only bring up the picture of a sister (Rachel, a later story calls her) whose son did Paul such a good turn in Jerusalem in a time of storm (Acts 23 : 16). This nephew was worthy of his uncle, and that is enough to say for his shrewdness and courage. There may have been other sisters and even brothers. We simply do not know. The curtain refuses to rise on this point. But we have caught some conception of the home in the city of which Saul was proud.

4. *The Date of Saul's Birth.*—The ancients did not have the same concern for minute chronology that

modern men show.   Luke (Luke 3 : 1 f.) does exhibit
an historian's interest in the time when John the Baptist began his ministry.   He seeks to locate the event
by the names of the rulers of the time.   In the Acts,
likewise, there is occasional allusion to men and events
that lie outside of the Apostolic story.   One is grateful
to Ramsay again for the vindication of Luke's trust-
worthiness as a historian.[1]   But it is to be borne in
mind that Luke does not profess to give the life of
Paul.   He takes up Saul, who is already a young man
(Acts 7 : 58), where he touches the story of Christianity
and follows him with more or less fulness to Rome
and there drops the narrative.   There are no clear
indications in Paul's Epistles, though hints are dropped
here and there.   He is Paul the aged when he writes
to Philemon (verse 9).   Unfortunately there is no absolutely certain date in Paul's entire career.   Even the
two foci (the coming of Saul to Antioch about the time
of the death of Herod Agrippa I and the famine, the
change of Roman Procurators at Cæsarea when Felix
is recalled and Festus succeeds him) are not fixed
points any longer.   If we knew for certain that the
one was A.D. 44 and the other A.D. 60, there would
be less difficulty in arranging approximately the other
chief dates in Paul's life.   For a discussion of the
matter, see Turner's article, N. T. Chronology[2] in

---

[1] Cf. "Was Christ Born at Bethlehem?"
[2] Cf. also, Ramsay's discussion of Pauline Chronology, "Pauline and Other Studies."

Hastings' "D. B." We may, with some hesitation, use these two dates as a working hypothesis for the division of Paul's life into three parts. Then the great missionary journeys come between A.D. 44 and 60. But even so, we have no clear light thrown on the length of Paul's life. Whether he was put to death in A.D. 64 or 68, he would still be an old man when he wrote the letter to Philemon. If, as is possible, Saul was thirty years old at the time of the stoning of Stephen, which would certainly be true if he was actually a member of the Sanhedrin (Acts 26 : 10), we must add to this the fourteen years (II Cor. 12 : 2) plus the three spent in Arabia and Damascus (Gal. 1 : 18). But these two periods cannot be insisted on minutely, since pieces of years might be counted at the beginning and the close. At any rate one will not be far astray if he thinks of Saul as five years the junior of Jesus. This would make his birth about A.D. 1. There is no straining of the facts if we imagine the boy John in the hill country of Judea, the boy Jesus in Nazareth, and the child Saul at Tarsus at the same time. Each faced the same world, but from a different point of view, these boys who were to revolutionize the world. John came out of a priestly atmosphere, and when his aged parents died took to the wilderness as a place for preparation for life's problems. Jesus lived on in the humble Nazareth home doing the work of a carpenter (Mark. 6 : 3) and waiting for the voice in the wilderness to call him to his destiny.

5. *The Boyhood of Saul at Tarsus.*—What was the
boy at Tarsus doing meanwhile? Unlike John, Saul
lived in a city. Unlike Jesus, his home was in one of
the great Greek cities of the world. Nathanael could
sneer at Nazareth (John 1 : 46), but Paul could brook
no reproach on Tarsus. He was proud to hail from
"no mean city" (Acts 21 : 39). How much right Paul
had to civic pride in the town of his birth Ramsay[1]
has shown at great length and with brilliant success.
Tarsus was the city of all the world best adapted for
the youth of the Apostle to the Gentiles. In Tarsus
was accomplished most perfectly that union between
east and west that Alexander the Great attempted
everywhere. The city remained Asiatic in character
while it appropriated the Greek qualities. Greek influence, indeed, dated back to the Ionian colonists,
but the Greek spirit did not obliterate elements which
survived even the work of Alexander. Under the
Romans it was a "free city" and the Jewish element
was a positive force in the life of the community.
There was a great university here also. It would be
difficult to imagine a city of that era more thoroughly
cosmopolitan and representative of life in the empire.
The absence of intense hatred of the Jews would open
the way for more sympathy on the part of the Jews
toward the best things in the Græco-Roman civilization. In common with the Hellenists in general Saul
spoke Greek in addition to his Aramaic, and seemed

[1] "Cities of St. Paul," pp. 85–244.

to find it not inconsistent with his Jewish scruples to witness the public games which he afterwards used so effectively as illustrations (I Cor. 9 : 24 f.). The middle wall of partition between Jew and Gentile did not extend to every detail of life, though in the main the atmosphere of his home in Tarsus was thoroughly Jewish, not to say Pharisaic. If he mingled to some extent in the life and play of Gentile boys in Tarsus, it is not so clear that he went to the Gentile schools. It was just here in the matter of education that the Pharisee would be more particular. As a boy he would learn the Old Testament story from his mother and from the synagogue teaching, which had become a great institution in Jewish life. Environment plays an important part in every human life. Heredity plus environment and the curious personal equation, added to the grace of God, explains the wonderful creature called a man. Saul would not have been quite the same man if he had been reared wholly in Alexandria or Jerusalem. Both of these centres of culture left their impress on Paul, as is seen in the use of allegory about Hagar and Sarah (Gal. 4 : 24) and the rabbinic refinement in the use of words (Gal. 3 : 16) and traditional interpretation (I Cor. 10 : 4). But it is easy to see that Saul of Tarsus was not cut out to be Philo, nor, indeed, Shammai. Tarsus left its mark upon him as a boy and made possible the more generous sympathies of his later life. It is interesting to observe how the comparatively few illustrations in his teaching are drawn chiefly from city life.[1] It is not, however, necessary to say that he misused the subject of grafting the wild olive, for he expressly explains that it is "contrary to nature" (Rom. 11 : 24). John and Jesus both revelled in the use of illustrations from nature with which they were so familiar. From one point of view it seems a pity for a boy to have to live in a city and miss the joy and freedom of the country. But Saul had some compensations. His life was to be in the great cities of the empire, and he had a natural bond of sympathy with city life and had less to learn in that respect. It is clear that his boyhood was free from the enervating dissipations of city life, and so he had strength of constitution to endure the terrific strain of missionary work, not to say persecution and imprisonment. One may imagine that the boy at Tarsus took some interest in athletics from his fondness for the figure. I Tim. 4 : 7 f. surely cannot be construed as condemnation of bodily exercise. He was a self-reliant boy, if we may judge from his advice to Timothy (I Tim. 4 : 12). What his day-dreams were we do not know, but so gifted a boy was bound to feel a call to higher service. He doubtless sympathized with the desire of his parents that he should become a Jewish rabbi, perhaps another Gamaliel. As a Jew, no higher glory was open to him than this, since the prophetic voice had ceased from Israel and the kingly sceptre was no longer in Jewish hands. The heel of Rome

[1] Cf. Reaker, "St. Paul's Illustrations."

was upon the world, the Mediterranean world, Saul's
world. Long afterwards he will look back upon
God's plan in his life and see that God had "separated"
him even from his mother's womb (Gal. 1:15) to make
a spiritual Pharisee of him, a Separate for the Gentiles, not from the Gentiles, charged with the revelation
of the Son of God in his very self. But it will take
time and a revolution in his nature before he can
see that foreordination. None the less we may conclude that the Tarsian Jewish boy was instinct with
life and eager to have a part in the great world that
surged all about him. If he felt the impact of his time,
he was anxious to play his part in his day. We may
suppose that already his conscience was active according to which he sought to live free from offence towards
God and men (Acts 24:16). But if, on the whole, the
life at Tarsus still remains obscure to us, it was not
obscure to Saul's later friends, for he was a young man
of prominence as his father was a man of position.
Paul does say that "from the first" his friends in the
Sanhedrin and others in Jerusalem, had knowledge of
him (Acts 26:5), but it is not clear that this knowledge
went further than his youth in Jerusalem (verse 4).
But from the time of his student days in Jerusalem he
was in the open so far as the Jewish world was concerned.
It will repay us to form a mental picture of the boy
that left Tarsus.

6. *At the Feet of Gamaliel.*—It was no mean ambition that Saul's parents had for him to receive his

theological education in Jerusalem. That city was the goal of Jews all over the world. Here was concentrated the history of the nation. Every hill and every valley teemed with holy associations. Saul had learned the outlines of that story, and he was coming to his own when he came to the Holy City. He was probably, according to Jewish custom, about thirteen when he came to school in Jerusalem, so that he could speak of his being "brought up" there (Acts 22 : 3). One cannot help thinking of the brief visit of the boy Jesus to the temple at the age of twelve. Each was full of zest in the problems of his people and his time. Saul probably did not astonish his teachers by the penetration of his questions and his answers in the same measure that Jesus did, but one cannot doubt the keenness of his interest in the new world that he had now entered.

But much as the city had to offer of historic attraction, the thing that stood out clearest in his after life was the fact that he sat at the feet of the great teacher of his time among the Jews (Acts 22 : 3). The temple had its wonders, that glorious temple of Herod still unfinished. But the greatest thing in the world is a man. It is a supreme moment in the life of any youth when he comes under the spell of a master teacher. This grandson of Hillel was the glory of the law and it meant much for Saul to come under his influence. His school (called the school of Hillel) was more liberal in some fine points than the rival rabbinical theological school of Shammai (contemporary of Hillel). For one thing Gamaliel was willing to read the Greek authors, and his pupil Paul will later show some knowledge of Greek literature. To be sure, Paul says, that he was "instructed according to the strict manner of the law of our fathers" (Acts 22 : 3), but he explains this later when he remarks: "After the straitest sect of our religion, I lived a Pharisee" (26 : 5). He does not say that he was brought up in the more rigid of the Pharisaic schools. From the non-Pharisaic view, however, it was strict enough. It was a life of complacent self-satisfaction to which he was reared (cf. Rom. 7 : 7) in bondage to the letter which killeth (II Cor. 3:6). One must not, however, get too extravagant an idea of Gamaliel's breadth of view and sympathy. It is true that he did protest formally in the Sanhedrin against the violence of the Sadducees towards the Apostles (Acts 5 : 34). But one is slow to believe that this action on his part was due either to any interest in Christianity or real concern for religious toleration, not to say liberty of opinion. When, later, Stephen had fired the Pharisees by his denunciation of mere ceremonialism and insistence on the spiritual nature of worship (cf. the experience of Jesus), there is no indication that Gamaliel raised a restraining hand to save him from the fury of his pupil Saul, and the Pharisees in the Sanhedrin (Acts 6 : 11 ff.; 7 : 57 f.). In Acts 5 : 35–39 he does warn the Sanhedrin to beware lest they be found fighting against God, a piece of advice not to be pressed too literally, as he did not later use it himself. It is evident that, while only the Sadducees were enlisted in the fight against the Apostles on the ground of the doctrine of the resurrection, the Pharisees were holding aloof, and in this very division lay the safety of the disciples, a point that Paul knew how to use on a later occasion (Acts 22 : 9 f.). But when Stephen stirred the Pharisees also, Gamaliel takes no interest in the matter.

Jesus did not come under the spell of the rabbinism of his time. In the Nazareth home there was less of the oral tradition (Midrash) and more of the spiritual teaching of the Old Testament prophets and psalms. Simeon and Anna breathed that atmosphere also, as did Zacharias and Elizabeth, as is shown by the report of their words. It is no reflection on theological education as such to comment on this fact. From the human point of view Jesus was free from this ceremonial perversion and had no cobwebs to brush aside. He sprang into instant opposition to the traditionalists of his time. It will not do to say that if Saul had not gone to Gamaliel's school of the prophets, he, too, would have been more open to the New Way. Peter and John were unschooled, and they, too, were slow to learn Jesus. There are difficulties of ignorance as truly as there are problems of knowledge. They are not the same in character, forsooth, but just as real in fact. One can see how Christianity gained by having this man of theological training, even though much of his knowledge was rabbinical rubbish. The Talmud itself, though written down much later (both Mishna and Gemara several centuries after Saul), yet gives us a fair specimen of the theological hair-splitting indulged in by the grave and reverend doctors of the law who dispensed wisdom in Jerusalem. Paul did have much to unlearn, much that he came to count only as "refuse" (Phil. 3:8), but great blessings resulted to him and to the cause of Christ. These more than made up for the loss, and may console any man who may have spent his time at a modern school of merely rabbinical methods and points of view, provided he gets over them.

For one thing, he gained a thoroughly trained mind. He was all in all the most gifted man of his time, leaving out of view, of course, Jesus of Nazareth. The skilful use of question and answer was not merely drill, though drill in school is not to be despised. He learned how to distinguish between things that differ (Phil. 1:10 marg.), a true mark of the justly educated mind. His ambition led him to surpass his fellow pupils (Gal. 1:14), and the result was that his brilliant intellect had received really magnificent training in mental gymnastics. Much that he had learned was really good in itself. He won familiarity with the letter of Scripture, a point about which some brilliant modern scholars are gloriously indifferent. He was to learn the spirit of Scripture-teaching later, but there was some good in the letter, provided it was not allowed

to kill. He gained, likewise, the art of disputation
which stood him in good stead on many an important
occasion as on Mars Hill, on the steps of the Tower
of Antonia, before the Jewish Sanhedrin, before Felix,
Festus, Agrippa, and perhaps Nero himself the first
time. Being well versed in rabbinical theology,
when he came to the side of Christ, he knew how to
parry all the points of his old friends the rabbis. He
knew the strength and the weakness of Pharisaism
and could speak as an expert on that point. Cf. "Tell
me, ye that desire to be under the law" (Gal. 4 : 21).
He knew only too well "the weak and beggarly rudi-
ments" of bondage to the ceremonial law (Gal. 4 : 9),
and his biting sarcasm will later sting his Jewish enemies to fury. But now he loved Pharisaism and lived
it with fierce conviction, a Hebrew of the Hebrews.

What did Gamaliel think of his brilliant pupil?
One would like to have a word from him. But the
position of leadership to which he will soon attain
shows that the master's approval rested on Saul.
Perhaps the old teacher looked proudly on the young
man from Tarsus as a possible successor. When Saul
left Jerusalem he was to all intents and purposes the
one young Jew in all the world who had most in pros-
pect before him. He had been educated as a rabbi
and the career of a rabbi lay before him. But that
was not all. Many a young rabbi lived in comparative
obscurity. This young rabbi had great friends at
Jerusalem who could help him to the highest places

if he proved worthy. We may imagine the joy of his parents as he returned home full of honor, the hope of Gamaliel and the pride of his home.

7. *Elements in Saul's Education.*—These have already been touched upon in the preceding discussion to a certain extent, but it is well to gather up the main outlines here. In fact scholars are not agreed as to this matter, some insisting that the influences that moulded him were wholly Jewish, others finding a rather large Greek side to his training, others even would add a positive Babylonian influence. It is not an easy matter to keep the balance in a matter of this sort. But after all the facts must decide.

To begin with, Paul shows in his Epistles a forceful and commanding style. His Greek is not, indeed, that of Demosthenes, and it would have been an anachronism if it had been. He uses beyond controversy the Koiné (κοινή) vernacular, as did other cultivated and uncultivated men of his day. The papyri show all grades of culture in the vernacular then as now. While his Epistles exhibit traits of the merely personal letter as in Philemon, the passionate appeal of non-literary correspondence, as in I and II Thessalonians, Galatians, II Corinthians, yet in Romans and Ephesians there is more literary style and conscious effort to express himself in accord with the greatness of his ideas. Cf. also I Cor. 13 and 15. He is an educated Jew who knew his Aramaic (Acts 22 : 2) and Hebrew, but who was also at home in the Greek of his time.

The few quotations from the Greek writers (Acts 17:
28; I Cor. 15 : 33; Tit. 1 :12) are not from writers of
the highest rank, and cannot be used as proof that
Paul was thoroughly familiar with Homer and Plato.
That matter may be left open to conjecture. What is
clear is that he could hold the attention of the cult-
ured Athenians so long as he did not offend them
by the doctrine of the resurrection.

In discussing the Hellenism of Paul one must remember that he was himself a Hellenist, not a Palestinian Jew. Besides, the Hellenism of Paul's day was
not the Hellenism of Aristotle's time.[1] The later
Hellenism and the later Judaism of the Dispersion
were not so far apart as their antecedents had been.
"In the mind of Paul a universalized Hellenism coalesced with a universalized Hebraism."[2] To be sure,
one must not make a real Greek out of Paul. But it
is, I believe, missing a part of Paul's nature to refuse
to see his bond of contact with the Greek world in
which he lived.

We know how proud he was of his Roman citizenship,
so that the Roman side of his training is not to be overlooked, though it was naturally slight as compared
with the Hebrew culture. He seems to have known
some Latin, as he managed his own case in the various
trials before the Roman courts.

[1] Ramsay, "Cities of St. Paul," p. 31. Cf. Hicks, "St. Paul and
Hellenism." Thackeray, "Relation of St. Paul to Contemporary Jewish Thought."
[2] Ramsay, "Cities of St. Paul," p. 43.

But it is quite within bounds to think of Saul's education as really cosmopolitan, as much so, indeed, as that of a young Jew who was loyal to his people could well have been. Besides the teaching of the rabbis, he probably read some of the Jewish apocalypses like the Psalms of Solomon, Book of Enoch, Testament of the Twelve Patriarchs, books which had a vogue at that time. Other books, like the Wisdom of Solomon, which reflected the Jewish Alexandrian Philosophy, he possibly read also. There is no reason to think that he was too narrow a Pharisee to be open to the various means of culture of his time. Fundamentally a rabbi, he was familiar with the apocalyptic method of teaching also (cf. II Thess. 2 : 3–10). But around this Jewish learning there gathered a certain amount of Greek and Roman culture which made him a real citizen of the world and a fit vessel to bear the Gospel to the Gentiles when Christ should lay his hand upon him.

If Christianity only possessed one so well equipped as this young rabbi! No one of the Twelve Apostles was his equal in mental gifts and culture. But he is far from any thought of Christ in his home at Tarsus. Brilliant, accomplished, masterful, ambitious, he is eager to be in the midst of the stirring events in Judea. He appears in Jerusalem again, possibly drawn thither by the attacks of Stephen on the citadel of Pharisaism. It is not improbable that he measured swords in debate with Stephen in the Cilician synagogue, where Saul would naturally go (Acts 6 : 9).   But, if so, he had a new experience.   He could not stand against this tornado of the Spirit.   Few things annoy a man of culture quite so much as to be overcome in public discussion whether by ridicule or weight of argument. An unanswerable argument is a hard thing to forgive. Stephen was all ablaze with passion.   Before him Saul's critical acumen and theological subtleties vanished.   Saul was beaten and his defeat rankled within him.   Such in brief is the picture that we may form of Saul and Stephen in Jerusalem.

CHAPTER II

SAUL THE PERSECUTING RABBI

"I verily thought with myself that I ought to do many things contrary to the name of Jesus of Nazareth" (Acts 26:9).

1. *Saul's First Taste of Blood.*—This form of statement may shock one a bit at first. It suggests that Saul became bloodthirsty in his persecution. That is true. He was, indeed, a most respectable persecutor, but blood was on his hands, and he afterwards recognized it with shame and humiliation. "And when they were put to death I gave my vote against them" (Acts 26 : 10). "And I persecuted this way even unto the death, binding and delivering into prisons both men and women" (Acts 22 : 4). He could never forgive himself for this lapse from the true moral standards. Paul was by nature a gentleman, and to think that he had led even lovely women to prison and death! "For I am the least of the Apostles, that am not meet to be called an Apostle because I persecuted the church of God" (I Cor. 15 : 9). The only consolation about it all that he could get was that he "did it ignorantly in unbelief" (I Tim. 1:13), but he could never think of himself as aught but the chief of sinners. In him as chief, Jesus set forth "an ensample of them that should

thereafter believe on him unto eternal life" (1 Tim. 1:16).
If Christ could save a sinner like Saul, he felt that no
one else need despair. Paul did not spare himself
later by the reflection that he thought that he had done
his duty to God in this matter. That is the excuse of
every persecutor. It is just his way of serving God,
to kill the heretics! Indeed, the conscientiousness of
Saul in the matter merely added to his later remorse.

So we know how Saul felt after he saw his persecution in its true light and how he felt before his conversion. When he stands by Stephen, keeping guard
over the garments of those who had stripped themselves
for vengeance on Stephen the traducer of the faith of
the Pharisees, he is full of self-complacency. His conscience gave him no trouble at all. The sense of sin had
not revived in him, and he felt very much alive (Rom.
7:9). He seemed to have abundant justification for this
first step in persecution. Pharisaism was the hope of
Israel and so the hope of the world. Had not Gamaliel
said so? When the real Messiah came he would be
a Pharisee, not this Jesus of Nazareth who had met a
just death on the cross for his opposition to the Pharisaic teaching. "Paul had been nurtured on the
Messianic Hope of Israel. What a caricature was
this of the glorious fulfilment for which devout Jews
had yearned."[1] And Stephen was actually repeating
the blasphemies of Jesus and seeking to subvert the
customs which Moses had delivered unto them! Jesus

[1] Kennedy, "St. Paul's Conceptions of Last Things," p. 82.

himself had dared to say that he would destroy the temple itself, and now Stephen is repeating that saying (Acts 6 : 14) and is depreciating the value of the temple in the worship of God (7 : 48).   He has actually charged us with not keeping the law, as if the Pharisees were not orthodox!   He even insults the Sanhedrin by accusing them of being "betrayers and murderers" of Jesus (7 : 52)! As if Jesus were not legally tried and condemned by Pontius Pilate the Roman Governor! No wonder the Sanhedrin are gnashing their teeth at this blasphemer and have stopped their ears to hear no more.   He actually imagines that he sees Jesus now!   We will rush upon him without waiting for a formal vote of condemnation.   Even Gamaliel does not protest.   Out of the city we shall go and stone him there as a common blasphemer.   So is justice satisfied and the temple preserved.

Saul did not, indeed, cast a stone at him.   He could not stoop to that, nor was it necessary for him to stain his hands with blood that far.   Perhaps he did not stop to analyze his ideas and emotions very closely at the moment.   It was mob violence, in fact, close to a modern lynching.   He could justify it if necessary, for Stephen deserved his fate!   Indeed, the Sanhedrin could no longer put one to death without the consent of the Roman Governor, and this it had been difficult to obtain in the case of Jesus.   On the whole, therefore, it was just as well to take the law into their own hands. The excitement and resentment of the moment had led Saul on along with the crowd. There may have been an unconscious personal element in it all. If Saul had gone down in defeat before Stephen in the Cilician synagogue, a touch of personal revenge came in also. This was Saul's answer to Stephen's unanswerable addresses. Thus the defeated rabbis had squared accounts with Jesus for that last debate in the temple. Stephen would never trouble Saul again.

Saul was not merely passive in the matter of Stephen's death. He was a scholar and a rabbi and so left the actual killing to others. But he was in hearty sympathy with the deed. "And Saul was consenting unto his death" (Acts 8:1). The word here used ($\sigma\upsilon\nu\epsilon\upsilon$-$\delta\omega\kappa\hat{\omega}\nu$) in its simple form is the one used of the Father's good pleasure in the Son (Matt. 3:17). It suggests complacent approval, and the preposition adds to the force of the verb ("perfective" use of the preposition). We may pause a moment, therefore, to contemplate the brilliant young rabbi who is now introduced to us for the first time in Luke's narrative. He was not the kind of a man to do things by halves. He had been drawn into the controversy against Stephen in behalf of Pharisaism. His whole soul was enlisted in the cause.

He probably did not at first expect to have a very active part in the matter. Stephen had been formally arraigned before the Sanhedrin, and witnesses had been secured to testify against him. It was Stephen's own speech which had precipitated the riot and the death in this form. But things had to take their course.

There was no need of Saul's going further in the matter. One mob did not matter so much after all, especially as it had the seeming approval of the members of the Sanhedrin itself.

2. *Saul's Leadership in the Persecution.*—Saul never sought to shift the responsibility in the matter to the Sanhedrin. He always confessed simply: "I persecuted the church of God, and made havoc of it" (Gal. 1:13), "I was before a blasphemer, and a persecutor, and injurious" (I Tim. 1:13). The wonder ever was to him how Jesus counted him worthy, putting him into the ministry. The narrative of Luke (Acts 8:1) seems to imply that the extension of the persecution to the other Christians was more a natural evolution than the result of preconcerted action. It is easier to start a fire than to put it out. It is the history of mob law everywhere. It is first just for this one man guilty of so grave a crime. Then it is for any one charged with that crime or even suspected of it. Then the vengeance of the mob vents itself on anybody suspected of any crime. The excuse against Stephen had been that he was a blasphemer against Moses and the temple. The charge against the rest of the Christians is that they are sympathizers with Stephen. They are guilty of the crime of being disciples of Jesus. Christ had sought to protect the Apostles when he was himself caught in the toils of hate and gave himself up to his destiny. (John 18:8). They had escaped persecution then, though Peter had quailed before the sneers of the

servants. Since the Ascension of Jesus the Apostles
had learned what it was to go to prison for Christ.
They had the new-found joy, "that they were counted
worthy to suffer dishonor for the Name" (Acts 5:41).
The death of Stephen had extended the persecution
to the deacons if we are justified in so terming the
Seven chosen in Acts 6:1-6.

But the persecution that arose on the very day of
Stephen's death was "against the church that was in
Jerusalem." There, for the first time, was a general
attack on the entire body of believers in Jerusalem.
This attack was so "great" that the bulk of them fled
for their lives *instanter* and were scattered throughout
Judea and Samaria. The Apostles stood their ground.
They had gotten used to going to prison. Besides, if
Stephen could die, so could they. It is not clear whether
the "devout men" who gave Stephen decent burial,
were believers or merely sympathizers who had courage enough to do that service to the first martyr of the
faith. The work of extermination was swift and seemed
complete.

But it is just at this point that Saul steps to the front.
He wishes no half-way measures. It is a great popular movement to stamp out the vicious heresy and
rescue Pharisaism from future peril. In every crisis
there is always a man who comes to the surface as the
man of the hour. It is not always true that a man
makes a crisis or the crisis the man. Sometimes both
spring up together and react the one on the other.

Saul "laid waste the church, entering every house" (Acts 8 : 3). Already the term church (ἐκκλησία) has left its merely etymological sense of assembly and taken on that of body. It was a church when out of service as well as when assembled. One can well imagine the dumb terror that entered into the hearts of the Christians who had remained in the city. It was bad enough to feel the senseless rage of a mob which spent itself in a day. But here was relentless hate that deliberately violated the precincts of one's home. The approval of the Sanhedrin (Acts 26:10) gave this high-handed action of Saul the semblance of legality, but it cannot mitigate the bitterness that filled his own soul as he dragged men and even women out of their homes to prison for the crime of Christianity.

One might palliate a spurt or two of this sort on the part of the hot-blooded young rabbi, who, like all persecutors, had his conscience and his prejudices sadly mixed. He "shut up many of the saints in prison" (Acts 26 : 10), and kept it up as long as there were any to seize. His activity in Jerusalem ceased only when the material there gave out. He had various means of refined cruelty for those who did not flee before this wolf who was ravening the fold. Some he simply punished in the synagogues (Acts 26 : 11). This he did "oftentimes," though the exact shape that his wrath took is not made clear. He even "strove to make them blaspheme" the name of Jesus. Let us hope that he failed in this attempt. One is reminded of the days

of Antiochus Epiphanes. Others were put to death
by formal vote of the Sanhedrin and with Saul's full
approval (Acts 26 : 10). It is a grewsome tale at best,
and the matter is not improved when Luke describes
Saul as "yet breathing threatening and slaughter
against the disciples of the Lord" (Acts 9 : 1). That
"yet" is quite significant. His thirst for blood was
not quenched while any Christians remained. True,
the Apostles were not seized then, though why they
escaped we do not clearly see. They remained boldly
behind and even untouched. There is sometimes safety
in boldness.

Saul himself has grown apace. He had in him the
material for an arch-persecutor if the occasion came.
He was made of the right stuff and his training under
Gamaliel gave help also. The touch of Hellenism in
him was not enough to withstand the lion of Pharisaism once aroused. One recalls also that the Athenians
demanded the death of Socrates and Antiochus Epiphanes sought to inject Hellenism into the Jews by com-
pulsion. Saul had been taught to regard the minutest
regulation and scruple of the oral tradition as on a par
with the very Word of Jehovah. The intensity and
ardor of his nature added fuel to the dry tinder of
rabbinism. Individual infallibility and conscientiousness make a dangerous combination. Once his blood
was up it was easy to spring from the place of helper
at the death of Stephen to that of leader in a great movement to rid the country of the disciples of the hated

Nazarene. One can well suppose that his former fellow-students rallied around the brilliant young leader. In all probability Saul led a student movement against Christianity with the sanction of the Jewish authorities. The Sanhedrin had itself tried to put down this heresy, but Gamaliel had put a stop to their proceedings. They now rejoiced in a Pharisaic revival as an offset to the rising tide of Christian power in Jerusalem. This tide had been neglected too long.

3. *Saul's Connection with the Sanhedrin.*—The question is raised at once whether Saul himself was a member of the Sanhedrin. If one takes the language used by him in Acts 26 : 10 ("I gave my vote against them") literally, then he was, of course, a member of this august body. It must be confessed that this is the obvious and natural way to take the language. There exists, so far as I know, no real obstacle in the way of such a fact. He was young, and yet he was probably over thirty. If he had to be married, as was the custom, we have no evidence to the contrary. His unmarried state later (I Cor. 7 : 8) can be explained just as well on the ground that he was a widower. It is to be said further that one small objection to Paul's comments on the subject of marriage would thus be removed. It is, of course, not impossible to think of a merely metaphorical use of the term "vote" in Acts 26 : 10. But, on the whole, it seems more than probable that he means to imply that he was a member of the Sanhedrin. It is not impossible that the rather familiar tone of Acts

22 : 5 is explained by this fact: "As also the high priest
doth bear me witness, and all the estate of the elders:
from whom also I received letters unto the brethren."
Observe that "the brethren" here are Jewish brethren,
not Christians.   Note also "brethren and fathers" in
verse 1.   If he was a member of the Sanhedrin, it is
possible that it was due chiefly to his activity in this
persecution as a reward of merit.   He may have been
promoted rapidly by reason of his unusual zeal for the
cause.

At first blush it seems a little strange that the Sanhedrin should here be exercising the power of death
when in the trial of Jesus it is expressly disclaimed by
them to Pilate (John 18 : 31).   We do not know, to be
sure, the exact date of the events growing out of the
stoning of Stephen.   There was some delay in the
appointing of a successor to Pontius Pilate, who was
recalled in A.D. 36.   But even before that time his
great unpopularity had broken his authority with the
people very largely.   It is entirely possible, therefore,
that the Sanhedrin may have taken the reins of authority back into their own hands in this time of confusion.   They could have evaded responsibility for the
death of Stephen, but not for those slain under Saul's
leadership since he expressly says that he "received
authority from the chief priests" (Acts 26 : 10).   But
Luke is so careful in other matters that one cannot
well doubt his comments here merely on the ground of
our ignorance of the true explanation.   He has been

vindicated on too many points already where quibbles of like nature were once raised against him.

But, whether Saul was an actual member of the Sanhedrin or not, he was in the closest touch with them now. He was, indeed, their spokesman. Perhaps Gamaliel felt that his hopes about Saul were already more than realized. He had known that a great future was before him. It had come more quickly than he had expected. He could rest in peace now. As President of the Sanhedrin (A.D. 30–51)[1] he was in a position to work in thorough accord with his great pupil who was now so active in Jewish public life.

4. *Saul's Fight to a Finish.*—He was "exceedingly mad against them" (Acts 26 : 11). Those not already dead he had driven out of town. That ought to have satisfied an ordinary man. But Saul was not an ordinary man. He "persecuted them even unto foreign cities." "Beyond measure" (Gal. 1 : 13) he was zealous in his persecution. No wonder that the poor fleeing disciples went as far as Damascus and Cyprus. The marvel is that they stopped at all. This Pharisaic war-horse sniffed the battle from afar. His very breath (ἐνπνέων) was threat and slaughter (Acts 9 : 1). He seemed to have paused a moment to survey the field of carnage. News came to him that a band of believers in Jesus had collected in Damascus. That was enough for Saul. He "went unto the high priest, and asked of him letters to Damascus unto the synagogues, that

[1] Pick, "What is the Talmud?" p. 31.

if he found any that were of the Way, whether men or women, he might bring them bound to Jerusalem" (Acts 9 : 1 f.).   Once in prison in Jerusalem the punishment (Acts 22 : 5) would be easy.   He was determined to finish the business while he was at it.

He was going with "the authority and commission of the chief priests" (Acts 26 : 12), and that authority would have been acknowledged beyond doubt if he could once have served his papers.   The Jew, like the modern Roman Catholic, owed a double allegiance, one to his state, the other to the ecclesiastical or temple authorities at Jerusalem.   It is not certain whether Damascus was at this time under Roman rule or under a governor of Aretas as was the case a little later (II Cor. 11 : 32).   The point is not material.   In either event the Sanhedrin claimed religious control over Jews, and Christians as yet were treated merely as a sect of Jews like the Sadducees or Pharisees.

Saul was now the typical heresy-hunter of all time. He has been carried on by the tide of events till he is the acknowledged leader of aggressive and triumphant Pharisaism.   He felt himself pitted against the very name of Jesus.   Brutal passion was linked with high motives.   He felt personal zest in his attacks on the followers of Jesus.   He had outlined a definite programme of extermination, and complete success was within his grasp.

It is idle to conjecture what might have happened if Saul had met Jesus in Jerusalem before his crucifixion.

The probability is that he would have joined the Jewish leaders in crucifying him, for Jesus opposed the precious theology which Saul had learned from Gamaliel. But, whatever might have happened then, the offence of the cross was insuperable. To Saul the cross was the very curse of God upon this Messianic pretender (Gal. 3 : 13). He richly deserved the shameful death that befell him.

Perhaps as Saul rode upon his way to Damascus his mind was full of thoughts about the great events that had recently occurred. The Christians were a stubborn set and were hard to teach the truth, the orthodoxy of the time. The death of Jesus ought to have been enough. But Stephen had gone the same way. It was a pity, for Stephen was a man of parts. After all, the leaders were the most responsible. He would take up the case of the Apostles when he returned to Jerusalem, for they had been neglected too long. It was too bad that these ignorant and misguided followers of Jesus had to be slaughtered like sheep. It was particularly bad about the women. He had shrunk back at that a number of times, but the miserable business would soon be over. Then he could return to the study of theology. There were some new apocalypses that he had not yet had time to read. Of course it was not worth while to make any serious investigation of the claims of Christianity. It was bound to be false since it was opposed to Pharisaism which was the test of all truth. Gamaliel was a great teacher. How fortunate he had been in his career so far, in his parents, his home advantages, his theological training, this very uprising which had given him his opportunity. He was now the victorious champion of orthodox Judaism. The path ran straight before him to glory and power. True, Stephen had said some things about Jesus that had a fascination for him at times when he had leisure for abstract thought. Some day he would look further into this question of the Messiah. Then at night, ofttimes, the wistful face of Stephen haunted him. Just before he died he really did look like an angel, and he spoke as if he were talking directly to Jesus. What if it should turn out after all that Stephen was right, that Jesus was really the Messiah, that all these disciples whom he had destroyed, men and women, were pious people? The faces of some of them were strangely ecstatic as they died! And why did they die so cheerfully? How could heretics have any consolation in the hour of death? But away with such thoughts which sting one like an ox's goad. The road to Damascus was indeed beautiful, but the noonday sun was growing very hot and the glare of the sand was painful. It would be pleasant to be at the journey's end. What a surprise he had in store for the heretics in Damascus! They could hardly know that he was coming. Damascus was a great and ancient city. He would be glad to see it.

CHAPTER III

SAUL'S VISION OF JESUS

"Saul, Saul, why persecutest thou me?" (Acts 9:4).

1. *The Challenge by Jesus.*—The darkest hour is just before the dawn. From the human point of view Saul was carrying everything before him. Unless his career was stopped the annihilation of Christianity may have seemed imminent to some of the disciples. And who was there who could stop his onward course? No one of the Apostles at Jerusalem seemed equal to the task, nor indeed all of them combined. No one of them could stand before Saul nor was equal in ability, training and experience. One may well contemplate this "if of history." What would have been the history of Christianity if Saul had not been converted? It would not have been exterminated. That much we know.[1] But the difficulties in its path would have been immeasurably greater than they were when he stepped out of the way. A man is sometimes more than a kingdom. Alexander was more powerful than all the hosts of Darius. If Washington had been on the

[1] "But the Good Shepherd had heard the cries of the trembling flock and went forth to face the wolf on their behalf." Stalker, "Life of St. Paul," p. 43.

side of the British, the whole course of American history might have been different.

Jesus had said that he would be with the disciples all the days (Matt. 28 : 20). They had never needed him more than now. It did seem to the despondent disciples as if Jesus no longer cared what became of his cause. Was he powerless to interfere? But just at this point he did interpose in a wonderful way. From every point of view we come here to one of the epochs in human history, not merely an epoch in the life of Saul. So many matters clamor for discussion at this point that only a selection of the most pressing and pertinent can be attempted. In the whole discussion one should keep in mind the larger aspects of the matter, not merely the personal experience of one man, important and vital as that is. If Jesus could reach out his hand in behalf of his disciples, now was the time and Saul was the man to lay hold of in this supernatural way.

We may pass by the abstract discussion of the possibility of miracles. The world has largely lost interest in that phase of the subject, and few, save the boldest materialists like Haeckel, have the hardihood to say any more what God can and cannot do. It is utterly unscientific to approach this great event from the point of view of the impossibility of the miraculous, as that term is used for the unusual interposition of God in human affairs. Indeed so strong and clear to many has come the conception of the immanence of God in nature that the absence of God would seem more of a miracle than his presence. And, after all, what we call the laws of nature are merely our notions or discoveries of God's ways, and these laws worked before we discovered them as do the many others that we have not yet found out.

But still we must squarely face the question, Did Saul see Jesus? That is a matter to be determined by historical evidence. We need not here enter into the metaphysical or psychical phases of the subject which are brought up by the word ὤφθη "appeared" in I Cor. 15:8, except to observe that it is the very same word that Paul uses about the appearance of Jesus to the Apostles and others after the resurrection (I Cor. 15:5–7). Luke uses the same word about the appearance of Jesus in Luke 24:34. It is no mere refinement of Paul's. What Paul's doctrine of the resurrection of the body of Jesus was is not the point at issue here. It is the personality of Jesus in visible and audible form that Saul claims to have met. The notion of a mere vision of Jesus, who had no real body, does not relieve the incident of its supernatural aspect. That, after all, is the *crux* of this problem as it is of the resurrection of Jesus himself, not to say the fundamental question of Christianity itself.[1] It is obviously true that the new knowledge in psychology decreases the difficulties in the way of our apprehension of the phenomena connected with Saul's conversion. We

[1] Cf. Orr, "The Resurrection of Jesus" (1908).

may not hope that the discoveries concerning the sub-
conscious mind or telepathy will relieve the incident
of all the supernatural element. But it is increasingly
hard on scientific grounds to deny the possibility of
the manifestation of God to man. What Paul means
beyond controversy is that he had a personal interview
with Jesus of Nazareth after his death. In that interview he heard the voice of Jesus and understood his
words in a conversation of some length (Acts 9 : 4–6;
22 : 7–10; 26 : 14–18). It was not a mere voice that Saul
heard. He claims that he saw Jesus (I Cor. 9 : 1).
There are difficulties of detail about the narratives in
Acts, but they are not specially material and have
possible explanations, such as the men standing speech-
less (Acts 9:7) and the falling down of all (Acts 26:14),
where two stages may be referred to, though we do
not know. In the contradiction between hearing the
voice (ἀκούοντες τῆς φωνῆς Acts 9 : 7) and not hearing
the voice (τὴν φωνὴν οὐκ ἤκουσαν Acts 22 : 9) the difference in case (hearing the sound with the genitive and
understanding the sense with the accusative) is in harmony with ancient Greek usage. They all beheld the
light, but Jesus spoke to Saul (Acts 22 : 9), not to the
men. They were all dazed by the brilliance of the light
that flashed at mid-day above the brightness of the sun
(Acts 26 : 13). It is admitted that the men with Saul
did not comprehend this event and that Saul fell to the
ground himself (Acts 9:4) from the glory of the light out
of heaven. When he rose from the earth, he was blind.

What happened to Saul on the road to Damascus? Only three alternatives are possible. Either Saul invented this story as an excuse for his change of attitude toward Jesus, or he was deceived by a wrong interpretation of a natural phenomenon, or he has told what actually occurred. I see no escape from these alternatives. We cannot throw on Luke the responsibility of making up the whole matter including Saul's speeches in Acts 22 and 26. For one thing, he did not even take the trouble to correct verbal disagreements. Another and much more important point is that Saul himself repeatedly affirms the heart of his story in his own Epistles. If we left Acts out entirely we should have substantially the same problem as before. The position that Saul deliberately made up such a story to justify his desertion of Judaism and espousal of Christianity is a psychological impossibility plain to any one familiar with human nature and the facts of Saul's life up to this point, not to say afterward. That he misinterpreted a natural experience is more worthy of discussion. But what sort of an experience? That he had an epileptic fit? Then how explain the light, the voice, the effect on the other men? That Saul was asleep and was awakened by a clap of thunder and a flash of lightning? But it seemed to have been a clear day, not to mention the detailed conversation and Saul's claim that he saw Jesus. If one supposes that Saul had worked himself into a fury over this business of persecution and suddenly went mad, he has more problems on his hands than he had before. If one imagines that Saul, who did have trances and dreams later, had a nightmare or a sunstroke, he likewise makes Saul read back into a mass of incoherence the most coherent and definite expression of his whole life. However possible such a thing might be for a mere neurotic, Saul's mental vigor and clearness remain indisputable and a protest against such playing with the deepest experience of a man like him. Add to all this the clearness of Saul's recollection of the interview (that it was in the Aramaic tongue) and Saul's instant apprehension of the momentous issues raised. Besides the whole current of his career was flowing in a consistent channel. Schmiedel, indeed, admits that Saul imagined that he saw Jesus. It was an hallucination, but Saul was sincere in his belief that he had had this experience. But here again Saul is the last of men to be the victim of a mere hallucination, especially on a theme so vital to his whole career. Baur ("Paul," Vol. I, p. 68) doubts the historic reality of the bright light, but at last confesses his inability to explain away the experience of Saul by mere dialectical or psychological analysis ("Das Christentum," etc.). No rational motive for a deliberate change has ever been suggested, and Saul was a rational man. I mean no rational motive apart from Saul's own statement of the case. Against his own wish and plan he was seized and turned round. Saul says that Jesus did it. No one has yet successfully explained away

Saul's own explanation of what occurred to him on the way to Damascus.

Saul was too clear-headed to quibble with Jesus about the use of "me" (Acts 9 : 4). He would have persecuted Jesus in person if he had had a chance. He was not now persecuting the disciples of Jesus for their own sakes. It was the teaching and career of Jesus that he was aiming at all the time. He did not yet know how true in the mystic sense it was that Jesus was identified with his people. "Caput pro membris clamabat" (Augustine). The matter was at bottom a personal one between Saul and Jesus. By the most unexpected turn in a man's career possible he suddenly was face to face with Jesus of Nazareth whose Messianic claims he had denied, whose name he had traduced, and whose disciples he had led to prison and death. The zealot for the traditions of the fathers was at once put on the defensive and challenged to give a reason for the faith that was in him and in particular for the excess of zeal shown in his persecution of the saints.

2. *The Quandary of Saul.*—It is a shock to have one's unquestioned beliefs suddenly challenged, especially if one had simply assumed them as true without any effort to formulate an explanation of them. Saul was no novice in Pharisaism. He knew what the rabbis taught. He knew the line of cleavage in theology that divided the Pharisees from the disciples of Jesus. If he had been asked at another time, he could have presented a reasoned, if not rational, justification

of the whole case of ceremonial religion against the emotional spiritual theology of the Christians. But he was manifestly caught at a disadvantage and there was no time for theological fencing. He was face to face with the eternal realities and the foundations of his theological prepossessions were crumbling all around him. It was idle to argue on minor points when the major premise was in ruins. He will not attempt to answer the "why" of this inquiry till he learns "who" it is (Acts 9 : 4 f.) that makes the demand. One thinks rapidly in an emergency. He speaks deferentially and the word "Lord" apparently implies more than merely the civil "Sir" of ordinary address which the word may mean. He is willing to admit the supernatural (perhaps angelic) visitation. Beyond doubt Saul was filled with awe and so was on the way toward agreement with the demands of the strange visitor.

Besides, the stranger had made use of a proverb that bore marvellously on his personal situation. "It is hard for thee to kick against the goad" (Acts 26 : 14). How came this visitor to know that Saul had had secret struggles, may, indeed, have been but just now struggling with them in an acute form? When, indeed, Saul himself at first may not have been fully conscious of it?[1]

3. *The Personal Issue Pressed by Jesus.*—The reply of the stranger repeats the charge of the first inquiry

[1] Bacon, "Story of St. Paul," p. 37.

"whom thou persecutest" (Acts 9 : 5). The repetition of the charge would not decrease the tension of the moment. His answer removes all doubt as to the personality of the speaker by the use of the name Jesus of Nazareth (Acts 22 : 8). He calls himself Jesus, the human name hated by Saul. He does not here claim to be the Christ (Messiah). It is not a time to raise theological discussion by the use of terms. It is the historic Jesus of Nazareth who here converses with Saul of Tarsus. He is confronted with his hitherto unseen enemy, and now he must explain why he hates him. While Saul hesitates, for he is in doubt for once in his life, Jesus bids him to rise to his feet. Jesus resumes the conversation, when Saul, in a conflict of emotion, asks what he is to do. Jesus tells him to go on to Damascus as he had planned. There he would find one who would tell him what to do (Acts 9 : 6). A new destiny is now "appointed" for him (Acts 22:10). For a while he must remain in darkness as to what that destiny is. In Acts 26:16–18 Paul, in his address to Agrippa, in the brief summary omits the mission to Damascus and puts in the mouth of Jesus the message of Ananias. But that is a mere detail and easily understood.

Jesus has sharpened the issue between himself and Saul of Tarsus. He assumes that Saul surrenders. What will Saul do now? The crisis of his life is upon him. He cannot turn to Gamaliel for advice, nor to his father and mother. Here in the open and practically alone with this wondrous Person he must decide. We may well imagine that he foresaw what would happen to him if he gave up to Jesus. He knew the Pharisees. He saw what he had to undergo. But was Jesus what he claimed to be? What must he answer to this Voice?

4. *The Surrender of Saul.*—Did Saul give up to Christ at this point, or was it only after his eyes were opened in Damascus that he was converted? There is no doubt as to the conviction at this point. The matter is not very material, but one is led to conclude that the surrender took place during the interview with Jesus from the question which Saul made to Jesus: "What shall I do, Lord?" (Acts 22 : 10). The temper of this inquiry is one of submission to the will of Jesus. He surrenders on the spot and at discretion. There is no reserve. He is the slave of Jesus from this time forth, to obey the commands of the Lord Christ. Light had shone into his heart, "the light of the knowledge of the glory of God in the face of Jesus Christ" (II Cor. 4 : 6). He had seen the face of Jesus before he fell to the earth and darkness came over him.

Stephen was right when he thought that he looked upon Jesus standing at the right hand of God. The spirit of controversy has left Saul. He wishes to know what Jesus wishes for him to do. "I was not disobedient unto the heavenly vision" (Acts 26 : 19).

This interpretation of the story is not without diffi-

culty, though the most probable on the whole. It is
hard to think of so radical a change in a man like
Saul taking place so suddenly. But a tornado had
swept over Saul and there was no room left for dispute
with the storm. Some light is thrown on the matter
by the words of Jesus about kicking against the goad
(Acts 26 : 14). They suggest a struggle in Saul's soul
that had been going on for some time. Our ignorance
of such a struggle does not controvert the words of
Christ on the subject. Saul does not contradict the
indictment of Jesus. Saul had failed in the moment
of his triumph. Persecution was futile. Saul's state
of mind may have been more ready for the capture
by Jesus than we know. Two explanations of the
possible preparation in Saul's own mind have been
offered. One (see Findlay, on Paul, in Hastings'
"D. B.") view is that the goad was Saul's struggle with
the law from the awakened sense of sin (Rom. 7 : 9 f.).
It was a bootless conflict with the commands of the
law. Pharisaism was not wholly satisfactory. The
other view is that Jesus had more fascination for Saul
than he had been willing to admit. Stephen had left
his mark upon Saul who was really to take up the
unfinished task of this exponent of spiritual religion.
In spite of his vigorous attacks on Christianity he had
had secret misgivings as to whether, after all, Stephen
might not be right. This explanation is well set forth
by Bruce.[1] The very vehemence of Saul's persecution

[1] "St. Paul's Conception of Christianity."

was partly due to the lurking doubt that Jesus might
be in truth the Messiah.

> "Who lights the fagots?
> Not the full faith; no, but the lurking doubt."

This inward struggle may very well have included
both of these elements. The sudden and penetrating
question of Jesus with this remonstrance served to
reveal Saul to himself. The inner light from Christ's
face exposed Saul's heart to his own gaze. Often the
man who shouts the loudest his own orthodoxy is a
heretic at heart. All that may be needed for crystalli-
zation is a jar of the glass. It is one of the causes for
gratitude that it was not psychologically impossible
for Saul of Tarsus to turn his face in full surrender to
Jesus of Nazareth.

But, when all is said, there remains the supreme
difficulty. Why did Saul surrender to Jesus? As
a matter of fact at bottom the surrender of Saul to
Jesus does not differ from that of others. Jesus assumes the mastery of Saul at once. Saul wavered
not for a moment afterward. His course had run
straight on and consistently up to this point. He all
at once wheeled right round and forever kept to the
new turn in his life. I have a notion that there is
something in this contact with Jesus that is not told.
Perhaps in the brief instant before darkness came Saul
saw the glory of God in the face of Jesus (II Cor. 4 : 6).
The transcendent, appealing, melting, powerful look

of Jesus, as in the case of Peter, may have broken every barrier down. The stern will of Saul gave way before the imperial will of Jesus. "It was by something which may perhaps best be called a divine contagion that the spirit of Paul was absorbed into the life of Christ."[1]

5. *The Temporary Darkness.*—No reason for the blindness is assigned other than the one given by Saul himself. "I could not see for the glory of that light (Acts 22 : 11). Luke (Acts 9 : 8) naïvely remarks: "When his eyes were opened, he saw nothing." He had spiritual light though physical blindness possessed him. The contrast of the helpless blind man led by the hand to Damascus with the masterful rabbi who was riding the spirit of persecution to victory is complete. Certainly the pathos of the situation is consonant with the sudden whirl in the fortunes of Saul, whatever may have been God's purpose in this affliction. The tables were completely turned. He was now himself led by the hand of Jesus (Phil. 3 : 12) and the spirit of persecution had died out in him forever.

Perhaps one object of the blindness to the outer world was to give Saul a better opportunity for mental readjustment. The affliction would be a perpetual reminder of the genuineness of his experience. The tornado had left his house of theology in a state of ruin. As he sat in the ashes of humiliation, he could see the

[1] Percy Gardner, "Historic View of the New Testament," p. 216.

Phœnix of a new theology rise. The vision of Christ had changed the whole world for Saul. All his anti-Christian premises and conclusions had vanished in a moment. As yet, and always, in fact, Jesus had come to him "as to the child untimely born" (I Cor. 15 : 8). At this juncture it was all so new and strange that he needed to feel his way and had to grope awhile. It was appropriate that these three days of blindness should be a time of fasting also (Acts 9 : 9).

It was fitting that he should go on to Damascus. His papers for the arrest of the disciples were now useless. But it would bring matters to a clearer focus for him to take his stand in Damascus with the very people whose destruction he had had in mind. He would never persecute again, though he would often be the victim of persecution.

6. *The Appeal to Ananias.*—It is, perhaps, needless to moralize on the reason for the use of a man like Ananias to induct Saul in a more formal way into the outward observances of Christianity. The miracle was necessary to halt Saul and turn his course. A miracle is not needed for the more humble duties that fell to the lot of Ananias, save the opening of Saul's eyes. This of itself is explanation enough for the fact that in these respects Saul followed the usual course of other believers in Jesus.

But even Ananias had to be made ready for Saul. The fame of the arch-persecutor had gone far and wide. It is the Lord Jesus who appears to Ananias to per-

suade him to receive Saul to his heart. This is evident
from the terms used in Acts 9 : 15 ff. The difficulty of
this appearance of Jesus is certainly no greater than that
to Saul and is free from the outward phenomena. But
the heart of the problem remains the same, which is
the manifestation of the Risen Christ to a mortal man.
That is a supernatural fact, not an ordinary experience.
There is, of course, the further difference that in the
appearance of Saul there was not a mere vision.
Ananias is not, however, thrown into the state of excitement that was true of Saul. He recognizes the
voice of the Lord, but is not willing to obey without
protest (cf. Simon Peter on the house-top at Joppa).
Evidently Saul, at the house of Judas (curious names
to be revived in Saul's experience, Judas and Ananias),
had made no proclamation of the fact that he was now
a follower of Jesus. The news of his mission had apparently come to Damascus ahead of him, and the fact
that he had papers from the chief priests for the binding
of the believers was also known. Ananias knew "how
much evil he did to thy saints at Jerusalem" (Acts 9 : 13).
This is an interesting colloquy where the servant shows
more anxiety for the safety of the saints than the Master
does. It was only after further assurance of the Lord's
purpose concerning Saul (Acts 9 : 15 f.) that Ananias
consented to do his part by Saul.

Saul, indeed, did not know of the reluctance of
Ananias to welcome him to the fold, this wolf suddenly
lying down with the lambs, for he speaks only well of

Ananias (Acts 22 : 12). But Saul himself had been granted a vision of his benefactor coming to him and laying his hands upon him that he might receive his sight again (Acts 9 : 12). Thus again, in a truly unusual way, a welcome was provided for Saul among the Christians of Damascus. If one is disposed to scout the possibility or probability of such care on the part of Jesus in such a matter, let him consider the sure fate of Saul in Damascus if he had come announcing himself a new recruit for the cross! No one would have believed this wolf in sheep's clothing! The disciples knew too well his teeth and claws.

But, once he started, Ananias opened his whole heart. He greeted him as "Brother Saul" (Acts 9 : 17), and explained to him that the same Jesus who had appeared to him had sent him. Thus Saul knew it was true, for he had not told his wondrous experience and yet it was known. Thus, at the very start, Saul's experience of grace in Christ was the open sesame to other Christian hearts. What exact relation existed between the laying on of the hands and the opening of Saul's eyes we may not settle. It was, indeed, a miraculous restoration, and synchronized, not his conversion, which had already occurred, but the bestowal of the Holy Spirit (Acts 9 : 17). It is one of the mysteries of the apostolic history how the bestowal of the Holy Spirit for service, not for salvation, was so often at the hands of men and accompanied by miracles. It does not, of course, follow that we to-day may not be

filled with the Holy Spirit for service save by the ac-
companiment of miracles and at the hands of others.
But it is a point on which later Saul will insist that his
apostleship is wholly independent of that of the Twelve.
They imparted nothing to Saul, he is careful to explain
(Gal. 2 : 6 f.). When he consciously receives his sight,
he looks up joyfully to Ananias who had brought him
this blessing (Acts 22 : 13).

The baptism of Saul, likewise, calls for a few words.
So far as the record indicates, there was no meeting of
the disciples in Damascus, if indeed a church had been
already organized there. It seems to be a meeting
between only Ananias and Saul at the home of Judas.
There would be no difficulty about the baptism, since
the Jews, like other Orientals, had bathing facilities
in the court. But the fact that Saul submitted to the
usual rite without protest shows how normally baptism
followed conversion. The use of "wash away thy
sins," in Acts 22 : 16, in connection with "baptize,"
cannot properly be insisted on as teaching baptismal
salvation, since the Oriental symbolism often put the
symbol to the forefront in descriptions when, as a matter
of fact, the experience preceded the symbol in order of
time. We know, in fact, that this was the case here, for
Saul not only was already converted, but had received
the Holy Spirit before his baptism (Acts 9 : 17 f.).
Saul now took food and was strengthened.

7. *The Call to a World Mission.*—Jesus had told
Saul that he would be told in Damascus what it was

appointed for him to do. He knew full well what he
had given up in choosing Jesus as Lord and Saviour.
He had suffered the loss of all things (cf. Phil. 3 : 4–9).
He gave up all that he held dear, pride of race, family,
creed, position, fame, leadership. These he will come
to count loss for Christ, and he will not complain. He
is indeed a new man in Christ Jesus with a new world
outlook (II Cor. 5 : 17). But Ananias was charged with
a new commission from Jesus, to take the place of the
papers from the Sanhedrin. Jesus had assured Ananias
that Saul of Tarsus, strange as it might seem, was
a "vessel of choice" for him. God goes to strange
places for his agents: to the wilderness for John, to the
despised Nazareth for the Messiah, to the fishermen
and the publicans for the Apostles, to the jail for the
dreamer, to the cobbler's bench for the great missionary, to the priest for a revolutionist against the papacy,
to the ringleader of the Pharisees for the spiritual
emancipator of Jew and Gentile. This quondam leader
of an inquisition is to bear the name of Jesus before Gentiles, kings, and the children of Israel (Acts
9 : 15).

Ananias is able to explain to Saul why Jesus has
called him, how "the God of our fathers hath appointed
thee to know his will, and to see the Righteous One, and
to hear a voice from his mouth. For thou shalt be
a witness unto all men of what thou hast seen and
heard" (Acts 22 : 14 f.). Thus, in few words, that
Saul never forgot, he hears his destiny proclaimed.

As he recites it elsewhere (Acts 26 : 18), he is to open the eyes of the Gentiles, just as his own have been opened, to turn them from darkness to light, that Gentiles as well as Jews may receive remission of sins. He is to be a minister and a witness of what he has seen and of what he will see (26 : 16). His theology and message will therefore be grounded in his own experience. A good part of this experience is yet to come and he will learn as he receives it, "for I will show him how many things he must suffer for my name's sake" (Acts 9 : 16), Jesus said to Ananias. Fortunately for Saul this revelation of his sufferings was not to come all at once. The time will come when his chief ground for glorying will be the sufferings that he undergoes for Christ (II Cor. 11 : 23–33), though he could ultimately glory in other things also. But the point to observe just here is that Saul was not drawn into the service of Christ under a misapprehension of what was before him. He knew what he was to receive in lieu of what he had given up.

One need not insist, indeed, that Saul fully understood the significance of his mission to the Gentiles, nor do we know how largely that aspect of his call bulked in his mind at the time. The work for the Jews was included also. The time will come when, by agreement, there will be a delimitation of the work in a general way (Gal. 2 : 9), though it was never meant to be absolute. It always remained to Paul one of the mysteries of grace how Jesus broke down the middle wall of partition between Jew and Gentile (Eph. 2 : 4–6), and in particular how to him, who was less than the least of all saints, was this grace given to preach unto Gentiles the unsearchable riches of Christ (Eph. 3 : 8). In this world-wide mission he came to find the very joy of work for Christ. He rose to his mission as God led him on.

Saul, therefore, had a commission from Christ as definite and clear as that given to the earlier Christians who likewise received it in their capacity as individual Christians as did Saul. The commission of Jesus to preach the Gospel to the heathen was not merely to the Apostles, but was given to all Christians. Not preachers alone have this obligation, but members of the body of Christ have the burden of sending the Gospel to all the world. This burden was rolled upon Saul at the start.

But more than this is true, though all phases of it do not come out here. Saul is called to be an independent Apostle to the Gentiles. This independence he will later have reason to insist upon when his apostleship itself is challenged by the Judaizers. In Gal. 1 and 2 he makes a formal defence of his apostleship as he does with even more passion in II Cor. 10–13. He will work in harmony with the other Apostles (Acts 15 : 22; Gal. 2 : 6–10), though on occasion he will resist Peter to the face (Gal. 2 : 11–21). It is purely gratuitous for one to say, as does Baring Gould,[1]

[1] "A Study of St. Paul," p. 83.

that Saul did not know till fourteen years after his conversion that he was to go to the Gentiles. Such juggling with the sources is wearisome. Not only was the call to go to the Gentiles clear at first, but it was repeated at Jerusalem (Acts 22 : 21) a few years later. Paul was always distinctly conscious that he had received this definite ministry from Jesus himself (II Cor. 5 : 18 f.; Gal. 1 : 1, 16). Jesus had said through Ananias: "I send thee" (Acts 26 : 17). Though he was not one of the Twelve, he was an Apostle in the real sense. He had seen "Jesus our Lord" (I Cor. 9 : 1). He had received his apostleship directly from Christ (Gal. 1 : 1, 11 f.). Ananias baptized him and conveyed to him the message of Jesus, but he did not get his apostolic authority from Ananias. It was a comfort to Paul that, as a rule, the Gentiles were loyal to him as the Apostle of Christ (I Cor. 9 : 2). He had the seal of his apostleship in the conversion of the Gentiles.

Paul's Epistles are full of expression of his fidelity to the call of Jesus. He tried to heed the voice of Jesus. He felt a woe upon him if he did not preach the gospel of Christ (I Cor. 9 : 16). He felt himself the ambassador of Christ (II Cor. 5 : 20). He never felt that he had succeeded as he could have wished (Phil. 3 : 13), yet it was his constant aim to realize Christ's ideal about him, to "lay hold of that for which also I was laid hold on by Christ Jesus" (verse 12). If his office as Apostle is grounded more in the inter-

nal revelation of Christ in him (Gal. 1 : 12, 16),[1] yet
it was far more than merely internal in its basis. If it
was *pneumatique* and *mystique*, it was also *historique*
and *traditionaliste* (Heinrich Bruders) in one sense only
of traditional, however. But the historic and the spiritual aspects of Saul's mission were always clear to him.
God gave him all the signs of the Apostle (II Cor. 12 : 12)
and in truth as to authority and work he was not one
whit behind the chiefest Apostles (II Cor. 11 : 5). But
he was not merely an official Apostle, he was also and
mainly preacher and teacher of Christ Jesus (I Tim.
2 : 7; II Tim. 1 : 11).

8. *Saul's Immediate Response to His Call.*—We
must remember that Saul is already under the guidance
of the Holy Spirit. The Spirit of Jesus will block his
way (Acts 16 : 7) as well as direct him where to go
(13 : 2 f.). It is not possible to think of the restless
Saul as idle in Damascus. His first experience as a
preacher of Jesus was at Damascus (Acts 26 : 20).
The circumstances were not particularly auspicious.
"And all that heard him were amazed, and said, Is
not this he that in Jerusalem made havoc of them that
called on this name?" (Acts 9 : 21). The Jews themselves would regard Saul as a renegade and a turncoat.
The disciples could not help being suspicious. Was
this a genuine conversion? Would it hold out? Why

---

[1] Neander, "Planting of Christianity," Vol., I., p. 86. Cf. ἐν ἐμοί
also in I Cor. 4 : 11. Thackeray, "Relation of St. Paul to Contemporary Jewish Thought," p. 8, suggests that this may mean
"in my spirit," but "in my case" is probably the true idea.

had he changed his position? What was his motive in it all? They had abundant ground for their amazement.

It was a new experience for Saul. Never was a first sermon a greater cause for embarrassment. No doubt Saul's voice sounded strange to himself as he heard it proclaiming "Jesus, that he is the Son of God" (Acts 9 : 20). That was a new note, one that he had never struck before. He did not know a great deal of Christian theology. He had, indeed, heard Stephen and others preach Jesus. But he keeps close to shore in this first discourse. He preached what he had learned from his own experience. That is the basis of Saul's theology. He was able to identify Jesus with the Son of God. He had grasped at the start the humanity and the deity of Jesus. All the great superstructure of his future teaching will rest on this basis. He knows by experience that Jesus is the Messiah of the Jews (verse 22).

His preaching was powerful at first. He was indeed already a man of education. He did not need to learn how to think nor how to speak. He is a master in speech by training and experience. So long as he confined himself to what he knew about Jesus he was on safe ground. One can well imagine the commotion that his advocacy of Christianity created among both Jews and disciples in Damascus. It would seem as if the Jews made reply to his onset, but were "confounded" as completely as Saul had once been by

Stephen. The resistance to Saul's main position put him on his mettle. He was no longer a mere theological hair-splitter. The days of quibbling had gone forever. He had had a great experience that could never be taken from him. Already he knew him whom he had believed (II Tim. 1 : 12).[1] He would as soon doubt his own existence as doubt that he had seen Jesus. Hence Saul grew in strength by practice in speech. Opposition roused him. He had a new passion that had never before gripped his soul. He could understand better how Stephen had been so masterful and mighty.

The persecution in its organized form had collapsed. It went down with the loss of its head. The church will soon have peace (Acts 9 : 31). Meanwhile Saul himself is the victim of resentful hate on the part of the Jews in Damascus. He has to face the question of going on in spite of their opposition, or returning to Jerusalem, or of retiring to a strange region for a while. There was nothing in Jerusalem to draw him now. Damascus was in a turmoil. It was time for him to take stock of his situation and see exactly how it was with him. Events had moved so rapidly with him. He had taken his stand for Christ. All the world would now know where he stood.

9. *The Apologetic Value of Saul's Conversion.*—If we leave the personal aspects of this great event, we

[1] "His whole theology is nothing but the explication of his own conversion."—Stalker, "Life of St. Paul," p. 45.

still have the effect of the change in Saul on Judaism and on Christianity. As for Judaism, it is not merely the collapse of the persecution that followed. There was much more. The whole situation was at once changed and Judaism was put on the defensive. The time will come when Judaism will rally again and turn on Paul with a vehemence and vengeance that will seem all too familiar to him (Acts 22 : 3–5). But for the present Saul had turned round and was preaching that they should repent and turn to God, doing works worthy of repentance (Acts 26 : 20), a proceeding exactly in line with that of John the Baptist, of Jesus, and of Stephen.

But it is Christianity itself that receives the greatest impact from this reversal in Saul's position. For one thing a new Apostle is gained on a par with the Twelve who will be an independent witness of the resurrection of Christ which is the fundamental proposition of apostolic Christianity. He is not only the most brilliant young Jew of his time, but is thoroughly equipped in Jewish theology and methods of discussion. His Roman citizenship and Hellenistic affiliations in Tarsus made him cosmopolitan in sympathy. He is an Apostle of a new type and will be able to preach Jesus to both Jew and Gentile throughout the Græco-Roman world. It will be small wonder if he becomes the chief personal force in Christianity, next to his Lord and Master.

It is hard to overestimate the apologetic value of

Saul's conversion to modern Christianity. The opponents of Christianity have always perceived that the resurrection of Jesus and Saul's conversion were the two great historical pillars that had to be overthrown. For this purpose every form of attack known to criticism has been resorted to, verbal disagreements, mythological parallels, scientific difficulties. Even the existence of Saul as an historical personage has been denied by the Dutch scholar Van Manen. Baur's admission of the four great Epistles (I Cor., II Cor., Gal., Rom.) left the real problems of Jesus and Paul just where they were before. In these very Epistles he repeatedly and pointedly asserts the fact of the resurrection of Jesus, a matter known to him by personal experience. It was necessary either to overturn these Epistles as genuine works of Paul, to find some other interpretation of his language or some defect in Saul's mental or moral endowment, or to accept Saul's testimony. The attempt has boldly been made to eliminate Paul's Epistles entirely along with the Acts of the Apostles. It is now possible to say positively that this attempt has failed. On the other hand, the majority of modern critics accept as genuine more Epistles of Paul than Baur did. But the acknowledgment of these Epistles as genuine makes it impossible to make a successful onslaught on Saul's integrity of mind or heart. The same moral passion blazes here that was once turned against Jesus. A wonderful mental clearness shines in Paul's writings that paralyzes any at-

tempt to make Saul appear a fool or a weakling. But
to cease to try to find some weakness in Saul's armor
would be to admit his account of his conversion and
the tremendous corollary that goes with it, the resurrection of Jesus and the truthfulness of Christianity.

The battle will never cease to rage around the question of Saul's conversion so long as Christianity has a
voice raised against it. But Saul's judgment about
the resurrection of Jesus was an historical judgment
based on his own experience in seeing Jesus and cannot
be lightly brushed aside as a mere "wonder," as Strauss
does in his "Leben Jesu." One has no right to say
that Saul was out of his body on this occasion as he
was later at Tarsus (II Cor. 12 : 2–5). He did not
tell what he heard at Tarsus. He never ceased telling
what he saw and heard on the road to Damascus.
Holsten's effort to explain Saul's vision of Jesus on
purely naturalistic grounds is not successful.[1] Saul
not only dared everything for the new faith that was
in him, but it is impossible to believe that this high
allegiance was due to an illusion. Of all the men of
his time he shows spiritual sanity and insight. The
very wealth of Paul's view of Jesus gives much trouble
to the merely naturalistic theologian.[2] The direct testimony of Saul to Jesus is not seriously impaired by
the attacks of Steck and Loman. Even Renan[3] calls

[1] "Zum Evangelium des Paulus und Petrus," (1868); "Das
Evangelium des Paulus Dargestellt" (1880).
[2] Weizsäcker, "Das Apostol. Zeitalter," etc., S. 120.
[3] Les Apôtres.

Gal. 1 and 2 "les deux pages les plus importantes pour l'étude du Christianisme naissant," and Pfleiderer[1] compares Paul to Luther in the boldness of his stand for Christ and its great results. Even a sorcerer could see that there was some vital relation between Paul and the Jesus whom he preached (Acts 19 : 13, 15). Saul stood forth in defence of Christ against Jew and Gentile. He stands still a tower of strength, a bulwark that cannot be moved. Saul's career makes it easier for modern men to believe in Jesus of Nazareth. If one thinks that the experience of Paul is so peculiar as to rob it of evidential value, he must remember that Saul was a religious genius of the highest order and just the man to have and to interpret such an experience.[2]

[1] "Urchristenthum," S. 1534.
[2] Sanday, Art. Paul in Hastings' "Dictionary of Christ and the Gospels."

CHAPTER IV

SAUL LEARNING CHRISTIANITY

"That I may know him and the power of his resurrection" (Phil. 3:10).

1. *Saul's Jewish Inheritance.*—This is the striking phrase of a recent German writer.[1] What of his old Judaism did Saul take with him into Christianity? It is a pertinent inquiry and doubtless Saul had a battle over just this matter. He was already a Jewish theologian of a high order of culture. He had formulated or rather followed a definite theological system. He had taken sides on many minor points. He was a partisan theologian, in a word a Pharisee of the type of Gamaliel. He was so fierce a rabbi that he had believed in persecuting those who disputed the tenets of Pharisaism. But we have already noted that he was also familiar with the apocalyptic teaching of the time. He uses in his Epistles later both the rabbinical and the apocalyptic methods of discussion, and naturally so for they were the current methods in vogue among the Jews.[2] But Sanday[3] well observes

[1] Köhler, "Zum Verständnis des Ap. Paulus" (1908), S. 2.

[2] On the place of eschatology and the apocalyptic form in Paul's religious thought, see chapter I in Kennedy's "St. Paul's Conceptions of Last Things." The Jew of the first century A.D. did, indeed, have some alien influences on him. He had passed through Egyptian, Babylonian, Persian, Greek rule. It would have been a marvel if no trace of that fact were apparent.

[3] Art. Paul, in Hastings' "D. C. G."

that Paul rose above these methods very largely and saw spiritual realities. In particular is this noticeable in his use of the Old Testament. With the average rabbi the comment on the Old Testament was more important than the Scripture itself. But this was not true of Paul. He knew the Old Testament and he will come to get at the heart of the Scriptures even though his method will at times be rabbinical or apocalyptic. But the right result is far more important than the mere method of argument. There was much in this body of Jewish theology that Saul did not have to surrender. The great spiritual realities about God and man remained the same. In the matters of dispute between Pharisees and Sadducees Saul remained a Pharisee, and on occasion could say so (Acts 23 : 6), especially on the point of the resurrection.

But one must not go to the extreme of finding in Saul's Pharisaism the roots of all his Christian theology. Pfleiderer[1] even traces Paul's doctrine of justification by faith to his Pharisaic notions! One could hardly go further astray, for the rest of Paul's life will be spent in the endeavor to show how hollow is the Pharisaic legal observance and how rich and vital is the grace of Christ in the heart (Rom. 9 : 31). Paul will indeed prove that Christianity is the real Judaism, the spiritual Israel, the true Israel (Rom. 2 : 28 f.), but he will have to learn how this is true. This interpretation is the very antithesis of that spirit

[1] "Paulinismus," S. 12.

which was satisfied merely with being the children of
Abraham.

The Judaism of Saul was not that of John the
Baptist nor of Jesus. It was not that of Philo. It
was really Palestinian traditionalism with some outside influences which tempered it and modernized it
to some extent. But his Judaism was hard enough to
amalgamate with Christianity. One has only to consider the struggle that Peter had towards the spiritual
and universal aspects of Christianity to sympathize
with Saul's limitations on this point. "He was changed
from an anti-Christian Jew to an anti-Jewish Christian."[1] This is rather an overstatement, for he loved
the Jews still, but he did oppose the current orthodoxy
of the Pharisees and of the Judaizers.

We know quite well what the Pharisaic notion of the
Messiah was. It is clear in the background of the Gospels as well as in such books as the Psalms of Solomon.
It is not necessary to draw that picture here in detail.
It is enough to say that while it had eschatological
features in some respects like that drawn by John the
Baptist and Jesus himself, at bottom it was widely
different. It concerned itself mainly with the temporal
side of life and the Pharisaic hope centred in a deliverer from the Roman yoke who would impose
Pharisaic ceremonialism upon the whole world. There
was terrific opposition on the part of the Pharisees

[1] Means, "St. Paul and the Ante-Nicene Church," p. 6. Cf.
Hilgenfeld, "Zeitschrift für Wiss. Theol.," B. XVIII., S. 162.

to the programme of Jesus in his teaching of a merely
spiritual Messiah who would reign in the hearts of men,
and in particular when that conception was embodied
in Jesus himself who had collided with the Pharisees
on various items of their theology, such as the Sabbath,
washing of hands, fasting, etc. Saul inherited this
antipathy to Jesus as the Messiah and was more
vindictive about it than any other Pharisee.

And yet God chose a Pharisee,[1] but a Pharisee who
had already learned the emptiness of mere legal cere-
mony and who could interpret that hollowness with
consummate skill after he had learned more completely
the difference between the letter and the spirit. He
was an expert in religiosity. He was to learn the heart
of religion.

Saul was already a theologian. He brought the
theologian's love of order and analysis with him. He
differs in the theological type of mind not only from
Jesus, but also from the other Apostles and New Testament writers. He will naturally become the first
Christian theologian.[2] Matthew Arnold[3] perceives Paul's
Judaism so clearly that he considers it impossible to
tell what he really meant in his Epistles. This is an
overstatement surely. He did have the "thought-
forms" of his time as every one has, but the kernel is
not hard to get out of the hull.

[1] Sabatier, "The Apostle Paul," p. 69.
[2] Means, "St. Paul and the Ante-Nicene Church," p. 3.
[3] "St. Paul and Protestantism," p. 23.

As already indicated, Saul was able to bring over the heart of Judaism to his Christianity. His Christianity will be rooted in his Judaism. In this he will not differ from Jesus, his new Master, who in the Sermon on the Mount carefully explains how his teaching seized the spirit of the Old Testament and realized that ideal while it was in opposition to some of the current interpretations and additions. Saul, though he has undergone a revolution in his whole mental make-up, never felt that he had deserted the true Judaism of Abraham, Moses, David, Isaiah. He longed to lead all Jews into the full fruition of their hopes. But the apprehension of this point of view lies in the future with Saul. He will admit that Jesus himself was born under the law.[1]

2. *Saul's Greek Inheritance.*—Did Saul have affinities with the Hellenism of his time? The question is hotly debated and has already been alluded to in this book. Sabatier,[2] for instance, says pointedly that "to seek the origin of Paul's Christian universalism in his Hellenism is, therefore, manifestly an entire mistake." Pfleiderer[3] even charges that Paul has "rabbinized" Christ and hence has obscured Jesus instead of revealing him. On the other hand, Rabbi Köhler[4] asserts that Paul was a Hellenist and no real

---

[1] Hilgenfeld, "Zeitschrift für Wiss. Th." (1894), S. 510.

[2] "The Apostle Paul," p. 69.

[3] "Influence of Paul on the Development of Christianity" (1885).

[4] Article Saul of Tarsus, "Jewish Encycl." So Fraedlaender, "Reliog. Beweg" ('05), rather overdoes the Hellenistic side of Paul.

Jew like Jesus! Paul, indeed, changed the whole character and course of Christianity, for Jesus had no notion of a break with Judaism. "Paul fashioned a Christ of his own, a Church of his own, and a system of belief of his own; and because there were many mythological and gnostic elements in his theology which appealed more to the non-Jew than to the Jew, he won the heathen world to his belief." The truth is between these two extremes.

As a Hellenistic Jew of Tarsus, Saul had been open to the best things in Greek culture without any forfeiture of his Pharisaic loyalty.[1] There has, indeed, been no such blending of Judaism and Hellenism as we find in Philo of Alexandria, nor indeed later in the Grecized Christianity of Clement of Alexandria. Ramsay[2] has shown us the right way in this matter when he asserts that it was a universalized Hellenism and a universalized Judaism that coalesced in the mind of Paul. He stoutly objects to Harnack's view that Paul's mind was wholly Jewish. He was mainly so beyond a doubt. Kennedy[3] well shows Paul's knowledge of the Greek ideas of flesh and spirit, not to say other psychological terms. Many arguments go to show the possibility of Paul's acquaintance with the Book of the Wisdom of Solomon, which had undoubted influence from the Greek philosophy.[4] The similarity

[1] Hicks, "St. Paul and Hellenism," Vol. IV., in "Studia Bibl. et Eccl."   [2] "The Cities of St. Paul," p. 43.
[3] "St. Paul's Conceptions of Last Things," p. 343 ff.
[4] Cf. Menzel, "Der Griech. Einfluss auf Prediger und Weisheit Salomos" (1889).

in idea and phraseology between Paul and Seneca has
often received discussion as by Lightfoot, in his "Commentary on Philippians." The real explanation is
probably due to the fact that both Paul and Seneca
drank from the same fountain of Greek philosophy.[1]
If Gamaliel, for diplomatic purposes, could read
Greek writers, his pupil could easily follow suit. One
need only mention further Paul's use of "knowledge"
and "wisdom" to see a real Greek influence. There
is, besides, a Greek clarity of mental vision which at
times reminds one of Plato.[2] If one wonders how a
Pharisee could ever have any contact with Greek
culture after the days of Antiochus Epiphanes, he may
recall two things. One is that the Maccabees themselves came to be called Philhellenes (cf. Aristobulus)
after the breach with the Pharisees. The other is that
Saul had lived in Tarsus, not Jerusalem. If God
called a Pharisee, he also called one who could speak
on Mars Hill and to the Greek world of his time.
Modern life is chiefly a blend of the Jewish contribution
to religion, the Greek contribution to culture, and the
Roman contribution to government. All these streams
had already met in Saul.

I do not enter into the discussion of Saul's contact
with the Babylonian and Persian mythology and

---

[1] Ramsay, "Cities of St. Paul," p. 34. Cf. also Fraedlaender,
"Der religiösen Bewegungen innerhalb des Judentums," etc.,
V., "Die Botschaft des Paulus."
[2] Cf. Köhler, "Zum Verständnis des Apostels Paulus," S. 9–13,
for a brief discussion of Paul's Greek inheritance.

mysticism. The Oriental cults all had a foothold in
Tarsus. The religion of Tarsus was a blend between
the Anatolian and Greek ideas,[1] but one cannot think
that Saul received any positive impress therefrom. In
his later years he will be all alert to preserve Christianity from the blight of incipient gnosticism, as is apparent
in Colossians, Ephesians and the Pastoral Epistles. But
we do not know that as yet Saul had come in contact with
this cult. Paul shows some knowledge of Roman law as
used in the Græco-Roman world in his use of the term
"adoption" (Rom. 8:15). "To the Jewish student and
the Greek cosmopolitan Paul there was added *the Roman gentleman*" (Findlay, Paul, in Hastings' "D. B.")

3. *The Original Christian Inheritance of Saul.*—
Here again I use a phrase of Köhler.[2] What had Saul
added to his Judaism and Hellenism in lieu of what
he had given up? We must not put into this conception
what Saul later learned of Jesus either by experience,
revelation or from other Christians. His entire
system of doctrine "simply means the exposition of the
content of his conversion, the systematizing of the
Christophany."[3] But the "system of doctrine" is in
the future, when we see him in Damascus. We do
not indeed know how much he really knew of the
message of Jesus to men. If, as a boy, he had heard
Jesus preach in the temple at Jerusalem, he gained

[1] Ramsay, "Cities of St. Paul," p. 137 ff., discusses the religion
of Tarsus.
[2] "Zum Verständnis des Ap. Paulus," S. 13.
[3] Holtzmann, "N. T. Theologie," Vol. II., S. 205.

little from that experience. If he heard Stephen in
the Cilician synagogue, he would by that time be able
to get a better idea of the Christian contention. One
can hardly imagine that he parleyed much with the
disciples whom he persecuted. But before the Sanhedrin, if they were all as skilful as Peter is reported in
the Acts (chs. 2–5) to be, they may have managed to get
in the heart of their belief about Jesus. Saul had seen
it all with eyes of prejudice and hate. How much of
that can he now recall as he seeks to readjust himself
to the new situation? A reinterpretation[1] and restate-
ment of what he already knew of Jesus was necessary
in the light of the profound spiritual experience of his
conversion. He "taught what he had first felt, and
he verified his teaching by experience."[2] He was not
an immediate disciple of Jesus, and so came to the interpretation of Jesus from the point of view of Luke rather
than that of John. He has seen the preëxistent
Christ as well as the historical Jesus, and both conceptions will remain with him.[3] In this picture of
Christ he has a standard by which to test all his future
thinking.[4] He is lifted into a mystic union with Christ
which will glow and warm his soul into intense intellectual activity.[5] "He stands almost by himself in

[1] Cf. Means, "St. Paul and the Ante-Nicene Church," p. 57.
[2] Sanday, Paul in Hastings' "D. C. G."
[3] Drescher, "Das Leben Jesu bei Paulus," S. 107. Cf. Stade's
"Festgruss," 1900.
[4] Titius, "Der Paulinismus," etc., S. 11.
[5] Aquelhon, "L'Homme Psychique d'après Saint Paul,"
1898, p. 63.

his manifestation of intellectual activity."[1] Whatever else Saul did or did not know about Jesus, he
knew the main thing at the very start of his Christian
career. Christ is henceforth to him the "Kern und
Stern" of his religious thinking and life.[2] It is a
wonderful thing to have a great experience of grace.
This was the true genesis of Saul's Gospel, the revelation of Christ in him (Gal. 1 : 16).[3] One has no right
to expect a fully developed creed a few days after
one's conversion. We shall soon see in Paul's sermons
as reported by Luke in Acts how clearly he apprehended
both the historical Jesus in the main outlines of his life
and the significance of Christ's life and death. For
the moment he is almost intoxicated with the glory of
the vision of Jesus. He can already see in the light of
the call to be the Apostle to the Gentiles the trend of
his theology. We need not credit him yet with full
knowledge of all that was to come. Some day he will
be "the Apostle $\kappa\alpha\tau'\dot{\epsilon}\xi o\chi\dot{\eta}\nu$, the disciple who raised the
Messianic faith, hitherto but the creed of a Jewish
sect, to the position of a world religion."[4] But the
revolution in Saul's theology has come. Hence it is
now merely readjustment and interpretation.

4. *The Years in Arabia.*—Luke passes by this part
of Saul's life. It is probably to be inserted between
verses 22 and 23 in Acts 9. Paul himself is not re-

[1] Means, "St. Paul and the Ante-Nicene Church," p. 2.
[2] Sturm, "Der Apostel Paulus," etc., S. 5.
[3] Sabatier, "The Apostle Paul," p. 71.
[4] Juelicher, "Introduction to the N. T.," p. 45.

ported as mentioning it in Acts 22 and 26. But for
Gal. 1 : 17 f. we should know nothing at all of these
"three years" or less in Arabia, a lesson for those who
draw large inferences from silence. The "three years"
include also a second stay in Damascus on his return
from Arabia. They need not be strictly full years, since
the first and third years may only have been parts
of years. We may conclude, however, that something
over twelve months at any rate was spent in Arabia
on Saul's sudden departure from Damascus.

We do not know what part of Arabia is meant,
since the term was very flexible then as now and
varied at different periods. He may, indeed, have
gone as far south as Mount Sinai, though one cannot
logically argue so from the mention of Mount Sinai in
Gal. 4 : 24. There might be an appropriateness in
the presence at Sinai, full of memories of Moses and
the law, of one who was to present grace and faith as
the message of the covenant antedating the law and
realized in Christ (Gal. 3 : 17). But that is idle conjecture.

We are left in ignorance, besides, both as to Saul's
motive for going to Arabia and his work there in the
meantime. He does tell one thing in Gal. 1 : 16:
"Straightway I conferred not with flesh and blood."
He did not wish to talk with men now, but with God.
One can sympathize with a desire at such a time to
get away from the stress and storm of Damascus.
He would at least be in new scenes and among strangers.

He could find desert places also in Arabia if he wished it, like John the Baptist and Moses long before. It is more than likely that he did for a while seek solitude for meditation and reflection. Jesus himself after his baptism spent forty days in the wilderness. Saul needed some time to see clearly his bearings, to commune with God, to grasp more adequately the significance of this whirlwind in his life. This much seems certain. Whether in addition Saul also labored for Christ in various parts of Arabia one cannot tell. If he did, as he himself says he labored later in Tarsus (Gal. 1 : 21, 23), we may conclude that he did missionary work in Arabia also.

5. *In Damascus Again.*—Here Luke goes on with the story (Acts 9 : 23-25). One is reminded of a similar probable combination of the narrative in Acts 15 and Gal. 2 concerning a visit of Paul to Jerusalem. If this arrangement of the story is correct, Paul spent "many days" in Damascus with the result of a plot on the part of the Jews to kill him. This would have come at once if he had not gone to Arabia. But the anger of the Jews toward the "turncoat" has not ceased. Saul now knows how it feels to be persecuted. He has his first experience in the very city where he had expected to make a finish of the business of persecuting the disciples. A very homely saying comes to one's mind at this point. We have a proverb about chickens coming home to roost. It is only poetic justice after all.

It was a delicate situation for Saul, when he learned of the plot. He could, of course, meet his fate like a man and a Christian as Stephen and others had done before him. He did not lack courage. But was it wise to sit still and be killed? It is a wise man who knows when to run and when to fight. On the whole Saul decided on flight. But the gates were watched day and night and flight was not easy. Saul now had friends who devised a plan of escape. His enemies had even stirred "the governor under Aretas the King" of Arabia against Saul (II Cor. 11 : 32). He had known himself how to get authority for his vengeance. It was not very glorious, but they let him down one night through a window in the wall in a basket! He did not tarry, one may be sure. Thus Saul left Damascus for good, he who had come not over three years ago with blast of trumpets and papers from the Sanhedrin. Where can he go now?

6. *Saul in Jerusalem.*—He could not be treated any worse in Jerusalem than he had been in Damascus Besides he must go to Jerusalem some day if he was not to be a sort of pariah in the ministry. The Apostles were there, and many other disciples had come flocking back to Jerusalem after the wolf ceased ravaging the fold. To Jerusalem then he will go.

But he feels no need of receiving the *imprimatur* of Peter or of any of the other Apostles. He is clear about his own call at the hands of Jesus himself. He has been baptized. He has received the special gift of the

Holy Spirit with the laying on of hands. Still, while he did not need or desire any apostolic ordination at the hands of those who had been Apostles before him (Gal. 1 : 17), he did owe a courtesy to those noble men chosen also by Jesus himself to push on the work of the Kingdom. He was free from jealousy. He wished to coöperate with them.

It would be pleasant to relieve their minds of any uncertainty about him that might linger. In particular he would like to pay his respects to Cephas, the leading spirit among them. What thoughts must have filled his mind as he retraced his steps to Jerusalem? Did he go back over the same road by which he had come three years before? If so, he passed the very spot, the never-to-be-forgotten spot, where he had seen Jesus face to face. That was henceforth his holy place.

Once in Jerusalem one can well imagine that he would be shy of approaching or seeing his old associates. The scorn of Gamaliel would be terrible to face. Still harder to bear would be the sneers of the lesser men who had once looked up to Saul as leader and hero. There was only one thing to do. He must go right to the disciples themselves and tell his story to them. Would they believe him? Did he first attend a public meeting of the disciples? If so, he noticed a peculiar dread of him. There was suspicion in the very atmosphere. "They were afraid of him, not believing that he was a disciple" (Acts 9 : 26). Could one well blame them? True, he now said that he was a fol-

lower of Jesus and he had taken a stand for Christ-
at Damascus, so a few reported. But all men knew
what he had done to believers right here in Jerusalem.
Can the leopard change his spots?

Barnabas was apparently at the meeting. Barnabas
was from the island of Cyprus and so a Hellenist.
He was somehow convinced of the sincerity of Saul's
conversion, though no one else was. It is a heroic
thing to take a stand by an unpopular man. Barnabas
championed the cause of Saul, and became the one
friend that Saul now had in Jerusalem, where once his
word was almost law. Barnabas took him straight
to the Apostles who were in town (Acts 9 : 27). As
a matter of fact, Paul himself declares that he saw only
Cephas and James, the Lord's brother, who was not
an Apostle in the technical sense (Gal. 1 : 18 f.). Now
that the persecution had ceased, the rest had probably
gone on mission work among the Jews in various parts
of the world. Barnabas tells these two the essential
parts of Saul's story, viz., his vision of Jesus in the
way, the message of Jesus to Saul or his call, the bold
preaching of Saul in Damascus (Acts 9 : 27). It was
enough. He had come primarily to visit (become ac-
quainted with, ἱστορῆσαι, Gal. 1 : 18) Cephas. Now
for fifteen days he had that privilege. He went in and
out freely with Peter, James, and other disciples. It
is pleasant to think of Peter and Paul here together
for two weeks in Jerusalem. Paul would naturally
be the learner and let Peter tell the history of Jesus

in particular as it was connected with Jerusalem.
There was Bethany; here was the road of the Triumphant Entry, down there was Gethsemane, where Peter
went to sleep; here Jesus was arrested; at this place the
trial took place and just here Peter had denied him;
and on yonder hill they crucified him; and in that
tomb they buried him; lo! here was the spot where
Jesus had appeared to Peter after his resurrection;
in this upper room he had appeared to the disciples
twice; up here on Olivet was the place where they had
caught the last glimpse of him as he went up on the
cloud. And Saul had seen him since then. These
great spirits held high converse with each other about
Jesus. Each was the richer for the visit of Saul.
Saul now had in simple outline at least the original
apostolic gospel. He knew the leading facts, the
cardinal events, in the earthly life of Jesus. He had
heard Peter preach in all likelihood during this time.
That was worth much.

And Saul had to preach himself. How could he help
it after all these new experiences? The people wished
now to hear him. Once he had opposed Stephen
(so it seems) in the Cilician synagogue. He will go
to this very synagogue and seek to undo some of the
mischief that he had then done. He will set himself
straight with the Grecian Jews for he is one himself,
and they are more open to new truth than the Palestinian Jews. Stephen had once had great power with
these Hellenists, but, alas! Saul had taught them how

to kill Stephen and other believers. They will not hear Saul's new doctrine. They will turn his old doctrine of persecution on himself. Damascus had cast him out and now Jerusalem will not hear him. What should he do? He can pray. So in a prayer in the temple he falls into a trance, and, lo! he sees Jesus again at his side. Jesus bade him leave. He can only acquiesce for he recalls how in every synagogue he had beaten those who believed in Jesus. They will now hear him in no synagogue. "Depart," says Jesus, "for I will send thee forth far hence unto the Gentiles" (Acts 22 : 21). They will hear. The brethren escort him hurriedly out of town before the plot is carried out. The way looks dark for Saul. Gone his power, his place, his friends, his fame, an outcast from Jerusalem! Whither shall he now go? In Acts 26 : 20 he speaks of preaching throughout all the country of Judea. This may have been on his way to Jerusalem, for now they sent him on to Tarsus (Acts 9 : 30).

7. *Back in Tarsus Again.*—A man can always go home. That is one good thing. It had probably been a long time since Saul had been to Tarsus, not since the death of Stephen, several years ago. There had been changes in the city, of course. Some people had died, but probably Saul's father and mother were still living, loyal Pharisees as of old. How had they regarded Saul's change of base? They must have heard if he had not himself written about it. as is likely. He was fond of writing letters, as we know, and it was

easy to have communication over the world, thanks to
the Roman order. But even so he had not seen them
since he had gone over to the side of Jesus. They had
taken pride in his prominence as a leader of the Pharisees. And now? He knew full well what the name
of Jesus had meant to them. What can he say? Let
us hope that he received a welcome. He was still their
son with all his gifts and graces. He was sincere and
honest. His father and mother knew that. He had
tried to do right as he saw it. Let us hope that they
heard his story and that they were led to the service of
Jesus. That would atone for his treatment in Damascus and Jerusalem.

We only know one thing for certain. He was not
idle during these years at Tarsus. He tells us himself
that he preached in the regions of Cilicia and Syria and
that the churches of Judea, to whom he was unknown
by face (save in Jerusalem), heard of his activity and
glorified God in him (Gal. 1 : 21–24). Saul found
pleasure in that. He was busy with his work of preaching Christ in the regions near Tarsus. Christ had
called him to go far hence to the Gentiles. Meanwhile there was work at home. In truth he was among
the Gentiles already. Did he preach to them? The
man who will not work for the lost at home will do
little for Christ abroad.

We are to think then of Saul as working and learning. He is learning by doing. He continued to have
unusual experiences. Christ did not desert him. In-

deed, during this period (he only speaks of it fourteen years afterwards, II Cor. 12 : 2) he had a wonderful rapture to Paradise in the body or out of the body, he cannot tell. He heard unspeakable words, and they will remain unuttered by him—unlike "special" secrets with many. The revelations were so great, indeed, that he was in danger of being exalted overmuch. But Jesus blessed him in giving him a thorn in the flesh. He had prayed to him for its removal, but instead he obtained grace to bear it, which was better (II Cor. 12 : 9). One cannot, of course, tell the nature of this experience. It was a supernatural revelation of Christ's glory. Nor do we know the precise nature of the thorn in his flesh. There is special consolation in our ignorance, for each can make a personal application. He comes out of the Tarsus period of his ministry, however, richer in experience than when he entered it. He is a stronger man and minister from every point of view. He has a "handicap" in the thorn in the flesh that apparently remained with him to the end. But he learned lessons of wisdom out of that.

8. *Saul as an Interpreter of Jesus.*—It is just here that Saul commands so much attention in modern times. His mission as Apostle to the Gentiles does concern us greatly also since we are in large measure the heirs of his European labors. He planted Christianity in the Roman Empire, and modern Europe has risen out of the ruins of that empire. But, important as the

official aspect of Paul's career is, it is in his claims as a
competent interpreter of the life and teachings of Jesus
that he stands or falls in the present day. The cry
"Back to Christ" is a reasonable cry, when one considers the dust of mediæval theology that has been
scattered over the story of Christ. Ecclesiastical
councils turned dogma into a club to use on the heads
of the recalcitrant. The schoolmen split hairs, like
their prototypes the Pharisees of old, to justify or to
evade the current dogma. The reformers set up new
dogma to crush the dogma of the schoolmen. The
hunger for Christ has become world-wide. Men could
see Calvin; but where was Christ? Men could find
Augustine; but where was Jesus?

It was not hard to find Paul in the New Testament;
but where was the historical Jesus? Has Paul given
us the real Jesus of the Gospels? Indeed, have the
Gospels represented or misrepresented Christ? Do
we have in the New Testament the Christ of dogma
or the Christ of fact? One cannot complain at questions like these. They are legitimate, if only the investigation be prosecuted in the right spirit and with proper
methods. The question as to the Gospel story demands a book in itself, but one may remark that the
gradual coming back of Harnack to the acceptance of
the genuineness of Acts is a symptom of the times.
The acceptance of the early date of the Gospels and
the probable order (Mark, Matthew, Luke, John)
simplifies the matter also. Two other documents are

fairly well worked out, one the Logia or Sayings of
Jesus, probably used by Matthew along with Mark.
Ramsay[1] accepts, in the main, Harnack's view in Sayings and Speeches of Jesus that this book of Logia or
"Q" corresponds to the original Aramaic Matthew.
The point of it all is that the result of historical research is to strengthen the historical basis of the Gospel
narratives.   John's story stands largely by itself, but it
stands.   From the Gospels we can form an adequate
picture of Jesus.

What about Paul?   Wrede[2] makes Paul's teaching
differ radically from that of Jesus.   He considers that
Paul brought his preconceived ideas of the Jewish
Messiah and clothed Jesus with them.   Thus the Jesus
of fact is not the Jesus of Paul's theology.   Indeed,
according to this view we must discard Paul as a competent witness in the apprehension of the historical
Jesus.   This is a serious charge to make.   But Wrede
is not by himself.   He is supported by Brückner.[3]
Nietsche, of course, ridicules both Paul and Jesus.
And Wellhausen[4] has to be reckoned with.   But Paul
has defenders of great ability.   Kaftan[5] answers
Bousset's notion[6] of Jesus that he unwillingly accepted
the rôle of Messiah.   He attacks vigorously Wrede's
views about Paul's perversion of Jesus.   Jülicher[7]
has a very able defence of the essential continuity of the

[1] "Luke the Physician," pp. 71–101.   [2] "Paulus."
[3] "Die Entstehung der paulinischen Christologie.
[4] "Einleitung in die drei ersten Ev.," S.
[5] "Jesus und Paulus."   [6] Jesus.   [7] "Paulus und Jesus."

Gospel and the Pauline conception of Jesus. Indeed, so clearly is this true that some critics even assert that all the New Testament is Pauline except the Petrine[1] books. If one rejects the Pauline view of Christ he must logically reject the Synoptic and the Johannine conceptions. At bottom they agree.[2] Kölbing[3] ably contends for the justness of Paul's picture of Christ. The discussion grows in interest[4] and Paul's position as a great exponent of Jesus is ably maintained.

Fraedlaender[5] sums the matter up by calling him "the congenial interpreter of the message of Jesus." Goguel[6] properly argues that with Jesus the concrete reality of the gospel is dominant, but Paul aims to interpret the facts of Christ's life and teachings. Saul did not invent a story of Jesus. He is not the originator of Christianity in any sense. He is not the second

---

[1] Sanday, Art. Paul in Hastings' "D. C. G."

[2] Cf. Warfield, "The Lord of Glory."

[3] "Die Geistige Einwirkung der Person Jesu und Paulus."

[4] Cf. Schaeder, "Das Evangelium Jesu und das Ev. von Jesus"; Resch, "Der Paulinismus und die Logia Jesu"; Goguel, "L'Apôtre Paul et Jésus"; Ruegg, "Der Apostel Paulus und sein zeugnis von Jesus Christus"; A. Meyer, "Wer hat das Christentum begründet, Jesus oder Paulus?" Feine, "Jesus Christus und Paulus"; Monteil, "Essai sur la Christologie de Saint Paul"; Moffatt, *Review of Theology and Philosophy* for July, 1908, and *Biblical World* for September, 1908; Knowling, "Testimony of St. Paul to Christ"; Knowling, "Witness of the Epistles." These will serve as specimens of the increasing literature on the subject. For further lists see *Theol. Rundschau* for 1902, 1905, etc.; *Amer. Journal of Theol.* for 1905, etc.; the "Brief Bibliography" in this book.

[5] "Religiösen Beweg.," S. 373.

[6] "L'Apôtre Paul et Jésus," pp. 98 f.

founder of Christianity. He built on the one foundation laid by Christ himself (I Cor 3 : 11). Paul built his theology around Jesus. This fact explains the genetic connection between Jesus and Saul. The differences in Saul's view are due to fuller expansion and adaptation with his own peculiarities of mind and method, (cf. James, Peter, John) not to difference in spirit or content.

But Saul was not an immediate disciple of Jesus. That is true. He is not, however, disqualified for apprehending Christ. If so, the mission of Christ would be a failure. No one has the right to say that Saul had no knowledge of the historical Jesus. If Luke could learn, so could Saul. Sanday [1] rightly argues that the allusions in Paul's Epistles (cf. I Cor. 11 : 23–25; 15 : 3–8) must be regarded as samples of Paul's knowledge of the details of the life of Jesus. He appeals to the words of Jesus; he understands the character of Jesus; he knows what the message and mission of Christ is.

One is not to suppose that Saul's theology did not grow with new knowledge and new experience. The orderly development of his theology can be traced in the four groups of his Epistles (I and II Thessalonians; I and II Corinthians, Galatians, Romans; Philippians, Philemon, Colossians, Ephesians; I Timothy, Titus, II Timothy), to adopt a probable grouping. In the first group he will contend with a perversion of the doctrines of the Second Coming, a matter prominent

[1] Art. Paul in Hastings' "D. C. G."

in the early apostolic preaching. In the second group he is in conflict with the Judaizers. In the third group the Gnostics have brought the person of Christ to the fore. In the fourth group ecclesiastical, pastoral and personal problems naturally concern the aged Apostle before his death. Each group suits the time and is vital with living issues. There is growth in grasp and power from the first to the second and third groups. In the fourth we see Paul in the contemplative mood of an old man. One is not to think of Saul as entering upon his career with a fully developed system. Indeed he had turned from a system to a person![1] He will inevitably have system in his theology, but only as that enables him to express his growing apprehension of Christ.

The death and resurrection of Christ is with Paul the heart of Christianity as it was in truth with Jesus himself when rightly understood. Saul, indeed, began with this basal truth vivified and glorified by his own great experience. His early preaching coincided with that of the other Apostles in proclaiming the Messiahship of Jesus.[2] The crucifixion of Christ had been the stone of stumbling for Saul. Now it is the rock of his faith. In the future Paul will go high and go deep, but he will never get away from the Cross as the centre of his message. Around this he will place the love of God, the grace of God, the deity of Jesus the Son of God, the sinfulness of man, justification by faith,

[1] Baring-Gould, "A Study of St. Paul," p. 89.
[2] Matheson, "Spiritual Development of St. Paul," p. 28.

sanctification in Christ, all the great doctrines of grace. They were all but the unfolding of the seed. He had seen the face of Christ.

The effort of Baur to pit Paul and Peter over against each other in bitter hostility has failed. He has admitted too much. One has only to compare the report of Peter's Sermoh in Acts 2 at Jerusalem with that of Paul at Antioch in Pisidia in Acts 13 to see how much they agree in all essential matters. If one is not willing to trust Luke as an accurate reporter, then compare I Peter with Romans. If one declines to acknowledge I Peter as a proper representation of Peter's views, then he has no right to set Peter over against Paul. In Gal. 2 : 11 ff. Paul did rebuke Peter for inconsistency, not for difference in theology. They had already agreed in their theology and shaken hands over it (Gal. 2 : 9). We need not refer to Acts 15 and II Peter 3 : 15. The Christ of Paul in all the main outlines is the Christ of the early apostolic tradition, of Mark, of Matthew, of Luke, of Peter, of James, of John, in a word, of Jesus himself as we know him through the first interpreters of Christ. Primitive Paulinism is essential Christianity. Paul's Gospel has become the standard of the Christian world because he had learned Christ as he really was and is, "even as truth is in Jesus" (Eph. 4 : 21). We may thank God for this man of a nature so intense and an insight so penetrating. Christ has never had another servant who so well conveyed the fulness and richness of that Gospel of the happy God which is the hope of the race unless John the Apostle be placed by his side, as he ought. One can feel the heart-throb of Paul in his letters and the rapier sharpness of his intellect, the passion of a great soul all ablaze with love of Jesus and the lost.

But no view of Paul's relation to Christ is adequate which overlooks the mystical side of his life in Christ. Christ lived in Paul and Paul lived in Christ (Gal. 2 : 20). For him life meant Christ (Phil. 1 : 21), no more, no less. He was Christ's slave. He did all "in Christ."[1] This intimate knowledge of Christ was part of the everyday experience of Paul. But he claimed for his message special revelation also. "When ye read, ye can perceive my understanding in the mystery in Christ" (Eph. 3 : 4). We can indeed. We are still reading and perceiving new things in that understanding.

[1] Cf. Campbell, "Paul the Mystic"; Deissmann, "Die Neut. Formel" "in Christo."

CHAPTER V

SAUL FINDS HIS WORK

"To preach unto the Gentiles the unsearchable riches of Christ" (Eph. 3 : 8).

1. *The Emergency at Antioch.*—Luke, in the Acts, has not traced the order of events in such a way as to make it perfectly clear how things went at this stage of the history. He left Saul at Tarsus and comes back to Jerusalem. Now the story of Peter is taken up. Did Saul preach to Gentiles in Cilicia and Syria? We do not know. He had been expressly directed to preach to the Gentiles. At any rate Luke tells in some detail the struggle that Simon Peter had in seeing that the Gentiles could be converted without first becoming Jews. Peter, like the other disciples, received the commission to go into all the world. But he did not at all understand that Gentiles must not first become Jews. It is an extremely interesting story how he was led gradually and with difficulty by his experience on the housetop at Joppa and in the house of Cornelius at Cæsarea, to see that God was indeed no respecter of persons and would save a Gentile *as a Gentile*. That was the new point which he "now" at last perceived (Acts 10 : 34). He had a hard time

convincing some of the saints at Jerusalem that his freedom with Cornelius was the work of the Lord. It was well that he had the six Jewish brethren along with him else it might have gone hard with him (Acts 11 : 2 f., 12, 18). Evidently the mass of the Church at Jerusalem were not ready for a missionary campaign except along lines of Jewish proselytism.

But the hand of God was moving again. Some of the disciples expelled from Jerusalem by Saul never came back. They went as far as Cyprus, Phœnicia and Antioch, but still spoke only to Jews, not willing to experiment with the Gospel unduly (Acts 11 : 19). But some of them were men of Cyprus and Cyrene, Hellenistic Christians, therefore. These, for some reason not told, ventured to try the Gospel on some Greeks at Antioch (11 : 20), perhaps to some devout Greeks, not yet proselytes, who had business and friendly connections with the Jews. Some of them, we know, attended the synagogue worship. The mss. vary about the word "Greeks" or "Grecian Jews," but I heartily concur in the acceptance of "Greeks" as the correct text. Otherwise the word "also" has little sense. It was no novelty to preach to Hellenistic Jews. That was going on everywhere and at Jerusalem itself (Acts 9 : 29). The same message of the Lord Jesus was preached to these Greeks that the Jews had heard. "And the hand of the Lord was with them: and a great number that believed turned unto the Lord" (11 : 21). This Gentile revival broke out of itself and without any knowledge of what God had done with Peter and Cornelius. These men of Cyprus and Cyrene were men of enlightenment. They seemed to realize no difficulty at all in the new situation. They had no desire to oppose the manifest work of the Holy Spirit.

2. *A Gentile Church at Antioch.*—A new thing had come into existence, unless, indeed, the household of Cornelius was organized into a church or the converts at Samaria had formed a church. At any rate, whether a new thing or not, the Gentile church at Antioch was a fact. It was all the more remarkable, too, because the Apostles had had nothing to do with it. They had sent Peter and John to Samaria to examine the results of the work of Philip there, and Peter himself had been the instrument used of God at Cæsarea. But here was a work that had sprung up independently and the brethren felt no need of help from Jerusalem. Slowly the leaven is working and the gospel is taking root in Gentile soil.

3. *The Mission of Barnabas.*—If the party of the circumcision (Acts 11 : 2) demanded an explanation of Peter for his conduct at Cæsarea, they would not hesitate to demand an investigation of the proceedings at Antioch. The precedent had already been set in sending Peter and John to Samaria. No issue then would be made in Jerusalem on this point, though apparently the Antioch saints had not asked to be investigated. But the report had come "to the ears of

the church in Jerusalem" (Acts 11 : 22). The proposal probably came from the Pharisaic party in the church there, for the experience of Peter at Cæsarea had revealed a serious cleavage of opinion among them on the missionary question.

But, whatever the impulse, a wise man was sent, a committee of one, Barnabas, the son of exhortation. He was just the type of man needed for this crisis, prudent and yet courageous, as was seen in his championship of Saul in Jerusalem. It is worth noting that none of the Apostles went, though Peter had received special preparation on the Gentile aspect of the situation. It is possible, of course, that he and the other Apostles were away from Jerusalem at the time. The fact that Barnabas was from Cyprus may have marked him out as the man to send. But already it is clear that the Apostles are not to do all the work in the Kingdom. Stephen and Philip had given ample proof of this, if any was needed. It is particularly added about Barnabas on this occasion that "he was a good man, and full of the Holy Spirit and of faith" (verse 24), those qualifications that fitted him for the really serious task imposed upon him. For actually what was he to do?

We know what he did do. He came, he saw the grace of God, he was glad. Evidently Barnabas was not of the Pharisaic party in the Jerusalem church. He exhorted them not to become Jews, but to cleave to the Lord. They had made a good start. They were just to go on as they had begun. The reason why he acted so wisely is found in the quotation from verse 24 which is introduced by "for." A smaller man could and would have caused no end of trouble here as to circumcision, baptism, ordination. The seal of God's blessing was on this work "and much people was added to the Lord." The thing to accent specially in the matter is that Barnabas rejoiced at the power of God which was at work among the Greeks. He himself had come from the island of Cyprus as had some of those who had first preached here. He was thus a Hellenistic Jew and had some sympathy with the Gentiles.

4. *The Insight of Barnabas.*—There had evidently been no thought in Jerusalem of sending for Saul of Tarsus. They had taken him into the fold, but had no notion of intrusting great interests to his care. He was too uncertain a quantity and too new a convert. He could wait. But Barnabas' hands seem to have been left free by the Jerusalem church. Indeed, they could not very well be tied. The church at Antioch did not have to take orders from the church at Jerusalem. The independence of the local church has an actual historical development in the difference of conditions between Antioch and Jerusalem.

Barnabas had the gift of understanding men. He had seen the good in Saul in Jerusalem. He has heard of the work that he had since been doing in Syria and Cilicia. He saw at a glance that Saul was the man to

keep up this work at Antioch, Saul and not the original
Apostles, who were all Palestinian Jews. Here was
a condition that called for a man of breadth of sympathy
and culture that only a Hellenistic Jew could have.
The door of opportunity was opening to the whole
Gentile world. There must be no mistake made at
Antioch. It perhaps never occurred to Barnabas to
go back to Jerusalem and ask the Pharisaic party
what to do in the matter. Perhaps one of them would
have liked to take the matter in hand.

The matter was urgent. So Barnabas went himself to Tarsus to seek for Saul. He found him. He
brought him to Antioch. The thing was done. The
problem was solved, for Saul was at Antioch. It is a
curious reflection that Saul is now here, Saul the very
man who scattered the Christians from Jerusalem
and so made possible this open door.

5. *The Man and the Hour.*—We have no remarks
on Saul's point of view. The story is all told from
the standpoint of Barnabas. But we know enough of
Saul's history to see that he knew that the hour of
destiny had struck for him. Here is a Gentile work
ready to hand in the greatest city of Syria, one of the
strategic centres of the world. It was the hand of
Providence beyond a doubt. He evidently came with
alacrity.

The man and the hour had met. It is a great thing
to be ready when the hour of opportunity comes.
Saul had been getting ready for this hour all his life,

most of the time unconsciously, part of it consciously.
In Tarsus and Jerusalem God had been preparing him
for work among the Gentiles as well as Jews. His
conversion and call had come some eight or ten years
ago. The call was as distinct as the conversion, but
still God had not opened wide the door for work among
the Gentiles. But he had not chafed nor had he been
idle. He had been driven from Damascus and Jerusalem. But they would listen to him in Cilicia and Syria.
So he had worked near home and God had blessed him.
Now he is ready by grace, culture and experience to
grapple with the new problems of teaching the gospel
to the Greeks. He had the zest that fires every true
missionary's heart. He is now in the prime of life,
about forty three or four years old, if it is about A.D
44 when he comes to Antioch. He has had a wondrously
checkered career so far. Will he justify Christ's choice
of him as the Apostle to the Gentiles?

6. *The Year at Antioch.*—Barnabas remained with
Saul at Antioch. He was the older and more experienced man. There was work enough for both of
them and Barnabas' heart was really in the new field,
the world-wide work of missions. He was not needed
in Jerusalem. The work of expansion and instruction
went on well.

There was a new spirit in Antioch. Jew was not
writ so large over the Great Commission here and it
could be read in a clearer light. Indeed, a new name,
that of Christian, is first given to the disciples here.

It probably arose in the effort of the Gentiles to distinguish this new religious body, which at Antioch, being a Gentile church on the whole, was not a sect of Judaism. They were followers of Christ about whom they preached and in whom they believed. The name comes from the Gentile point of view and may have been first given as a nickname in sport or derision. But it has stuck. In the first century, however, it is not so common, occurring only three times in the New Testament, the usual name being believers, disciples, saints. Manifestly no great point was made of the name. Gradually new issues come to the surface at Antioch which promises to be a rival of Jerusalem.

7. *The Mission to Jerusalem.*—There was some intercourse between Antioch and Jerusalem. Some prophets from Jerusalem (Christian prophets apparently) had come and predicted a great famine, which soon came. This famine accented the poverty of the Jerusalem saints. They had already been drained to the bottom in previous efforts (Acts 4 and 5) to relieve the necessities of the great number of poor people in the church there. Barnabas himself knew all about the financial situation in Jerusalem, and was probably one of the generous givers at that time (Acts 4 : 36 f.). Possibly he suggested a collection from this Gentile church for the great Jewish church. That would greatly help the Pharisaic party to understand how Gentiles could be converted. There

was no pressure, but each gave according to his ability
(Acts 11 : 29).

Barnabas and Saul took the contribution. This
gives Saul another opportunity to visit Jerusalem.
The Apostles were apparently absent in the mission
work, since the money was taken to "the elders"
(Acts 11 : 30), officers of the church now for the first
time mentioned. The term occurs in connection with
the Jewish synagogue and also popular assemblies in
Egypt (see papyri). These same officers are afterward termed bishops and pastors.

We do not know the exact relation in order of time
between this visit of Barnabas and Saul and the death
of James and imprisonment of Peter "about that time"
(Acts 12 : 1). It may have been before the persecution by Herod, during it or afterward. If it was
after the persecution the Apostles may have been
absent from the city. Ramsay puts the famine and
visit of Barnabas and Saul in 46 and the persecution
in 44.[1]

If the Apostles were absent on the occasion of this
visit, one can the better understand why Paul later,
in enumerating his interviews with the Apostles to
establish his independence of them, should not allude
to this visit at all (Gal. 2 : 1). That Paul is thinking
of the Apostles in Gal. 2 : 2 is manifest by the word
"them" which refers to the Apostles who were mentioned
back in Gal. 1 : 19. But if the Apostles were in the

[1] "St. Paul the Traveller," p. 49.

city, the visit was not to them and still may not have been in his mind in Gal. 2 : 1 f.

We are not, indeed, told what reception Saul had in Jerusalem at this time. Barnabas was the one who had to explain to the Pharisaic party what had taken place at Antioch. He seemed entirely successful, for John Mark returned with him and Saul to Antioch (Acts 12 : 25 correct text). It was a wonderful story that Barnabas and Saul had to tell. It had fired the imagination of one recruit who would go with these returned missionaries as they went back to Antioch.

There is a lull for the moment. Antioch is the city of opportunity. Will Antioch be worthy of it? Will she be the centre of a world-wide expansion or will the work stop here? Jerusalem had missed her day with Christ and without him. It was not exactly stagnation at Jerusalem, for the new civil persecution under Herod Agrippa I. had led to the death of James the Apostle and to the capture of Peter. The brethren had met at the house of John Mark's mother to pray for Peter, and James, the Lord's brother, had come to the front in the church there (Acts 12 : 17).

CHAPTER VI

PAUL THE MISSIONARY LEADER

"Now Paul and his company set sail from Paphos,
and came to Perga in Pamphylia" (Acts 13 : 13).

1. *The Call to a World Campaign.*—The call had
in reality been given a long time ago. Jesus had himself given it to the disciples three times after his
resurrection. Peter had been led to see a great light
on the subject of the conversion of the Gentiles. The
church at Jerusalem had acquiesced in the manifest
work of God at Cæsarea and at Antioch. The Apostles
themselves may have been on various mission trips to
the Jews scattered abroad. It was clear that Greeks
could be saved. The Jewish Christians were willing
for them to be saved without becoming Jews, provided
the Lord did it. He must be responsible for that breach
in the middle wall of partition between Jew and Gentile.

Saul himself had received a clear and definite call
to the Gentile work, and he is now engaged in it along
with Barnabas. They have both shown their fitness for
leadership in an advance movement among the Gentiles, if one is to be made. In the list of prophets and
teachers at Antioch (Acts 13 : 1) the name of Barnabas heads the list for obvious reasons, while that of

Saul comes last for reasons not so obvious. It is not safe to call Barnabas a prophet and Saul a teacher, nor indeed to say that Saul was the least influential in the list. Luke has not explained his reason for this order, and so we pass it by.

But the impulse towards a missionary campaign on an extended scale did not come from any of these brethren. The Holy Spirit spoke to the prophets and teachers, whether to the church is uncertain (owing to the ambiguous phrase "in the church"). The words of the call do not specify where Barnabas and Saul are to go nor indeed definitely what the work is. But they are called directly for the new enterprise. The call was acknowledged by both Barnabas and Saul. Was it the first time that Barnabas had received such a call?

2. *The Acquiescence of the Antioch Church.*—This is all that we are entitled to say for them. It is not absolutely certain that "they" of Acts 13 : 3 includes the church as a whole, but it is probable. If so, we do find approval by the church of this great missionary enterprise. It is the glory of the church at Antioch that they put no stumbling-block in the way of Barnabas and Saul, but wished them well. That was certainly more than the Pharisaic party in the Jerusalem church would have done. But Antioch, not Jerusalem, is the new centre from which the gospel starts on its world conquest. Christianity continually finds new centres as the old ones prove unworthy—Jerusalem, Antioch, Ephesus, Alexandria, Rome, not to go further.

There is no evidence that the Antioch church gave anything for the support of Barnabas and Saul. The church as a church did not originate the campaign nor finance it. They prayed for Barnabas and Saul and bade them God-speed. They were "sent forth by the Holy Spirit" (Acts 13 : 4). It was an heroic task for these two men to go out into the heathen darkness. They knew that Jesus would be with them. But already Herod Agrippa I. had killed James. Who could tell what fate awaited them? It is always a solemn thing to stand by the fountains of historic movements. Here was the genesis of the mission work on a large scale. God was in it, though some Christians were not.

There is no evidence that the laying on of hands in verse 3 was ordination. Both Barnabas and Saul had been effective preachers a number of years. It was probably more like a consecration service or farewell service.

3. *The Leadership of Barnabas.*—One need not be surprised at the fact that Barnabas is at the head of the new campaign. He was the older man and had had charge of the work in Antioch. He had asked Saul's help in that field. One must not let the after development of Saul obscure the real situation at this stage. Luke is a true historian and preserves the right perspective. Saul had had a marvellous experience, but none the less as yet he had not won the place in the kingdom now occupied by Barnabas. There was

in this matter no reflection on Saul at all, even though he had received a direct call from Jesus to the Gentile work. Besides, the Holy Spirit had expressly named the order "Barnabas and Saul" who were to be separated for this work. It was all very simple, and certainly Saul would feel no jealousy toward Barnabas who had done so much for his ministry.

The reason for the presence of John Mark in the company is not made perfectly clear by Luke (Acts 13 : 5). The term "attendant" is rather vague. Was he, as has been suggested, a synagogue minister? Perhaps he had wished to go on with Barnabas and Saul, having come with them from Jerusalem. A certain youthful spirit of adventure may have led him on along with a real desire to be useful in the cause of Jesus. He was kin to Barnabas anyhow and agreeable to Saul.

4. *Cyprus: Leadership of Paul.*—The reasons for going to Cyprus are fairly obvious, though Luke does not announce a formal programme for the expedition. As Barnabas was the leader, he probably desired to go to Cyprus because it was his old home and because there were already some Christians on the island. There were Jews there besides, and it was near. These reasons that lie on the surface may have been reinforced by others.

They landed at Salamis, on the eastern shore facing Syria. No details of the work are given by Luke save the fact that they "proclaimed the word of God in the synagogues of the Jews" (Acts 13 : 5). They had been sent forth to preach to the Gentiles, but they were not told not to preach to the Jews. Besides, a number of Gentiles would have more or less connection with the Jews in business and worship. If this nucleus of devout Greeks could be reached, it would be easier to get hold of the other Greeks. The conduct of the Apostles at this place, for Barnabas is an Apostle in the etymological sense of missionary, will be repeated uniformly whenever Jews can be found who will listen. The Jews and their Gentile friends form a nucleus accessible to the new faith. We are not told what the success was at this point nor in the long journey afoot across the island.

But at Paphos, the seat of the licentious worship of Aphrodite, a more detailed picture is given. Two men of prominence, typical of the times, are here. One was the Jewish sorcerer, Elymas Barjesus, who reminds us of Simon the sorçerer, with whom Simon Peter had a sharp collision (Acts 8) at Samaria. The case of the seven sons of Sceva, a Jew, in Acts 19 : 14 is parallel. If it seems queer that Jews should have taken to the magic art, one has only to reflect that in Christian lands soothsayers and mediums still flourish and live on popular superstition.

The other man of distinction was the proconsul of the island, Sergius Paulus. It is now common knowledge how Luke's accuracy in the detail of the term proconsul rather than propraetor has been vindicated

both by coin and by better understanding of Dio
Cassius. Cyprus at this particular time was a sena-
torial province. This official was also "a man of
understanding" in spite of his being under the influence of the Jewish sorcerer. He showed intelligence clearly in sending for Barnabas and Saul and
wishing to hear the gospel preached. To-day some
men imagine that they display intelligence by refusing
the preaching of the word. But the false prophet had
no notion of seeing his hold on the proconsul loos-
ened. So he withstood Barnabas and Saul, trying
to undo what they had already accomplished with
him.

It was a crisis. Saul is the one who sees the issue
at stake. It is interesting to note how Luke here, for
the first time, brings in Saul's Roman name Paul, perhaps suggested to him by the conflict over the Roman
Sergius Paulus. It was common in that cosmopolitan
age for men to have one name from one nation, the
other from another. Thus Cephas was Aramaic,
but Simon, Greek, like Salome Alexandra. John
Mark had both Aramaic (Hebrew) and Roman names
like Saul-Paul. As a Roman citizen Paul had always
probably had both names. Luke may have had an
artistic purpose in using Paul from now on.

Paul is filled with the Holy Spirit, and with penetrating gaze challenges this "son of the devil" and pronounces the curse of temporary blindness upon him.
The result was all that was needed to confirm Sergius

Paulus in the faith. He is astonished. He had never seen Elymas do it in this wise.[1]

And now it is "Paul and his company," according to Luke, who set sail from Paphos. Was anything said about the leadership? One hardly thinks so. Indeed, Barnabas may still have felt himself in charge of the work. Occasionally after this Luke will speak of Barnabas and Paul, but usually it is Paul and Barnabas. But the inevitable had happened. Paul was the man of initiative and energy. He had the gift of leadership and exercised it as the occasion rose. The rest followed naturally. Barnabas gave no sign of jealousy nor did he probably have any such feeling. He could easily be proud of Paul. If Barnabas led the way to Cyprus, probably Paul suggested the mainland of Pamphylia.

5. *Perga: John Mark's Desertion.*—Perga was in Pamphylia, a rough province in many ways. It now became apparent to Mark that he had enough of this tour if Paul meant to push on up the mountains to the high table-lands of Pisidia. There were some privations in Cyprus, but here perils of rivers and perils of robbers loomed before his imagination. Did the change in leadership affect Mark at all? Barnabas will not hold Mark's return to Jerusalem against him, but Paul will not forget that "he went not with them to the work" (Acts 15 : 38). It is a serious indictment against a man that he will not stand to his task. Per-

[1] Cf. Stalker, "Life of St. Paul," p. 79.

haps Mark had excuses enough. He was going back home. His mother may not have been willing for him to come anyhow. He was really not much needed, for Paul did all the preaching. His work was only of a subordinate nature. The positiveness and intensity of Paul later, when Barnabas proposes the name of Mark again, suggests that Paul may have said some sharp things to him as he left and certainly felt them. Paul met Perga as well as Mark, but he and Barnabas went on over the mountains while Mark sulked and went home.

6. *Antioch in Pisidia: a Specimen of Paul's Preaching.*—Pamphylia was probably the objective point when they left Cyprus, though, for some unexplained reason, no actual work was done there at this time. They push on to Pisidian Antioch, which is about 3,600 feet above the sea. They are now in the Roman province of Galatia. It is the southern part of the province which embraced part of Phrygia, Pisidia, and Lycaonia. The northern section of the province of Galatia covered Galatia proper, the old home of the Celts (Gauls), who invaded this region and gained a foothold, and the northern part of Phrygia. It is still a debated question in what sense Luke uses the term Region of Galatia in Acts 16 : 6 and Acts 18 : 23 and what is Paul's usage in Gal. 1 : 2. The question is of too technical a nature for minute discussion in this book. It is possible, indeed, that Paul may include the whole province in his use of the term. If so, the

Epistle would be addressed to all the churches in the province. Luke may be using the term in the ethnographic sense like Pisidia, Lycaonia, Phrygia, Mysia. As matters now stand one cannot be dogmatic. Ramsay, in all his books on Paul,[1] has set forth very ably the South Galatian view that both Paul and Luke mean only the region included in Phrygia, Pisidia, Lycaonia (Acts 13 and 14) and that Paul never entered Galatia proper, the old ethnographic use of the term (North Galatia). But the view that Paul entered North Galatia, that Luke so means in Acts 16 : 6 and 18 : 23, and that Paul addressed his Epistle to the real Celts of that section still has able advocates. On the whole I cannot see that this natural way of interpreting both Luke and Paul is overthrown, though admitting fully the doubt on the subject.

So then Paul and Barnabas are in the Roman province of Galatia, whether or not Paul ever entered the old Galatia. Paul is in one of the great cities of this ancient region. He will tap the centres of life along the great roads that run east and west. It will mean much if the gospel can be firmly planted in the great province of Galatia. This southern part was a hive of life. Antioch in Pisidia was the centre of a vast region.

We do not know how long Paul and Barnabas had been in the city before they addressed the Jews in the

[1] See especially "St. Paul the Traveller" and "Historical Commentary on Galatians."

synagogue. It may not have been the first[1] Sabbath. They sat down in orderly worship as other Jews did, but could not conceal the fact that they were strangers. The invitation to give the Jewish brethren "a word of exhortation" (Acts 13 : 15) could not be resisted. Paul stood up according to the Greek fashion, and Luke even comments on his gestures.

We are grateful for this specimen of Paul's preaching. He is now an experienced preacher, but as yet we have had only fragments of his discourses given, the mere theme or the main points. But on this occasion the line of argument is presented to us in some detail. It is easy to say that Luke has just made up this address after the fashion of Xenophon and Thucydides. But we know that Luke made use of documents in his Gospel (Luke 1 : 1–4). Paul may have made notes for this address and preserved them for Luke. Surely Luke was with Paul enough to have access to any papers which he kept. We may accept the report as a substantial presentation of Paul's address. As the first of Paul's discourses we may note some details.

The first thing that impresses one is the fact that Paul here occupies the same point of view that he had in Damascus when he first began his ministry (Acts 9 : 20) when "he proclaimed Jesus, that he is the Son of God." So here also are found the resurrection of Jesus (13 : 30 f.) and the Sonship of Jesus (verse 33). The Messiahship of Jesus is proven by

[1] Ramsay, "St. Paul the Traveller," p. 99.

his resurrection from the dead (32, 34). Paul grasps
clearly the human and the divine aspects of Christ's
person. He does not here allude to his own experience in seeing Jesus alive after his death, but he
rather appeals to the common experience of many
in Jerusalem who were still alive (verse 31). Perhaps
this was due to the fact that Paul was a total stranger
to the audience and his own experience as yet would
carry little weight.

But around this central theme Paul built up a skilful argument. Like Stephen, whose successor he is
in many ways, he first recounts the history of the chosen
people from Moses to David (17–22). He then announced the wonderful fact that the Messianic King
promised to David's line has come and that his name
is Jesus (verse 23), and he is a Saviour to Israel. He
outlines briefly the mission and message of John the
Baptist (24 f.) in perfect accord with the Synoptic
account of the Baptist as the forerunner, preacher of
repentance and baptizer, unwilling to pose as the
Messiah himself. Evidently Paul had been learning
the historical facts about the origin of Christianity.
He then appeals to the Jews and the proselytes (in a
loose sense of that term) from the Gentiles, and an-
nounces "to us is the word of this salvation sent forth"
(26). The dreadful story of the death of Jesus at
the hands of the Jewish rulers and of Pilate is briefly
told (27–29). The resurrection is discussed more at
length as the heart of the great message (30–37) and

in accord with the Scriptures. "Therefore," says
Paul, the first of those logical "therefores" so common in his Epistles, "through this man is proclaimed
unto you remission of sins" (38). This "therefore"
points to the atoning death of Jesus who is shown to
be the Messiah and Saviour by his resurrection. But
this is not all: "And by him every one that believeth
is justified from all things, from which ye could not
be justified by the law of Moses" (39). This sentence
is pregnant with meaning. This salvation is personal
("by him") and not by a mere creed or ceremonial
observance. It is open to all ("every one") both Jew
and Greek. Belief or trust is the basal demand, not
works of the law. Full justification is realized as a
fact, not a mere hope. The Mosaic law had not
brought actual justification. Here is the kernel of Paul's
theology as we have it expounded in Galatians and
Romans. It is clear that he has rightly apprehended
the teaching of Jesus as set forth by Christ himself, by
Peter on the Day of Pentecost, and by Stephen. Paul
will learn more, but he will not need to unlearn this.
He closes the sermon by a passionate appeal from
Hab. 1 : 5 (40 f.).

The sermon, as a whole, is a masterpiece of skill
and adaptation in a difficult situation. His addresses
will all repay study, as reported in Acts, for this adaptation to time, place, audience. Instance, besides this
one, that at Lystra (Acts 14 : 15–17), at Athens (Acts
17 : 22–31), on the steps of the tower of Antonia (Acts

22 : 3–21), before Felix (Acts 24 : 10–21), before
Festus (Acts 24 : 10 f.), before Agrippa (Acts 26 : 2–
23), before the Jews in Rome (Acts 28 : 17–28). His
addresses were never "misfits." It is small wonder
that on this occasion the effect was very great. The
people begged a repetition of "these words" on the
next Sabbath.

But the new preacher was entirely too successful
from the point of view of the Jews, and especially
the rulers of the synagogue, who had asked Paul to
speak at first. They did not relish the whole town's
coming out, including Greeks of all sorts. Paul had
let the bars down for the Gentiles to come right into
the Jewish synagogue. They came, but the Jews were
filled with jealousy and openly contradicted Paul and
even blasphemed or railed (marg.) at him (Acts 13 : 45).

The issue had come at last. Paul and Barnabas
wished to preach the Gospel to both Jew and Gentile.
Paul had done so. But these Jews at Antioch in
Pisidia would have no Messiah like that, nor message
for the 'am-ha-'aretz. Paul and Barnabas were quick
to grasp the new turn of affairs. "It was necessary
that the message of God should first be spoken to you.
Seeing ye thrust it from you, and judge yourselves
unworthy of eternal life, lo! we turn to the Gentiles"
(13 : 46). Every word cut like a knife. They justify
their conduct by an appeal to Scripture (Is. 49 : 6),
a passage evidently not familiar to the Pharisaic rabbis. But here is a platform upon which Paul will

stand in his presentation of the gospel for the whole world. The Jews have the right to a hearing first. But the Gentiles shall not have the door of hope shut in their faces.

It was a crisis in the world campaign. But the path was plain. What would be the result? That must take care of itself. God took care of it. The elect among the Gentiles believed with gladness and glorified God (Acts 13 : 48 f.) and the word of the Lord spread throughout all that region. Evidently Paul and Barnabas remained here some time and worked among the Gentiles. But success merely angered the Jewish rulers all the more. Paul and Barnabas paid no attention to them. But the rabbis found a way to reach the magistrates of the city,[1] not officials of the province. They managed, by means of some female proselytes, to get hold of some "devout women of honorable estate" who persuaded[2] the magistrates to expel Paul and Barnabas from the city as disturbers of the peace. The rabbis and the women had their ears. Paul and Barnabas had to obey the city magistrates and depart, but they "shook the dust of their feet against them" as they went (verse 51). But the rabbis cannot undo what Christ has done for the Gentiles at Antioch.

7. *Iconium: Division Among the Gentiles.*—At Iconium they were in the same Region as Antioch.[3]

---

[1] Ramsay, "St. Paul the Traveller," p. 105.
[2] Conybeare and Howson, "Life and Epistles of St. Paul," p. 81, Vol. I., Scribner's ed.
[1] Ramsay, "St. Paul the Traveller," p. 109.

Here they boldly entered the synagogue of the Jews and had great success with both Jews and Greeks (14 : 1). Here also the disbelieving element among the Jews resisted Paul and Barnabas. History often repeats itself as in the work of Jesus in different parts of Palestine. The new thing at Iconium was that the Greeks themselves became divided, part holding with Paul, part with the hostile Jews (14 : 2–4). Signs and wonders were wrought here, but still the multitude was divided. At Antioch the Jews had finally gotten the Greek women and magistrates to drive Paul and Barnabas out of town. One must remember that then, as now, the Jews had financial influence. But here at Iconium the opposition takes the form of a mob, and both Gentiles and Jews make an "onset" on the Apostles, to treat them shamefully and, if possible, to stone them. But discretion was the better part of valor and Paul and Barnabas fled (14 : 6). The Jews had carried their point again.

8. *Lystra: The Fickle Populace.*—Here a new region[1] is entered, that part of Lycaonia, comprising Lystra, Derbe and a "cityless" section. At Lystra no mention is made of a synagogue nor indeed of any Jews. It is a Gentile atmosphere into which they enter. The excitability and fickleness of the Lycaonians have been often commented upon, with which one may compare the changeableness of the Galatians (Gal. 1 : 6), who may, indeed, be the same people.

[1] Ramsay, "St. Paul the Traveller," p. 110 f.

The healing of the lame man led the multitude to take
Barnabas for Jupiter and Paul for Mercury. They
manifestly took Barnabas as the major god and Paul
as his spokesman. They had a myth about such divine
visits to their country. They know Greek as well as
their own Lycaonian dialect. Surely, Paul and Barnabas have popularity to spare when the priest of
Jupiter gravely proposes to offer sacrifice. The address of Paul (and Barnabas) was noble in its tone,
and skilful in turning their thoughts to the living God.
He has to appeal to these men from the point of view
of nature, presenting God as creator and preserver of
all men (14: 15-17). His Hellenism stood him in good
stead now as he sought a standpoint from which to
reach such a crowd. Even so, he had difficulty in
restraining the multitude (verse 18).

A god one day, a mere man the next day stoned
and left for dead. Thus the crowd changed under
the subtle persuasion of the Jews, who had come on
from Antioch and Iconium, flushed with victory, and
determined to kill Paul at any rate. They did stir
this Greek crowd. One may wonder how Jews could
be successful with Greeks, but they knew what arguments to make. They dragged Paul out of the city
and left him as a dead man. The real disciples in
Lystra, for there were some (Timothy, for instance,
whose father was a Greek and whose mother was a
Jewess), gathered in a circle around the body in sorrow. Probably Timothy was in that circle. So near

did Paul come to the end of his career on his first missionary tour. But he rose from the ground and went on his way. He had once had a share in the work of the mob that stoned Stephen. Now he knew what it was to be stoned himself by the fury of a mob.

9. *Derbe: The End of the Tour.*—Not a single detail is given of the work in this city except that much success was achieved (Acts 14 : 21). Probably persecution arose here likewise. It was now time to go back home. How shall they return?

10. *Strengthening the Churches.*—Much had been accomplished, if it could be made permanent. Organization was needed with officers. Words of encouragement and advice would be helpful. But how could they return in safety? Ramsay[1] suggests that new magistrates had now come into office in all the cities where they had been, and hence they could come back to them in safety. It is with grateful hearts that the Apostles retraced their steps. They could exhort with power how "that through many tribulations we must enter into the Kingdom of God" (14 : 22). They prayed and they fasted. A church with elders is established in each city, Gentile churches these, for the Jews had given little response to the message. When Perga was reached they hurry on to Antioch, skipping Cyprus.

11. *Report to the Church at Antioch.*—They had a wonderful story to tell. They had "fulfilled" (14 : 26)

[1] "St. Paul the Traveller."

the work to which they had been committed at Antioch. It was not exactly as they had hoped. The Jews had not responded to the message as they had wished. But the Gentiles had heard with open hearts. God "had opened a door of faith unto the Gentiles" (14 : 27), which would never be closed again. The church at Antioch was a Gentile church, and they heard with satisfaction this report of the first returned missionaries of the world. The work among the Greeks had now been launched upon a great scale and God had set the seal of his blessing upon it. Paul and Barnabas deserve some rest with the disciples. The missionary work with Paul is now not a theory merely, but a glorious fact. The Gentiles know the love of Jesus and they will never forget him. One of the greatest revolutions in human history has come about. Jews and Greeks are now members of the body of Christ. Will they dwell in peace together?

CHAPTER VII

PAUL'S DOCTRINAL CRISIS

"That the truth of the Gospel might continue with you" (Gal. 2 : 5).

1. *The Doctrinal Issue Raised by the Judaizers.*—
The indignation of the party of the circumcision in the church at Jerusalem over Peter's conduct at Cæsarea in going into a Gentile's house (Acts 11 : 3) had subsided when they saw that Peter had done this by divine direction (11 : 18). They acquiesced in the conversion of the Gentiles and held their peace for the present. Events at Antioch had already led them to send Barnabas up there, but Barnabas, instead of reporting to the Pharisees, went on saving the Greeks. The fires of prejudice were not quenched, but were only smouldering. Barnabas and Saul had prudently brought a contribution from the church at Antioch to the poor saints in Jerusalem. But this formal campaign on the part of Paul and Barnabas among the Greeks was more than the Judaizers had bargained for. They saw visions of Gentile Christians who might outnumber the Jewish Christians, take charge of Christianity, and divert it from Judaism. News had come to Jerusalem of the great success of Paul and Barnabas. The

matter had already been overlooked too long. Some
of the Judaizers decided to save the Kingdom by going
up to Antioch and laying down the law to Paul and
Barnabas. They had not obtained the consent of
the Jerusalem church, the mother church, for this
Gentile propaganda.

The term Judaizer is applied technically to those
Jewish Christians who felt that the Gentiles could not
be saved without becoming also Jews. The Gentiles
must be Judaized as well as Christianized. Christianity was not adequate of itself. Judaism must be added.
Now, originally, before the vision on the housetop at
Joppa and the work at Cæsarea, this had apparently
been Peter's view also. It was clearly never the view
of Jesus who had other sheep not of the Jewish fold
(John 10 : 16). In enjoining his followers to make
disciples of all the nations he had not said that they
were to be circumcised or Judaized (Matt. 28 : 19 f.).
But the disciples were Jews first, then Christians.
When Christianity diverged from Judaism, as it did
in the conversion of the Gentiles, they had, some of
them, difficulty in shaking off the Jewish point of view.
Some of them continued more Pharisee than Christian.
There was already a party of the circumcision (Acts
11 : 2), a Pharisaic party inside the Jerusalem church
(Acts 15 : 5). Here is the origin of the first cleavage
among the early Christians. It springs out of the
mission problem as have so many divisions in the centuries since due to the prejudices of race, creed or

custom. It is the spirit of Pharisaism *redivivus* in Christianity. Pharisaism had killed Jesus, but not Christianity. That attack was from outside the fold. Now the Pharisaic ceremonialism lifts its hand from inside the walls to smite the spiritual conception of religion. It is the eternal conflict between the spirit and the letter, a battle that rages to-day in every Christian land.

Paul knows this spirit of intolerance better than the Judaizers themselves. He had once been its foremost exponent. It is a curious turn of the wheeel of fortune that the man who rejoiced in the death of Stephen for preaching spiritual worship independently of the temple should be the man who will wage the great battle for Gentile freedom. Stephen fought the fight for the spiritual conception of religion against the Pharisees (as did Jesus). Paul has to fight for the spiritual gospel against the Judaizers. The regulators from Jerusalem came up to Antioch and put the matter bluntly: "Except ye be circumcised after the custom of Moses, ye cannot be saved" (Acts 15 : 1). There was the Christian law laid down for the Gentiles by disciples from Jerusalem! If they were right all the work of Paul and Barnabas at Antioch and on the recent mission tour was for naught. They should go back and Judaize the saints. Would Paul agree to that programme? He had not so learned Christ. Could he be mistaken? If these men were right, Christianity was small gain. He would not go back to the husks

of Pharisaism after renouncing it at so great cost.
These things were gain to him once, but not now.
He did not believe that Peter and James held such
views. He was sure that this was not the real spirit
of the Old Testament teaching concerning the Messianic reign. There was only one thing to do. It
would cause discussion. This was plain. But he
would resist any attempt to bring the Gentiles under
the bondage of Mosaic ceremonial law, not to say
Pharisaism. He knew the emptiness of tithing the
mint and anise of rabbinism. He loved his Greek
converts too much to see this calamity befall them.
And he loved Christ too much to see him so misinterpreted. The church at Antioch stood with Paul
and Barnabas. Would there be a split on the issue?
Will the church at Jerusalem side with the Judaizers?
That would be a great misfortune.

2. *The Appeal to Jerusalem.*—It was a solemn
moment. The issue of Paul's life was upon him.
Had he and Barnabas faltered, a Judaized Christianity
might have conquered the world instead of a Pauline
or spiritual conception of the kingdom (Rom. 14 : 17).
It is a great mark of the true statesman to see the real
issues involved in a controversy. Paul and Barnabas
showed themselves equal to this great occasion by seeing at once that the very essence of Christianity was
at stake. Spiritual Christianity was meeting the icy
hand of formalism and traditionalism. It was Christianity by itself or Christianity plus ceremonialism.

Paul was a man of peace, but not peace at any price, not peace at the cost of principle. The pathos of Christian history is that not long after Paul's great victory was won this very perversion of Christianity did triumph. But his victory was not in vain. The inspiring record of what he here won is a constant challenge to men to win and maintain spiritual freedom. He will have to fight the battle again in the letter to the Galatians, and that Epistle was Luther's bugle-note in the Reformation.

We do not know at whose suggestion the appeal to Jerusalem was made. "Paul and Barnabas and certain others of them" were appointed to take the matter up with "the Apostles and elders" in Jerusalem (Acts 15 : 2). It was the action of the church (verse 3), but most likely Paul really proposed the matter. He tells us himself (Gal. 2 : 2) that he "went up by revelation." He had probably gone to the Lord about this great question, and this was the answer, to consult the Jerusalem brethren. It is not necessary to make an elaborate discussion of the reasons for taking Gal. 2 and Acts 15 to refer to the same visit to Jerusalem. That is still the position of most scholars.[1] There are difficulties in this view, but not insuperable ones, and fewer than in any other. Thus we take it that Luke gives the story of the conference in its general aspects, while Paul gives the story of the private conference which really gave shape to the public

[1] Cf. Findlay, Paul in Hastings' "D. B."

meeting. It is to be recalled that Paul wrote first and that in his Epistle he is discussing the independence of his authority. It was in the private meeting that this issue came up. Luke in all probability never saw the Epistle to the Galatians, and wrote obviously and naturally about the general subject. There is surely no real contradiction in Paul's remark about a special revelation to him and Luke's mention of the action of the church.

But why go to the Jerusalem church at all? Was not the church at Antioch independent of the church in Jerusalem? They had not asked the consent or advice of the Jerusalem church in the matter of Barnabas and Saul's going on the mission tour. Why do it now? Was there not danger of having a yoke put upon their necks? A number of common-sense reasons occur to one. There must be no cleavage between these two great churches on this subject. There must be no schism, not two denominations, one Jewish, one Gentile. Besides, these Judaizers belonged to the church at Jerusalem. They had tried to get the church at Antioch to take sides against Paul and Barnabas. It would be only fair to see if the Jerusalem church would not take a stand with Paul and Barnabas against their own Judaizing members. Moreover, the other Apostles, the Twelve, were members of the church at Jerusalem. This fact would necessarily give great weight to the opinion of the mother church in the present emergency. A concordat, in which the great

Jewish church and the great Gentile church agreed, would settle the matter with all sensible men. Paul would take pains to make it plain to the Apostles and all concerned that he did not come to Jerusalem to receive orders from anybody. He came to confer with them as equals about this great question of Gentile liberty in the churches.

To Jerusalem then both sides go. Paul and Barnabas tell the story of the conversion of the Gentiles as they pass through Phœnicia and Samaria and cause great joy to the brethren (Acts 15 : 3). Already there are churches here. Naturally no objection to the Gentile cause would be raised in these parts.

3. *The First Public Meeting in Jerusalem.* — A general meeting was called (Acts 15 : 4) to hear the story of Paul and Barnabas. They knew how to tell it and it had a wonderful effect on the audience. Already it was plain that the church at Jerusalem sanctioned the work of God by the hands of Paul and Barnabas. But the Pharisaic party were not going to surrender without a fight. They "rose up" saying: "It is needful to circumcise them, and to charge them to keep the law of Moses" (15 : 5). There it was! The church had the *ipse dixit* of the Pharisaic Christians. It would be presumption to oppose the position of these intensely orthodox brethren. They sat down. Somebody must have moved to adjourn, a very convenient parliamentary device at times, unless James adjourned for dinner or pronounced the benediction.

In verse 6 we are told that they "were gathered together to consider of this matter," a reference to a second meeting. But the issue was sharply joined in public at Jerusalem. What will Paul do now? He tells us himself.

4. *Paul's Stand for Gentile Liberty.*—He probably called a meeting of the Apostles present and the elders, the leading spirits in the church. He did not wish an unseemly public wrangle with these Judaizers. He was no more concerned about them. He had said his say to them at Antioch. Peter, John and James, in particular, were the men that he wished to see. If he and they saw eye to eye, it mattered little about the rest. He had no reason to suspect the position of these great exponents of Christianity, but there was nothing like talking things over in private. In a public debate there were all sorts of chances for misunderstanding. It was plain that the Judaizers had made some impression by their bold, positive stand for traditional Judaism. Paul never showed greater wisdom than when he gathered these "pillars" of the church and "laid before them the gospel" which he preached among the Gentiles (Gal. 2 : 2). These men knew what Jesus preached, if anybody did. He had no fear of the outcome. He did not acknowledge their superiority to him at all, nor had he received his message from them (2 : 6). He was sure that they would understand his message, that they were not Judaizers. He was right. "They perceived the grace that was

given" unto Paul (2 : 9), and they shook hands all round as equals who agreed on this great issue of Gentile freedom. Paul had carried his point. Paul's own apostleship is thus freely acknowledged by the other Apostles, though it will be later attacked by the Judaizers. The rights of Gentile Christianity are freely admitted.

It seems clear that there were some timid brethren in the private meeting, perhaps some of the elders, who were willing to make a compromise in order to hold on to the Judaizers. Paul sharply resented the idea of surrender to these Judaizers, "false brethren" he even calls them, for the sake of peace, "who came in privily to spy out our liberty which we have in Christ Jesus" (verse 4). They took special umbrage at the fact that Paul had brought along with him Titus, a Greek Christian, who had not been circumcised. He had with him a live specimen to illustrate the point in dispute. It was proposed that the principle could be discussed to better advantage if Titus were first circumcised. But Paul stood his ground firmly and refused (verse 5, thus reads this somewhat involved sentence). "The truth of the gospel" was at stake in the case of Titus. The apparent inconsistency of Paul in circumcising Timothy will be treated later.

Paul and the leaders did agree on a general sort of division of work. Paul and Barnabas would devote themselves specially to the Gentile work, while James, Cephas and John would labor especially among the

Jews. But the matter was not an absolute division,
as the future showed. It was hinted (2 : 10) that Paul
and Barnabas should continue to remember the poor
at Jerusalem as they had been doing. Had they forgotten it this time? Paul will one day remember this
point with a great collection. They are now ready
for another public meeting. Probably the programme
of the proceedings was agreed on in the main, for
everything will now go smoothly. There is wisdom
for brethren in responsible positions in the kingdom.

5. *The Victory Over the Judaizers.*—It was a victory,
not a compromise, as can be shown. One must not
overlook the "much questioning" (Acts 15 : 7) which
came first in the second public gathering. It would
appear that full opportunity was given for the Judaizers
to say all that they wished. After all desire for public
controversy had been satisfied, Peter "rose up" and
spoke. The Judaizers would probably look with suspicion on him since his experience at Cæsarea, but,
still, they had not given him up. He was the great
speaker among the Twelve, and the Judaizers had probably tried to use his name against Paul as they did later
in Corinth. His opinion is bound to carry weight.
He reminds the audience how this is not a new matter
at all. He had himself been before the church once
on this very point. They had all agreed that the conversion of Cornelius was the work of the Lord, as shown
by the bestowal of the Holy Spirit. They had not demanded that Cornelius should be circumcised. Besides,

they had not as Jews been able to bear this yoke of the law. Why impose it on the Gentiles? As Jews they had to believe just as the Gentiles (15 : 7–11). Every word told in favor of Paul's contention. Peter and Paul agree here as they do later in their Epistles on the doctrines of grace and Gentile liberty.

Peter's speech made a profound impression. Nobody seemed willing to answer it. Finally, Barnabas and Paul (probably in this order, verse 12) told their story again, to refresh the minds and hearts of the brethren.

After a further pause James, the leading elder and apparently the President of the Conference, arose and addressed the body (15 : 14–21). Every one would wish to hear his opinion, for he was regarded as thoroughly Jewish. The Judaizers had hoped to win him, as they later will use his name to frighten Peter (Gal. 2 : 12). He seems deliberate and begs for attention. He refers to Symeon's (note the Jewish form of the name as in 2 Pet. 1 : 1) speech with approval. At once then he takes sides with Paul and Barnabas. He does a characteristic thing for a Jew. He shows how this whole matter of the incoming of the Gentiles was foretold in the Prophets (Am. 9 : 11 f.). That is enough for him after all that they have heard of God's blessing and what they knew already of the work of God at Cæsarea. He is ready with his "judgment." It is in favor of letting the Gentiles alone (verse 19). He offers a suggestion that this body send an epistle to the Gentiles expressing their opinion that they be careful to avoid a great sin to which they were specially subject and respect the Jewish feelings on two other matters. There was no need to worry about Moses. That was a Jewish, not a Gentile problem, and the Jews had synagogues everywhere. As yet the Jewish Christians had not ceased to worship in the synagogue (cf. also Jas. 2 : 2).

It was a powerful plea that covered the whole ground and brought matters to a focus. The wonderful part about it was that the verdict was unanimous in favor of the resolution, if one may so call it, of James (verse 22). One can hardly suppose that the Judaizers voted for it. They probably remained in sullen silence, completely overcome, and in utter defeat. The proposal of James about a letter was agreed to, and two leading brethren, Judas and Silas, were appointed with Paul and Barnabas to convey the decision of the conference to Antioch and Syria and Cilicia. The epistle is not in the form of a command. James had used the word "judgment." The word "seemed good" is the term used in the epistle itself (verse 28). They claim the guidance of the Holy Spirit in the conclusions reached. The epistle disclaims responsibility for the troublesome and arrogant attitude of the Judaizers (verse 24) and is very full of appreciation of the work of Paul and Barnabas (verse 25 f.). No demands are made of the Gentile Christians outside of the well-known Christian principles, except these "necessary" things (verse 28). Fornication was a dire peril in the Gentile world, and they needed warning on that point (cf. the Epistles later also). The question of meats offered to idols is not on the same plane, but can become in certain phases of it a very serious matter (cf. I Cor. 10 : 14–22). It will give Paul trouble in the future. He did not regard this decision as a "law," for in I Cor. 8–10 and Rom. 14 f. he discusses the matter in its fundamental aspects. Some phases of the subject were open to question. But he has won the great thing. It would not be wise to stickle over a small point. Besides, idolatry was another ever-present temptation to the Gentiles (I Cor. 10 : 14). The matter of "things strangled" was a concession to Jewish feeling that the Gentiles would not complain of. In fine, the Gentiles were not to become Jews. That was the great thing. They were to be careful about fornication and idolatry, their great temptations, as they ought to do. They could well afford to respect Jewish feeling in a matter like things strangled. There is the spirit of concession here and love, but not of compromise of principle. As to the actual working out of the matter of meats offered to idols that lies in the future. All this is very subordinate and relatively unimportant in the light of the victory for Gentile freedom, for spiritual Christianity, so gloriously won.

One will be pardoned a word as to the prominence of James in this work. The epistle sent is much like his speech and may have been written by him. It has often been noted how both speech and epistle resemble the Epistle of James written by the same noble man, and probably just before this conference. He makes no attacks on real Judaism, but he takes his stand with Paul and Peter for liberty and progress.

6. *The Reception of the Victory at Antioch.*—They were naturally jubilant in this Greek centre that the Jerusalem church had taken their view of the situation (Acts 15 : 30–35). It was, indeed, a "consolation" not to have a schism, for the Greeks would not become Jews. Judas and Silas were prophets and gave vent to many words. It was a good time all round. They at last returned to Jerusalem, while Paul and Barnabas and many others went on preaching the Word.

7. *Peter's Temporary Defection at Antioch.*—It is Paul who tells this painful incident (Gal. 2 : 11–21). He does it only to show his independence of the other Apostles, not to cast reflection on Peter. But it was the sequel of the battle for Gentile freedom, indeed the same struggle renewed in another form. In the course of time Peter came up to Antioch to see how this great work went. The wonder is that he had not come sooner. But he was now publicly aligned with Paul and Barnabas and he could come with no possible misunderstanding. Peter's impulsive nature went the whole way this time. He "ate with the Gentiles." He had done this with apologies to Cornelius (Acts 10 : 28; 11 : 3), but now he made no excuses about it.

He acted just like Paul and Barnabas. The Jerusalem conference had not passed on the question of social usages between Jewish and Gentile Christians. So the Judaizers have fresh cause for a quarrel if they wish it.

Perhaps news of what Peter is doing comes to Jerusalem. The Judaizers are quick to see the chance to reopen the controversy which had not been settled to please them. As before, so now they come up with assertion of infallibility and authority. They claim to be "from James." The claim need not be true because they made it. We know that James had agreed with Paul at Jerusalem. It is possible, of course, that some of the brethren may have asked James before they left if he thought Jews ought to have cordial social relations with Gentiles, and may have received a negative reply. We know that later (Acts 21 : 20 ff.) he is anxious for Paul to disabuse the minds of the brethren of the charge that Paul opposed the maintenance of the Mosaic customs on the part of Jewish Christians. But I do not believe that James sent a message of condemnation of Peter's conduct in eating with the Gentiles.

But, when confronted by the Judaizers with the threat to tell James about it, Peter changed his conduct, though not his convictions. It was a piece of cowardice, like his dreadful denial of Jesus to the servants of the high priest. "He drew back and separated himself, fearing them that were of the circumcision." He was

not brave enough to face possible social ostracism
in Jerusalem or another trouble in the church there
(Acts 11 : 3). Paul felt very strongly on the subject.
He charged Peter with hypocrisy and not standing to
his real convictions. Peter "stood condemned" when
Paul "resisted him to the face." Poor Peter. He can
now answer neither Greek nor Judaizer.

The worst of it was that all the other Jews followed
Peter's example. If it was wrong for Peter, it was
wrong for them. Paul and Barnabas stood alone.
They had lived with the Gentiles apparently on the
tour as well as in Antioch. But soon Barnabas also
deserted Paul. It was the first break that had come
between Paul and Barnabas. This was a cut, indeed,
to the quick. It was hard to stand up against Peter
and call him "Judaizer" "before them all" (2 : 14).
He expounded to Peter the fundamental gospel principle of justification by faith (15–21) to help him see
his inconsistency. It was Paul *contra mundum*. Suppose he had faltered? The victory of Gentile freedom
would have been seriously endangered if not lost.
Eternal vigilance is indeed the price of liberty. But
Paul's boldness won back both Peter and Barnabas.
They afterward are on friendly terms with Paul.
This passage in Galations really presents the essential
ideas of the Pauline theology which Paul explained to
Peter, "for if righteousness is through the law, then
Christ died for naught" (verse 21). If Moses must be
added to Christ, Moses is greater than Christ. Indeed

Christ in that case made a useless sacrifice of himself. The Judaizers, in truth, "belonged more to Moses than to Jesus."[1] Peter had to face "the overwhelming dilemma" that either faith in Christ was sufficient or it was not sufficient.[2] In fact, he had already faced that question (Acts 15 : 10 f.). Paul now sharply brought him back to the light.

8. *The Controversy Reopened.*—The Judaizers are greatly encouraged at the momentary sympathy on this point which they had obtained from Peter and Barnabas. They see a new line of battle. It is to isolate Paul, to drive a wedge in between him and the Jerusalem Apostles. They will claim at Corinth to have letters from the Apostles (II Cor. 3 : 1). They will undertake some missionary work on their own account, "a counter-mission."[3] They lost at the Jerusalem conference, but they have made headway at Antioch. They will appeal to Paul's own converts on the field and seek to shake his authority with them. They will use the concessions at Jerusalem to Paul's hurt. Henceforth a double campaign will be waged over the world. Paul and his coadjutors will carry the gospel from province to province in the Roman Empire. The Judaizers will follow in his train and dog his steps, maligning his name and preaching the gospel of ceremonialism, while Paul proclaims the gospel of grace. Paul will win the lost to Christ. The

---

[1] Sabatier, "The Apostle Paul," p. 126.
[2] *Ibid.*, p. 131.   [3] *Ibid.*, p. 135.

Judaizers will seek to save the saved, to rescue them from Paulinism and save them to Pharisaic orthodoxy. They will have only too great success in Galatia and Corinth. Paul will go on with foes in front and in the rear.

CHAPTER VIII

PAUL ANSWERS THE CRY OF EUROPE

"Come over into Macedonia and help us" (Acts 16 : 9).

1. *The Break with Barnabas.*—The missionary fever soon returned to Paul. He must go out again. So he proposes to Barnabas that they visit the churches which they had established. Manifestly Paul and Barnabas are on good terms again. Barnabas has come back to Paul's view in the matter of social relations with the Gentiles. Paul was too great a soul to cherish against one a temporary lapse like that. He had confidence in Barnabas, as in Peter, in spite of their faltering before the Judaizers. It is possible, however, that Barnabas was a little sensitive on the score of Paul's rebuke. It had, perhaps, brought up sharply the whole story of Paul's forging ahead of him in the work. But the recent unpleasantness made it necessary for Paul to take the initiative. They do not now wait for another revelation of the Holy Spirit to spur them on. Barnabas agreed and all seemed well.

But Barnabas made an unfortunate suggestion, that they try Mark again. One can see very easily how Barnabas would wish to give his kinsman another chance. He would reason that he was young, that the

experience had taught him a lesson, and that he felt
sure that Mark would be faithful this time. Paul
undoubtedly wished Mark well, but he did not wish
to experiment with him a second time. The risk was
too great in a work of this nature. Let Mark first
show himself a man by sticking to his work. Judgment of men is a very difficult matter, but very essential
to success. People inevitably have the right to differ
about personal likes and dislikes. One need not decide who was right here, Paul or Barnabas. There
was something to say on both sides. The contention
between them was "sharp," as is common in personal
matters. It is a sad story at best. If it were the only
case in Christian history! "They parted asunder one
from the other" (Acts 15 : 39). Henceforth Paul and
Barnabas never work together.

They will work separately. They agree to disagree.
They drop the matter and do not nag each other.
Paul will later allude to Barnabas (I Cor. 9 : 6) in a
most pleasant way, showing that he bore no resentment
and that Barnabas was still at work. Luke drops
Barnabas from his story, for he will follow Paul. One
could wish for more knowledge of this generous spirit
who did so much for Paul and for Christ. It is
always pathetic to see estrangement come between two
who have been so much to each other.

Barnabas takes Mark and goes to Cyprus, his old
home. Mark will learn his lesson. He doubtless was
humiliated by Paul's refusal to take him along. But

it did him good.   Later he will be of service to Peter
(I Pet. 5 : 13) and to Paul (Philem. 24; Col. 4 : 10;
II Tim. 4 : 11).   A young minister can overcome his
failings.   Mark the inefficient becomes Mark the useful to Paul for ministry.   But the world looks drear
for Barnabas and Mark as they leave Antioch.   The
sympathy of the church is with Paul (Acts 15 : 40).

2. *Paul's New Campaign with Silas.*—Silas (Latin
Silvanus) had shown himself in full sympathy with
Paul at Jerusalem and Antioch.   He was a prophet
and apparently of more age and force than Mark.   Indeed, he takes the place of Barnabas, not Mark.[1]   Paul
turns to the other part of the former tour, since Barnabas had gone to Cyprus.   They pass through some of
the churches of Syria as they go by land on toward
Galatia by a more direct way than in the former trip.
Both here and in Cilicia Paul had already labored so
that he will have a cordial welcome (Gal. 1 : 21 f.).
He strengthened the churches.

Ramsay[2] suggests that Luke fails to make any com-
ment on the realm of Antiochus between Cilicia and
Derbe (in Galatia) since it was "non-Roman territory
and out of Paul's plans."   Already, according to
Ramsay, Paul has the purpose of converting the
Roman Empire to Christ.

3. *Lystra: Finding of Timothy.*—No incident is
mentioned at Derbe when Paul comes upon the track

---

[1] Ramsay, " St. Paul the Traveller," p. 177.
[2] Ramsay, "St. Paul the Traveller," p. 179.

of his previous journey, but at Lystra Paul finds another companion for his work. Timothy was a child of Paul's in the Gospel (I Tim. 1 : 2). His mother, a Jewess, had also believed, but his father, a Greek, is not said to be a Christian. Already Timothy has a good reputation both in Lystra and Iconium (Acts 16 : 2). It is a great thing to discover a preacher. Paul made no mistake in choosing Timothy to go with him. He will never flicker as Mark had done. This young man will be one of the chief joys of Paul's ministry. Timothy agrees to go, but Paul first has him circumcised so that he will not be obnoxious to the Jews. The case is not similar to that of Titus, who was a pure Greek. Timothy, being half Jew and half Greek, was in an anomalous position. So he became a Jew also. No matter of principle was involved in his case and prudential reasons ruled.

4. *Paul Lives up to the Jerusalem Agreement.*— They proceed on the journey and deliver "the decrees to keep which had been ordained of the Apostles and elders that were at Jerusalem" (Acts 16 : 4). They had been duplicated so that a copy could be left in each church. The decree or decision would come in well if any effort should be made to enforce Judaism on them. Paul delivered this document after he had had Timothy circumcised, evidently seeing no contradiction between the two. The epistle was not meant as a law to bind the Gentiles. It was rather a charter of freedom from Judaism. The Gentile Christians

were already, of course, opposing idolatry and fornication. They show no reluctance to agree to Jewish feeling about meats offered to idols and things strangled. The trouble at Corinth about meats offered to idols comes after the Judaizers have been there and brings up aspects of the subject not contemplated in the Jerusalem epistle. But Paul is not allowing the fact that the Judaizers had reopened the controversy at Antioch on the ground of social relations with the Gentiles to keep him from loyal adherence to the agreement made in Jerusalem. Ramsay[1] thinks that the Judaizers will later use these decrees and Paul's circumcision of Timothy as an argument for their contention. Hence he thinks Paul soon ceased to say anything more about the decrees. The Galatians were led to desert Paul, he argues.

5. *Hedged in by the Spirit of Jesus.*—"And they went through the region of Phrygia and Galatia, having been forbidden of the Holy Spirit to speak the word in Asia" (Acts 16 : 6). Few historical statements in Acts have caused more comment over the geographical details. The natural way of taking this passage is that Paul has in verse 5 finished the region of Lycaonia (South Galatia), and had planned to go into Asia (Roman province) to the west, probably aiming to go on to Ephesus. But the Holy Spirit forbade that. Hence he turned north-west through the Phrygio-Galatic region. This is the normal way to understand

[1] "St. Paul the Traveller," p. 182 f.

the correct Greek text. He went on into another part of the province of Galatia after leaving South Galatia. It is still a question whether "the region of Phrygia and Galatia" means the Phrygian part of the Galatic province rather than the Phrygian part of the Asian province, in addition to Galatia. The margin of the American Revision has "Phrygia and the region of Galatia," which would imply two separate parts rather than two names for one region. According to this view Paul went north through the Phrygian region after leaving Lycaonia and went on into Galatia proper (old Galatia). According to the other view he may not have touched old or North Galatia at all, or he may have gone through only the western side of Galatia proper. This latter modification (North-western Galatia) is the view of Findlay in his article on Paul in Hastings' "D. B." It is just one of those questions that may never be settled satisfactorily, though a turn of the spade some day may put the matter at rest. Ramsay has ably advocated the position that Paul never entered Galatia proper (North Galatia) at all, but only Lycaonia, Pisidia, and Phrygia. Then he wrote only to the churches of South Galatia. This view has many attractions, but still has grave critical difficulties in its way. To be sure, Paul may have gone on this trip to Galatia (the western end) and still have written only to South Galatia. But it remains true that the incidental manner in which Luke, in Acts 16:6 f., mentions the journey suits best the accidental way

in which Paul comes to preach to the readers of the
Epistle (Gal. 4 : 13).   But the question is too large
for minute discussion in this volume, though I still
think that Paul probably had the real Galatians in
mind in his Epistle, to whom he went for the first time
in the second missionary tour.   We know from the
Galatian Epistle that he had success with them and
was kindly treated by the volatile Celts (Gal. 4 : 14 f.).

Luke seems to hurry over this portion of the trip
in the desire to reach Troas.   Ramsay[1] may be right
also in suggesting that the desertion of the Galatians
led Paul to say little about them to Luke.   Findlay
finds the explanation of Luke's silence about the
North Galatian work in the fact that it was off the
main line and a sort of "parenthesis" in Paul's labors.
It is clear that the northern part of the province of
Galatia (or north-western) was reached, because Paul
tried to go on into Bithynia.   Here he was debarred
again by the Spirit of Jesus.   Two rebuffs on the same
trip would have discouraged some men.   Paul was not
allowed to go west into Asia, nor north into Bithynia.
But he had no notion of turning back home in disgust.
He pushed on to the north-west through the edge of
Asia by Mysia to Troas.   He was pressed by the Spirit,
not backward, but forward.

6. *The Macedonian Call and Luke.*—Troas was full
of memories of Europe which it faced.   This region
was that of Priam and Agamemnon, of Xerxes, of Julius

[1] "St. Paul the Traveller," p. 183 f.

Cæsar, of Alexander. Once the European conqueror of Asia stopped here, but Conybeare and Howson[1] do not put it too strongly when they say that we are more concerned with the memories of Paul than of Alexander. In a sense Alexander's conquest of Asia made possible Paul's conquest of Europe for Christ. The triumph of the Greek culture had unified the world. Roman sway had conserved the Greek culture. Both Roman power and Greek culture are the servants and agents of Paul as he stands upon the shores of the Ægean Sea and faces the problem of Europe. It is one of those eras in history which give one pause. One can but wonder what might have been the result if Paul had not pushed on to Troas, but had turned back to Cappadocia and Pontus, to Armenia and Babylonia, to India and China. Others might in time have carried the gospel westward, as some did to Rome. But if the stamp of Paul were removed from Macedonia, Achaia, and Rome, Christian history would not have run the same course.

Paul had visions at great crises in his ministry. It has been suggested that in this vision the man of Macedonia was in reality Luke who lived in Philippi. A merely natural explanation will hardly meet the demands of the language in Acts 16 : 9, though Luke may have had his home in Philippi and may have spoken to Paul on the subject of the needs of Macedonia. The vision was clearly a call of God to Paul.

[1] "Life and Epistles of St. Paul," p. 280 of Vol. I Scribner's edition.

What should he do? It was a venture to go to a new continent among a strange people. He had no examples to guide him. But it was in line with his mission to the Gentiles.

Paul took the brethren into his confidence. He told Silas, Timothy, and Luke. We have not had Luke's presence in the story before and it is revealed here by the use of "we" and "us" (Acts 16 : 10). Where Luke joined the party we are not told. It is possible, though pure conjecture, that this "beloved physician" (Col. 4 : 14) may have saved Paul's life during his sickness in Galatia (Gal. 4 : 13). But the appearance of this Gentile Christian (one of Paul's new converts?) on the scene is an event of the first importance in the life of Paul. He will not, indeed, be with Paul constantly, though he is in the story in Acts steadily, from Acts 20 : 5 to the end, as well as from 16 : 10 to Philippi (the "we" sections). He is with Paul in Rome in both of his imprisonments (Col. 4 : 14; II Tim. 3 : 11). He is Paul's best interpreter (after his own Epistles) as well as one of the historians of Jesus. He brings a literary quality to the study of original Christianity, in the case of both Jesus and the disciples, that is extremely valuable. He is, in truth, the first church historian as Paul is the first Christian theologian. But he never obtrudes himself. We merely know that now he is giving us what he has learned first hand by his own experience.

The problem raised was not merely one of revelation,

though it was that. It was one of reason also. It was
an issue that had to be faced with the best judgment
to be had. It called for sober criticism. It did not
occur to Paul to go back to Jerusalem to get an opinion
on the vision from the brethren there. He acted on the
judgment of those with him. The result of the investigation was the conclusion (συμβιβάζοντες) that
God had called the whole party ("us") to preach
the gospel in Macedonia. Duty followed interpretation.

They start and make a straight course to Samothrace.
The next day they are at Neapolis (Newtown), the sea-
port of Philippi. It is a quick trip. The thing is done.
This Rubicon has been crossed. A great forward
step in the history of Christianity has been taken. It
is a noble company, these four, who step upon virgin
soil and grapple with the tremendous problem of
establishing the gospel among the mighty Greeks in
their own home. Macedonia and Greece are practically one from this point of view. The history of
Europe will largely turn upon the success of this campaign. The Greeks were the teachers of Rome. Ramsay observes that in saving the Roman Empire for
Christ Paul was really preserving it from decay by
putting a new vital force within it, a force that made
for peace and for progress.

7. *Philippi: Lydia and the Jailer.*—Paul is now in
the Roman province of Macedonia, the land of Philip,
of Alexander the Great, of Aristotle. The city of

Philippi was a colony of Rome (Acts 16 : 12). It had been started as a military post and was still largely so, though commercial interests were large. Luke does not claim that Philippi was the first city (Acts 16 : 17) in the province, for Thessalonica would challenge that claim. Even in the district Ramsay[1] thinks that probably Amphipolis still had the lead of Philippi in public opinion, though Philippi was "first by its own consent" and was rapidly forging ahead. Ramsay thinks also that Luke, being a citizen of Philippi "had the true Greek pride in his own city" and took Philippi's side in the rivalry between them. Did Paul know of the famous battle here in B.C. 42, when Brutus and Cassius went down before Antony, Octavius and Lepidus (the second triumvirate)? He is on historic ground.

Where should Paul begin the European campaign? He seems to have waited some days (Acts 16 : 12) to find out where he could take hold. The Jews seemed to be few, since it was largely a military city. No synagogue is mentioned. But Paul knew well what the habits of the Jews were. Their ablutions required water. Did Luke give Paul any clew? At any rate they went out of town, down by the river-side (Gaggitas?), "where we supposed there was a place of prayer." It was not a very encouraging field for a beginning. Besides, they found only a handful of women. Compare Jesus at Jacob's Well in John 4:6. Paul made

[1] "St. Paul the Traveller," p. 206 f.

the best of the situation. Curiously enough, Lydia
was herself from Thyatira of the province of Asia,
in which province Paul had recently been forbidden
to labor. God opened the heart of this Jewish mer-
chant woman, as well as the hearts of her employees.
The work of Christ in this great European campaign
begins with a handful of humble women. Thank
God that the women can be enlisted for Christ even
if gold still grips the souls of men. Her home was
opened to the brethren, and the place of prayer by the
river became Paul's pulpit for Philippi.

It was not long before trouble came. It is impossible
for a minister, who is always loyal to Christ, to keep out
of trouble. Ramsay[1] considers the girl who was converted under Paul's preaching merely a ventriloquist,
but one who herself believed that she had "a spirit of
divination." The trouble with this otherwise possible
explanation of the "python" is that Luke represents
Paul as addressing the spirit and ordering it to come
out of the girl (Acts 16 : 18). We have thus a case
parallel to the demoniacs who bore testimony to Jesus.
But, whatever the explanation, her masters ceased to
make money out of the poor girl's misfortune. They
seemed to have organized a regular company that
traded with her gift of divination. Paul and Silas
had touched the pockets of these men, and they rose
in wrath against the new preachers who had interfered
with their vested rights. The lottery, the saloon, the

[1] "St. Paul the Traveller," p. 215 f.

gambling hells of modern life have all made like complaint against courageous ministers of Christ.

The attack seems to have been rough, for they
"dragged" Paul and Silas before the rulers (ἄρχοντες)
or magistrates (στρατηγοί prætors). Luke uses both
terms, the general and the Latin, perhaps using the
mixed language of conversation.[1] It is an old and ever
new story that here follows. These infamous men
blandly pose as Roman patriots and seek to arouse
Gentile prejudice against Paul and Silas as Jews, not
knowing any special difference between Christians
and Jews. They say nothing, of course, about their
private grudge, but their patriotism is for revenue only.
The "trouble" to the "city" was what had come
to the masters of the girl. But the demagogues had
all too much success with the rabble, and the magistrates, like Pilate before them, yielded to popular
clamor and ordered the prisoners, after a flogging, to
stocks and the inner prison.

That night in the Gentile prison was a new experience for Paul. He was to have many more like
it in the future. The joy of Paul and Silas is noteworthy. Paul will one day write out of a prison in
Rome to the church at Philippi an Epistle full of
cheer. Ramsay[2] explains that an earthquake would
easily open an Eastern prison, while the prisoners

[1] Ramsay, "St. Paul the Traveller," p. 217. Ramsay thinks
it uncertain whether these "Masters" were themselves Romans
since the majority of the population were Greeks.
[2] "St. Paul the Traveller," p. 224 f.

would be overawed by the effect of that portent. Paul
is quick to seize the opportunity of the jailer's conviction, to win him from suicide to salvation.

The magistrates possibly felt that Paul had caused
the earthquake. At any rate, they wish to be rid of
these strange prisoners. It is not clear why Paul did
not claim Roman citizenship before the flogging. No
explanation is given by Luke. In the heat and excitement of the moment it is possible that Paul may
not have thought of it till later. Indeed the mob and
the magistrates gave Paul no time for explanation. He
will appeal to it in Acts 22. But, at any rate, Paul shows
plenty of independence when the magistrates wish him to
help them out of their dilemma. Silas is called a Roman
citizen also by Paul (Acts 16 : 37). Ramsay[1] thinks
that Luke has mistranslated Paul's Latin to the
magistrates when he claimed his Roman citizenship,
since the condemnation of a Roman citizen would not
alleviate the flogging, but make it worse. On the other
hand, the argument in Paul's mind may have gone thus.
It is unlawful to flog any one uncondemned; besides,
it was done publicly; then again we are Romans and
it was unlawful to do it at all; to cap it all they have
put us into prison. The argument about "Romans"
thus is not the first one, but toward the end. It is
the magistrates who are now afraid. They show proper
courtesy now. Paul and Silas leave Luke and Timothy
behind in Philippi with a church fully established.

[1] "St. Paul the Traveller," p. 224 f.

8. *Thessalonica: The Excitable Populace.*—Thessalonica is the capital of the province of Macedonia and the most important city that Paul has come to since Antioch.[1] It is the Roman administrative city and a great commercial emporium (the present Saloniki). The Jews are strong here. In their synagogue Paul preached on three successive Sabbaths (compare the two at Antioch in Pisidia (Acts 13 : 44). One is constrained to think from Paul's remarks in I Thess. 1 and 2 that he preached in the city much longer than this. Perhaps Luke's account is confined to the work in the synagogue alone.

Paul's preaching followed the familiar line of argument for Jews in an appeal to the Scriptures to prove that the Messiah was to suffer, to die, to rise again; that Jesus did all this; therefore Jesus was the Messiah. Thus we have (Acts 17 : 2 f.) only the premises and the conclusions, not the details, for which one may turn to the sermon at Antioch in Pisidia. Some impression was made on the Jews and a great one on the "devout Greeks," especially the women. One is reminded again of Antioch in Pisidia where the women were turned against Paul. In Thessalonica, however, the jealous Jews adopt bolder methods. The rabbis collect some "vile fellows of the rabble" ("toughs" from the outcast sections of the city) and engage them to "set the city in an uproar." They do it to perfection, and drag Jason and others, in lieu of Paul and Silas, to the

[1] Findlay, Art. Paul in Hastings' "D. B."

"politarchs," Luke's strange term for the rulers of the city now amply confirmed by inscriptions. Jason and his party of disciples are gravely charged by the rabbis and the hired rabble with having turned the city upside down, the very thing which the rabble had been employed by the rabbis to do! One might imagine himself back in Jerusalem at the trial of Christ, for the charge is filed against the disciples that they preach Jesus as King "contrary to the decrees of Cæsar" (Acts 17 : 7). The Jews were not notorious for loyalty to Cæsar, and these hired "hoodlums" were not loyal to anybody. In Philippi money was behind the cry of patriotism. In Thessalonica the motive is jealousy. These Jewish leaders "troubled the multitude and the rulers of the city" by their specious charges. But the orthodoxy that resorts to such demagoguery is rather lurid and spectacular, to say no more.

None the less, Jason and the rest were put on their good behavior. They apparently felt that Paul had better leave town. So they "sent away Paul and Silas" probably against Paul's own desire. The riot had been really very dangerous. Paul will later allude to these "Jews" (he lays the blame on them, not the politarchs) who "drove out us," "forbidding us to speak to the Gentiles" (I Thess. 2 : 15 f.). But a great work has been done in Thessalonica.

It is possible that the stress put by Paul here on the second coming of Christ may have played into the hands of the Jews in stirring up the mob against Paul.

They may have charged that Paul proclaimed that Jesus would soon come and supplant the Roman Cæsar. He did, indeed, preach to them about "the man of sin" "setting himself forth as God" (II Thess. 2 : 3 f.). "When I was yet with you I told you these things" (verse 5). It was not difficult for the Jews, who did not like the current emperor-worship any more than Paul, to turn his strong words on this subject against him and all the disciples. The excitability of the mob at Thessalonica, under the lead of the Jews, throws a side-light also on the volatile misconceptions of the disciples there about Paul's real statements as to the second coming of Christ. He had exhorted them to look for that coming and to be ready for him. He would come suddenly as a thief in the night (I Thess. 5 : 2). But some of them had claimed that Paul taught that Jesus' coming was "just at hand" (a point which he later expressly denies, II Thess. 2 : 2), and hence it was useless to work. These pious enthusiasts Paul exhorted while with them to be quiet, to attend to their own business and to work with their own hands (I Thess. 4 : 11): He has no sympathy with the type of piety that makes one unfit for work (II Thess. 3 : 10). Evidently Paul is not a socialist in the strict use of that term. This is not the last time that Paul will be misunderstood while present and absent.

But the work at Thessalonica was a great achievement. This strategic city with a live church in it

served as a sounding-board to echo forth the gospel
to all the region round both in Macedonia and Achaia
(I Thess. 1 : 7 f.). Paul tells us much of the consolation and joy that he found in the church at Thessalonica (I Thess. 1–3) so that one must expand a good deal
the brief narrative of Luke in Acts 17 : 1–10. The
pastoral side of Paul's work is prominent in the Epistles
to Thessalonica.

He carefully explains to them the substance and
spirit of his message, as well as the love which he still
bore them, and his exemplary conduct while with them.

9. *Berœa: Search of the Scriptures.*—If Paul and
Silas had to flee from Thessalonica by night (cf.
Damascus), they had reward in Berœa. They begin
with the synagogue of the Jews who differ from the
Jews in Thessalonica in a readiness to investigate the
Scriptures to see if the new doctrines were true. That
shows an openness of mind towards new truth that
entitles them to the term "noble" (Acts 17 : 11).
Timothy had now rejoined Paul and Silas (17 : 14).
The story of Thessalonica is, in a measure, repeated
here, for the Jews of Thessalonica follow Paul to
Berœa as those from Antioch in Pisidia went to Iconium.
It does not seem to have been necessary to get "hoodlums" to raise a mob for Paul's benefit in Berœa,
though that is possible, "stirring up and troubling
the multitudes" (17 : 13). The "brethren" (17 : 14)
sent him on to the sea. Silas and Timothy remain
in Berœa, while Paul goes on to Athens with instructions

for them to rejoin him there speedily, apparently with news from Thessalonica and Berœa. In Athens Paul waited for them (17 : 16). From I Thess. 3 : 1 it looks as if Timothy, at any rate, came on and was sent back again by Paul to Thessalonica. If so, when Luke in Acts 18 : 5 speaks of Silas and Timothy coming down from Macedonia to Corinth, he is alluding to the second coming, not to the first at Athens (cf. Paul's allusions to the visits to Jerusalem in Gal. 1 and 2).

10. *Athens: Idolatry and Philosophy.*—One need not suppose that Paul was insensible to the glory and greatness of Athens. But his mission to Europe was that of ambassador for Christ. He was, indeed, in the chief seat of ancient culture of all the world. The University of Athens had rivals now in Alexandria, Rhodes, Tarsus and elsewhere, but none of them had the glory of Athens. The great historians, orators, poets, generals, statesmen, philosophers of Athens were known all over the world. Paul was distinctly open to Hellenic influence, Jew though he was. The architecture, the sculpture, the beauty of Athens had been unrivalled in the crowning age of sculpture and architecture. The golden age of Athens was far in the past, but the glory still lingered over the Acropolis (as it does yet over its ruins). Paul had time enough to enjoy them, if he willed.

But the sculpture faded before the multitude of idols. The glorious Parthenon was itself the home of the worship of Minerva. The learning, the phi-

losophy of the city was under the spell of idolatry.
The city, this glorious city, was given over to idols
(Acts 17 : 16). That fact stared him in the face. He
had seen idolatrous cities before, even of the baser sort
as Antioch in Syria and Paphos in Cyprus. His very
spirit was provoked to see this city, the home of so
much that was high and noble, given over to false gods.
There were gods at every turn; some thirty thousand
in all were worshipped in Athens.

He must speak. In the synagogue he spoke to the
Jews on the Sabbath. On other days he had a word
with chance comers in the agora (17 : 17) where teachers of every philosophy and religion dispensed their wisdom to any who would listen. Paul was just one more
in the vast army of these lecturers who had come to
the world's intellectual centre. Ramsay[1] conceives
that Paul's debate with the Epicurean and Stoic philosophers in reality took place in the University of
Athens. That view gives more dignity to the matter.
These two schools of practical philosophy were dominant in the world of that time. Socrates turned the
trend of thought from mere cosmological speculation
to man himself. Plato had taken the cue from his
master and lifted philosophy to a high plane of abstract
thought with many noble ideals. Aristotle was en-
cyclopædic and combined the outward and the inward,
and systematized methods of thought and expression.
Zeno and Epicurus represented a recoil from so much

[1] "St. Paul the Traveller," pp. 241 ff.

speculation to a practical view of life. The one (the Stoic) aimed at conquest over evil by self-control that hardened into pride, despair and pantheism. The other (the Epicurean) was atheistic, light-hearted, flippant, selfish, and degenerated into mere love of pleasure. But they held the field, not only at Athens, but in all the great centres of life (Jerusalem excepted). They were ready to defend their views to any new-comer. Some of them cannot conceal their fine scorn for Paul "this babbler" (seed-gatherer like a sparrow picking up crumbs in the agora, or σπερμολόγος). Others are more polite, but equally obtuse, for they think that Paul preaches two gods (one Jesus, the other the resurrection).[1] The Athenians made gods out of the abstract virtues. Evidently Paul was not meeting with much success with the philosophers. One recalls Christ's difficulty with the Jewish rabbi Nicodemus.

They take him to Mars Hill! Why? Clearly not to be tried, though one is reminded of Socrates, who was charged with teaching strange doctrines. Was it merely idle curiosity to pass away the time? They were, true to their nature, always ready for something newer than the last fad if for nothing serious (17:21), a touch true to life in Athens as drawn by Plato himself. This motive was undoubtedly present. But was there any more serious purpose? Ramsay[2]

[1] Cf. Shakespeare, "St. Paul at Athens"; D'Ooge, "The Acropolis of Athens" (1909).
[2] "St. Paul the Traveller," p. 247.

makes out a pretty good case for the idea that Paul
was really brought before the Council, not for trial,
but to see if he was entitled to a lecturer's certificate
so as to have proper standing as a lecturer on religion
and philosophy along with the Stoics and Epicureans.
The matter is not entirely clear. It is possible, though
slightly artificial. But, in any case, the tone of the
audience is contemptuous, while formally polite
(17 : 19 f.). It is, however, an inspiring moment
when he stands on Mars Hill, facing the noble temple
of Minerva on the Acropolis, with members of the
Council present along with Epicurean and Stoic philosophers, to speak about Jesus of Nazareth in the midst
of Greek culture. We have seen Paul in various trying situations before. He has not yet met one that
called for more resource and readiness. He will need
not only his Jewish training and Christian experience,
but all his knowledge of Greek life and thought. He
has never addressed an audience whose world outlook
(*Weltanschauung*) was so utterly different from his.
Can he so put Christianity as to be loyal to Christ
and at the same time win the attention of this assembly?
There is a curious Attic flavor to the address of Paul
here which every Greek student appreciates. Paul
seems to respond to his atmosphere in his very language,
and Luke has the same feeling about it.

The address is a masterpiece of real eloquence on
the greatest of themes. He skilfully introduces the
subject of God after passing a compliment on their

religiosity (verse 22 f.). He waves aside the worship
of idols by an argument from nature and represents
God as near those who are groping in the dark toward
him (cf. in Rom. 1 and 2, the other side, the heathen
going away from God). He presents God, the living
God, as the centre of life and the Father of all men,
as spirit and to be worshipped in spirit. This God commands repentance from sin and will judge all by the
man whom he has sent and has raised from the dead.
The sermon ends abruptly. Paul probably had more
to say about Jesus, but he could not go on. Some
laughed in his face, others politely excused themselves,
a few believed; Paul abruptly went out from among
them (17 : 33), probably disappointed at such treatment.

But he had been faithful to Christ and the truth.
He had condemned idolatry and exalted God. He
had preached sin, repentance, judgment, Jesus and
the resurrection, as much as they would hear. He
had not preached philosophy instead of the gospel.
He had only alluded to their philosophy indirectly to
turn their thoughts to God. He had preached a great
sermon, but little was accomplished by it. Probably
he was mortified as many a preacher has been since,
at the result of his efforts. What shall he do? If
Athens will not listen to him, will any city in Greece
do so? Will they follow the example of Athens? It
matters not. He will stick to the preaching of the
Cross. He will preach Christ crucified whether the
philosophers will have it or not (I Cor. 2 : 2). Let the

Cross be foolishness to the Greek as it is a stumbling block to the Jew in every city. Paul knows that it is both the power of God and the wisdom of God (I Cor. 1 : 23 f.). He will preach the word of the Cross. The day will come when the disputer of this world as well as the scribe will both be made foolish before God (I Cor. 1 : 20). The Greek philosopher and Jewish rabbi do not use the same weapons in debate. Perhaps Paul was at a loss to know how to measure swords with this new variety of word-mongers. He was a greater philosopher than all of them in reality, but they could not grasp the range of his spiritual vision. Paul was not driven out of Athens. He was laughed out. They would not even persecute him.[1]

11. *Corinth: Sudden Wealth and False Culture.*—Will Corinth prove a more promising field? It could hardly be worse. Athens was old and self-confident, volatile and scornful. Corinth had been utterly destroyed by Mummius and lay in ruins for a hundred years, till Julius Cæsar restored it. Now it is a great and flourishing commercial metropolis, rich and wicked. Like other "boom" towns, Corinth has a veneer of culture and an imitation of philosophy. The false in taste was in the ascendant. There are difficulties in abundance in Corinth, but they are not exactly those of Athens where the whole life was dominated by the critical and philosophical atmosphere of the

---

[1] "Nowhere else had he so completely failed."—Stalker, "Life of St. Paul," p. 97.

University. Christianity and culture are not in opposition. They are in reality at one. But an arrogant
philosophy can be very scornful of spiritual matters.
But in a city like Corinth the false culture did not have
a firm hold on all. There were many who would be
open to something better, who even hungered for the
realities of life.

The Jews are strong in Corinth, and Paul found,
as usual, the synagogue at his service. The presence
there of Aquila, of Pontus, and Priscilla his wife, was
due to the expulsion of the Jews from Rome by the
Emperor Claudius (Acts 18:2). They are of much
interest in themselves, for they will come across Paul's
path a number of times and always in a helpful way.
Whether they were already Christians or became so as
the result of Paul's labors we do not know. What is
stated by Luke (18:3) is that they, like Paul, had the
trade of tent-making. That was a common bond,
besides that of Christ. So they dwelt together, while
Paul reasoned in the synagogue on the Sabbath. Here
is a noble picture of Paul, who had been begged to leave
Philippi, driven out of Thessalonica and Berœa,
laughed out of Athens, yet pushing on alone to Corinth,
supporting himself, making new friends, winning a
place for Christ among Jews and Greeks in that great
city.

He had moments of depression, but he held on. He
was longing and looking for the coming of Silas and
Timothy from Thessalonica. The arrival of Timothy

and Silas gave Paul great joy (I Thess. 3 : 6), for now he knew that the church at Thessalonica was standing fast in the Lord. Now he really lived (verse 8). The immediate effect of these new helpers was that Paul devoted himself with fresh energy to the word (Acts 18 : 5). They may have brought a supply of provisions from the church at Philippi, as had happened several times while Paul was in Thessalonica (Phil. 4 : 16). At any rate, Paul would need to make fewer tents and could preach more sermons.

The new power in Paul's preaching caused resistance among the Jews. The story of Antioch in Pisidia, Thessalonica, Berœa is, in a measure, repeated, but with a difference. The modification is that Paul now stands his ground. As at Antioch in Pisidia, Paul turns dramatically from the Jews to the Gentiles. Ramsay[1] admits that Paul's manner was not very conciliatory when he was angry, and calls the shaking out of the raiment a "very exasperating gesture." In the trial of Jesus the Jews took the blood of Jesus on their heads. Here Paul says: "Your blood be upon your own heads" (Acts 18 : 6). He was clean. It was probably exasperating to the Jews for Paul to hold his preaching services in a house "hard by" the synagogue. The sense of rivalry would thus be keen. Corinth, like Philippi, was a colony, and Titus Justus has a Roman name, though he had probably been an attendant on the synagogue worship (Acts 18 : 7). The conversion

[1] "St. Paul the Traveller," p. 256.

and baptism of Crispus (ruler of the synagogue) and his household would add to the bitterness. It would be like the pastor of a church of one denomination joining another next door.

The vision of the Lord to Paul and the message not to be afraid show that resentment was sharp (18:9 f.). Perhaps but for this message Paul might have left Corinth as he had done in other cities and not without reason. He had been told by Jesus to leave Jerusalem. But now he holds on till the outbreak comes and many days after, probably two years in all (18 : 11, 18).

The coming of Gallio, brother of Seneca, to Achaia as proconsul (so after 54 A.D.) had an important bearing on Paul's career in that there is developed under him "the imperial policy in its relation to Paul and to Christian preaching." [1]   In Galatia and Asia Minor, where Paul had been the victim of persecution, his case had only come before the city magistrates or a mob had driven him off as in Lystra. The various city magistrates had all felt the force of personal intrigue or popular clamor. Here, however, the proconsul himself is appealed to, who either had a more liberal and just temper or took more pains to separate the Jewish ceremonial quibbles from Roman provincial law.[2] As a result the Jewish conspirators fail utterly in this case against Paul, while Sosthenes, the new ruler of the synagogue, himself gets the beating that he had meant

[1] Ramsay, "St. Paul the Traveller," p. 257.
[2] Ramsay, "St. Paul the Traveller," p. 258.

for Paul, gets it from the mob which the Jews had so successfully used against Paul, while Gallio, like Nelson, has a "blind eye" to the work of the mob. The result of Gallio's refusal to punish Paul was to give him and his preaching a standing before Roman law that it had not had heretofore, a very important matter. It was a virtual edict of religious freedom for Christian preachers as a sect of the Jews at any rate, for Gallio did not go into the differences between Paul and the Jews.

12. *Paul's First Epistles: I and II Thessalonians.* —It was probably before the latter part of Paul's stay in Corinth that he wrote the Epistles to the Thessalonians. It was soon after Timothy and Silas came. These are the first of Paul's thirteen Epistles preserved in the New Testament. As already mentioned, these Epistles fall into four groups:

I and II Thessalonians.

I and II Corinthians, Galatians, Romans.

Philippians, Philemon, Colossians, Ephesians.

I Timothy, Titus, II Timothy.

The order here given is not known for certain. Some critics put Galatians as the very first on the list, but on insufficient grounds, in my opinion. Others would place it between the Thessalonian Epistles and I Corinthians. The position of Philippians is not clear, whether before or after Colossians and Ephesians. But these two matters of doubt do not greatly affect the working scheme here presented.

Paul had written other letters before these, as might be expected in an age of letter-writing.[1] In II Thess. 2 : 2 Paul warns his readers against forgeries, and in 3 : 17 tells them how to tell a genuine letter of his. Evidently he had already written more than one when men were trying forgeries of them. There is a difference between a merely personal letter and a formal and stately epistle that one writes for public perusal or for permanent preservation. Paul's Letters vary from Philemon, which is almost wholly personal, to Ephesians, which is almost wholly general. Those addressed to churches necessarily have a more formal character, but a personal tone is found, or, at least, personal items. The numerous papyri letters of the early Christian era illustrate well Paul's correspondence with the churches and individuals. He seems to allude in I Cor. 5 : 9 to an epistle which is now lost. A good illustration of the doctrinal epistle (cf. Romans) is found in Acts 15, the epistle from the Jerusalem conference to the Church at Antioch and the Gentile Christians generally. It was distributed as Paul's Epistles came to be (Col. 4 : 15 f.).

The Thessalonian Epistles were probably written during the period A.D. 52–3, and represent an important stage in Paul's spiritual and doctrinal development. One can trace with reasonable correctness the fundamental principles of his Christian theology prior to

[1] Cf. Deissmann, "Bible Studies"; Milligan, "Commentary on Thessalonian Epistles."

this time from the account in Acts. But it is significant in the study of any great man when one comes
upon documents by the man himself, especially if they
be letters where a man gives his real sentiments with
freedom. The ecclesiastical nature of these letters
does not keep Paul's own personality out of them.
His very heart is poured out in gratitude or concern,
for the disciples who were his crown and joy.[1]

The doctrinal theses of Paul's later and more ex-
tensive Epistles are here, the love of God in Christ,
his death on the Cross for sin, justification by faith,
obedience, judgment, the second coming of Christ.
But the remarkable element here is that the Thessalonian Epistles are largely taken up with the second
coming, a subject not mentioned by Luke as belonging
to his preaching so far, and which is not treated at
much length by Paul elsewhere save in I Cor. 7. One
is hardly prepared for its prominence just here in
Paul's teachings. But it is to be remembered that it
was present in the teaching of Jesus and in the early
apostolic preaching. Local circumstances or Paul's
own mood may have brought the subject to the front
at Thessalonica. It was misunderstood and demanded
further explanation. The explanation in the first
Epistle was still misunderstood and called for a second
Epistle. Thus the subject gained a rather larger proportion of attention in these Epistles than seemed to

[1] On the pastoral side of Paul's work, see Chadwick, "The
Pastoral Teaching of St. Paul."

have been true of Paul's preaching as a whole.   But
one cannot deny that Paul, like Jesus, urged the disciples to be in an expectant attitude and ready for the
Lord to come at any time.   The collision at Thessalonica with the city authorities may have led Paul to
feel strongly that the Roman Emperor was the man
of sin who set himself up to be worshipped instead of
God.   There is no doubt at all that Paul was right in
his perception that this emperor-worship was the great
foe of Christianity, the real Anti-Christ.   Paul saw
it thus early as John will discuss in Revelation this
titanic struggle between Christianity and imperial
Rome.   The history of Christianity in the first three
centuries amply vindicated the foresight of both Paul
and John.

The thing here to observe about these Epistles,
as about all of Paul's Letters, is that they spring out
of actual historic circumstances and were written to
meet immediate and pressing needs.   They possess
the element of life and hence are powerful to-day.
They are not artificial or merely literary performances.
Paul wishes to instruct the Thessalonian Christians,
to cheer them, to rebuke them, to lead them to juster
conceptions of the Christian life, to holier living.
Paul's Letters are echoes of his preaching to which he
alludes in these Epistles.   They teem with suggestions
that are rich to-day for every soul that loves Christ.
I cannot here give a minute analysis or exposition of
Paul's Epistles.   That would be to write a commentary,

One may be referred to my "Student's Chronological New Testament"[1] for my analysis of Paul's Epistles in their historical setting.

But at Corinth we see Paul fully conscious of a great message to men. He speaks with the note of authority and power. This gospel (II Thess. 2:14) which he said he had preached in Thessalonica was, indeed, the gospel of God (1 Thess. 2:2, 8, 9). He feels that he is preaching the word of God both at Thessalonica (1 Thess. 2:13) and at Corinth (I Cor. 2:4). He feels emboldened to "command" the church at Thessalonica (II Thess. 3:4, 6, 12) as he had done while with them (verse 10). He even threatens those who obey not his Epistles (II Thess. 3:14). He enjoins that they hold fast to his instructions both by word and epistle (II Thess. 2:15). He is now an experienced preacher of Christ and the proven Apostle to the Gentiles who knows that the hand of God is with him. Along with the clear doctrinal grasp of Christ's person, mission and message there breathes in these Epistles the same deeply spiritual note so really Pauline. Experience precedes theory with Paul.[2] He leaves Corinth the masterful exponent of the Risen Christ with a vision of a world empire for him. He now knows that Christ can conquer Cæsar's realm. Findlay[3] justly conceives that Paul has been making "an

[1] Fleming H. Revell Co.
[2] Sabatier, "The Apostle Paul," p. 114.
[3] Art. Paul in Hastings' "D. B."

interested study of the Roman Empire and its relation
to the Kingdom of Christ." As he approached Rome
he felt its grandeur and was repelled by its idolatrous
Cæsar-worship.

13. *The Return to Antioch.*—I pass by the detail
about the cutting of the hair at Cenchreæ (Acts 18 : 18)
in fulfilment of a vow. The Greek is ambiguous.
Whether it was Paul or Aquila cannot be determined.
Paul was still a Jew and had himself no objection to
observing the Jewish ceremonial law on the part of
Jews as is made clear later (Acts 21 : 26). Paul had,
on the voyage to Ephesus, the pleasure of the com-
panionship of Priscilla and Aquila. The noble wife
of Aquila is often mentioned before him. They were
both congenial spirits to Paul.

They actually sailed, of course, from Cenchreæ,
the harbor of Corinth. Did Timothy and Silas remain in Corinth or come on to Ephesus? Did Timothy go back to Lystra and Silas to Jerusalem? It
may seem remarkable that, after being forbidden on
the outward journey to come to Ephesus in the province
of Asia, Paul should now boldly proceed there. It is
plain that the prohibition was temporary and for a special
purpose. That purpose has now been realized, the
proclamation of the Gospel in Macedonia and Achaia.
Aquila and Priscilla will remain in Ephesus till Paul
returns there and is ready to leave (I Cor. 16 : 19),
over three years in all.   Paul has a brief ministry with
the Jews in Ephesus, but hurries away to Jerusalem,

hoping to return "if God will" (Acts 18 : 19 ff.). The Textus Receptus for verse 21 explains that Paul was anxious to reach Jerusalem for the feast which may have been the passover. If so, in the spring of A.D. 54 (or 53) we may think of Paul's taking ship to come to Cæsarea on his way to visit the Church at Jerusalem (Acts 18 : 22).

It is not absolutely certain that Paul went up to Jerusalem, but that is the natural meaning of "went up" and "went down." It had been some four years since Paul had his battle for Gentile freedom at the Jerusalem Conference. They had been years of great progress for him and the cause of Christ among the Gentiles. He has a more wonderful story to tell than ever. Did he see Peter, James and the other "pillars" at Jerusalem? One cannot tell. The apparent brevity of his stay indicates that the Apostles were chiefly away. Did Paul meet the Judaizers again? Probably their leaders were in Galatia or on the way to Corinth to regulate Paul's Gentile converts. They will soon begin to give Paul serious trouble all along the line of his great tour. But he "saluted the church" and, after an uneventful visit, went on his way home to Antioch. That was his real objective point. Here he was sure of a great welcome. He could now rest awhile and take his bearings. What had Barnabas accomplished meanwhile? One wishes that he knew.

CHAPTER IX

PAUL THE TEACHER OF THE CHURCHES

"Besides those things that are without, there is that
which presseth upon me daily, anxiety for all the
churches" (2 Cor. 11 : 28).

1. *The Statesmanship of Paul.*—It will come out
at every turn in this chapter as we see him carry on
his heart the burden of the churches. He has now
taken the whole world into his vision, and, wherever
the body of Christ suffers, Paul suffers (II Cor. 11 :
29). His horizon has broadened till it compasses the
whole Roman Empire. At Ephesus he will fight the
opposition of Jews and the rage of the silversmiths who
are losing the trade in their shrines; he will throw
his soul into the solution of the troubles at Corinth;
he will superintend the collections for the poor saints
in Jerusalem, a collection that has included Galatia,
Asia, Achaia and Macedonia in its scope before he
leaves Ephesus (I Cor. 16 : 1 f.; II Cor. 9 : 2; Acts
19 : 22); he is planning for a trip to Macedonia,
Achaia, Jerusalem, Rome (Acts 19 : 22). At Troas
Corinth will still be a burden as will be the case in
Macedonia. In Corinth he yearns after Galatia, where
the Judaizers have been playing havoc; after Jerusalem,
where the opposition has crystallized against him;

173

after Rome, where he has not yet been and where the Judaizers have gone on ahead of him; after Spain that great Western empire ripe for the gospel of Christ (Rom. 15 : 28). His sweep of sympathy is that of the Christian statesman who loves the whole world.

It is just during this period that the difficulties thicken in his way. He has now three sets of enemies to fight in detail or together, as Jesus had to meet the combination of Pharisee, Sadducee, Herodian, and finally also the Roman Pilate drawn in (cf. Nero with Paul). Paul has to meet the Jew, the Greek and the Judaizer, and finally the Roman. But during this period (A.D. 54–57) the Romans are not hostile to him, thanks to Gallio's decision in his favor. Nero has succeeded Claudius, but Nero's golden *quinquennium* was the very time when Paul is struggling with the problems of the mission churches, bringing order out of chaos with some of them, indoctrinating all of them. He has to fight Jew and Greek on the ground at Ephesus, while the Judaizer has followed his trail (and that of Apollos at Corinth) and sowed discord with marvellous success. The false brethren let their dogs loose on Paul's heels while he drives back the wolves in front. The perils from his countrymen, from the Gentiles, from the false brethren (II Cor. 11 : 26) were the perils that affected him more than shipwreck, hunger and cold. The hostility of the Jew gave him anguish of heart (Rom. 9 : 2). The Judaizers he spurned as "false apostles," like Satan, coming as angels of light

(II Cor. 11 : 13 f.). The Gentiles rage at him like wild beasts (I Cor. 15 : 32). But he loves both Jew and Gentile and tries to be all things to all men to save some (I Cor. 9 : 20–22).

The grandeur of Paul's nature comes out in this gigantic struggle which he wages with the forces of evil thus massed against him. He has friends, indeed, though some of them are treacherous. He has joy in the churches, though some of them are fickle. The other Apostles have followed the agreement made in Jerusalem and are endeavoring to win the Jewish world to Christ, though with comparatively poor success according to Rom. 9–11. Tradition reports them in various parts of Egypt, Arabia, Mesopotamia, India, and Peter writes to the various provinces of Asia Minor (I Peter 1 : 1 f.). But Paul is not entirely alone, though no other figure of like stature stands by his side as he directs the great campaign in the Roman Empire. He has faithful lieutenants who are loyal to him, men like Timothy, Titus, Erastus, Aquila (with Priscilla), Sosthenes, Apollos, Tyrannus, Sopater, Aristarchus, Secundus, Gaius, Tychicus, Trophimus, Luke, the household of Chloe, Phœbe and the noble array of coworkers whose names occur in Rom. 16. There were others also (see I Cor. 16), but these are enough to show the strong personal ties that Paul had made all over the world. These helpers were his stay and support as he strengthened the work at Ephesus, managed the great collection, wrote his Epistles, sent

committees or embassies, sought to strengthen the
cause and extend the sphere of the Gospel everywhere.
"He was, indeed, born for conflict," and "without
these great troubles we should never have known Paul
at his greatest, nor guessed how tender his heart was,
how heroic his faith, how vigorous his mind, how in-
finite the resources of his strong and supple genius."[1]
Paul appears in his true glory now, but he himself
sees only the face of Jesus. "For the love of Christ
constraineth us" (II Cor. 5 : 14). He glories in his
weaknesses that the power of Christ may rest upon him.
"When I am weak, then am I strong" (II Cor. 12 : 10).
The passionate love for Christ and for lost souls has
him fast. He is willing to be thought beside himself
(II Cor. 5 : 13) if so be he succeeds in his ambition to
please Jesus.

Findlay[2] has a remarkably vigorous paragraph
about "the period of his struggle with the Judaistic
reaction in the Church, and of the four great evangelical
Epistles which were its outcome. The evangelist
becomes the controversialist; the church founder must
defend the churches of his foundation. The apologetic
and doctrinal interests now predominate in St. Paul's
work; he is employed in consolidating the conquests
already won." The Judaizers have made an impression outside of Jerusalem. They have led many
of the Gentiles to believe that Paul was unsound, that

[1] Sabatier, "The Apostle Paul," p. 136.
[2] Art. Paul in Hastings' "D. B."

the Judaizers alone were the exponents of true Christianity, that they have the sanction of the real Apostles. In a word, they are Judaizing the Gentile Christians. The Jerusalem agreement has been set aside. Paul confronts the whole array of them with a lion's courage and vanquishes them in the greatest struggle of his career. His great Epistles "are the crushing and terrible blows with which the mighty combatant openly answered the court intrigues of his enemies. The contest is in reality a drama, which grows larger and more complicated as it advances from Galatia to Rome." [1]

2. *Paul Leaves Antioch Again and for the Last Time.* —Like a whaler he yearns to set forth once more. He is too far from the centre of his great mission conquests. He must be in the thick of the fight. Antioch is now a seasoned church and does not need him so much. His objective point is Ephesus, to which place he had promised to return. He proceeds "through the region of Galatia and Phrygia" (Acts 18 : 23). Ramsay[2] here understands Luke to describe two regions, the Galatic and the Phrygian. Thus Paul went through the province of Galatia and that portion of Phrygia west of Galatia (really in Asia). This interpretation leaves undetermined what portion of the province he traversed, though Luke's phrase in Acts 18 : 23 natu-

---

[1] Sabatier, "The Apostle Paul," p. 136. Cf. Lock, "St. Paul the Master Builder," pp. 38–67.
[2] "St. Paul the Traveller," p. 211.

rally implies that he revisited the churches of Lycaonia
and Phrygia, at any rate, "in order." This would include Galatia proper if he had gone there on his previous
visit. This is the third time that Paul has come to the
province of Galatia and the second time to Galatia
proper, if we follow the North or North-western Galatian
theory. It was during this visit that Paul probably
arranged the collection in Galatia for the poor saints
at Jerusalem (I Cor. 16 : 1). The Judaizers followed
him and got in their mischievous work in Galatia
after Paul had left it.

3. *Three Years in Ephesus.*—It was most likely in
the early summer of 54 (or 53) that Paul reached
Ephesus. He was probably here less than three full
years (cf. Acts 19 : 8, 10, 21 f.; 20 : 31). It was in
the spring of A.D. 57 (or 56) that he left Ephesus
(I Cor. 16 : 8). In this great metropolis of the province
of Asia and of the whole of Asia Minor, Paul plants
himself. The city was a strategic one from every point
of view. The gospel is already well established in
Central Asia Minor. He passed "through the upper
country" on his way to Ephesus (Acts 19 : 1), an expression in harmony with the North Galatian construction. The silversmiths will charge that "not
alone at Ephesus, but almost throughout all Asia,
this Paul hath persuaded and turned away much
people" (Acts 19 : 26), a testimony to the power of
his ministry in Ephesus. Luke himself remarks that
as a result of Paul's labors here "all they that dwelt

in Asia heard the word of the Lord, both Jews and Greeks" (Acts 19 : 10). Paul will later write to Colossæ and Laodicea (Col. 4 : 16), cities in the Lycus valley, a portion of the province which he had not visited (Col. 1 : 9). Later, Timothy will be located here to superintend the mission work in this vast region (I Tim. 1 : 3). John the Apostle seems to have spent the closing years of his ministry in Ephesus and neighborhood. The Book of the Revelation of John is addressed to a circle of seven churches in this province of Asia (Rev. 1 : 11), a list which by no means includes all in the province. It is clear, therefore, that Paul made no mistake in choosing it for his present head-quarters.

We not only have Luke's historical account in the Acts of the Ephesian ministry, but a report of Paul's own summary of his labors there given in an address to the Ephesian elders at Miletus on his way to Jerusalem (Acts 20 : 17–35). The so-called Epistle to the Ephesians was probably a general letter for other churches (Col. 4 : 16) also and is devoid of personal details. But the address at Miletus throws a clear light back upon Paul's work in the city of the goddess Diana. He sketches with tenderness and pathos the elders' knowledge of his life in Ephesus, his loneliness of mind, his tears, the plots of the Jews against him. He is glad to recall his courage in public and private teaching. He had faithfully told them the whole counsel of God. He had done his duty by them. He had preserved his manhood by self-support for his own necessities and for the help of those with him. He had not been a covetous preacher. He had been an example to them of helping the weak. He had remembered and practised the word of the Lord Jesus about the joy of giving. This is a farewell sermon a year after he had left the Church, an address to other preachers. It is wonderfully pertinent to-day. It will help us get Paul's own point of view about his work in Ephesus.

Paul just misses Apollos when he reaches Ephesus. This brilliant young Alexandrian disciple of John the Baptist had become an accurate and powerful expounder of Christianity before he reached Ephesus (Acts 18 : 25), but he was ready to learn more accurately at the hands of Priscilla and Aquila. He was teachable as well as mighty in the Scriptures, and eloquent. It was doubtless a pleasure to Aquila and Priscilla to write to the Corinthians a note of introduction (Acts 18 : 27; cf. II Cor. 3 : 1). As an Alexandrian Jew he powerfully confuted the Jews in Corinth, perhaps with more success than Paul had (Acts 18 : 28). He was a noteworthy successor to Paul and "helped them much." Paul will meet Apollos when he returns to Ephesus. Aquila and Priscilla meanwhile give Paul a joyful welcome.

The case of the twelve misinformed disciples of John the Baptist whom Paul met on his arrival illustrates well the complicated development that went on after the death of John and Jesus. The most of

John's disciples who survived were probably merged into the Christian body, but some held aloof, as we know was true, for a good while after this period. Some of these may have regarded Christianity as a rival, while others were merely in ignorance of the relation of the Baptist's work to that of Jesus. The present group were evidently friendly towards Christianity, but ignorant of the basal elements of John's own preaching. They had not heard of the Holy Spirit, of Jesus, of repentance. John taught all these subjects. They had not really received the baptism of John except in name, a very different example from that of Apollos. Paul baptized them, therefore, in the name of Jesus (Acts 19:5), showing that the full name of the Trinity was not always used. The essential name for Christian baptism was that of Jesus. But note Paul's question in verse 3. Then followed the laying on of hands, speaking with tongues, and prophecy, common experiences of the early Christians.

When Paul had stopped at Ephesus, on his way to Jerusalem, he had been received kindly by the Jews and even invited by them to stay longer. So he renews his work with them, showing that Aquila and Priscilla had kept on good terms with the Jews of Ephesus. He now spends three months teaching the Kingdom of God in the synagogue. But the inevitable breach came when Paul began to get solid results from his work. When they spoke evil of "the Way," he took the disciples away from the synagogue, but without any special dramatic act as at Corinth or at Antioch in Pisidia. They went to the school of Tyrannus. One of the school-teachers (a Greek) had become a disciple. Paul was not over-particular as to the place where he should preach. He would take the Jewish synagogue, a place of prayer by the river-side, a jail, Mars Hill, the home of a disciple (Titus Justus), a school-house, anywhere. But now a cleavage has come and Paul addresses himself more directly to the populace. After school-hours were over (about the fifth hour[1]) we are to think of Paul's addressing the people in the school-room of Professor Tyrannus ("King"). This went on for two years till the riot broke it up.

It is a remarkable incident Luke records in Acts 19 : 11–20. He calls the miracles "special," quite aware of the unusual character of such cures from the use of handkerchiefs or aprons. One is reminded of the cases in connection with Peter's shadow and the hem of Christ's garments. It is evident that the historical evidence for such instances is hardly on a par with that for the more usual miracles. And yet one must not fall into the error of thinking that no difficulties exist about the narratives of the more common miracles. If the event is really supernatural, the humble channel of an apron need not of itself debar belief. Ramsay[2] cites the sudden change from "seven" sons to "both" as discrediting the story. But Moul-

---

[1] Ramsay, "St. Paul the Traveller," p. 271.
[2] "St. Paul the Traveller," p. 272.

ton[1] has produced papyri examples of the use of
ἀμφότεροι (both) in the sense of πάντες (all). One is
not yet able to throw any light on Sceva as a "chief
priest." The failure of these strolling Jewish exorcists
greatly increased the influence of Paul for Christ.
The burning of the magical books set a good example
for all time. The price was high, but not too high, if
it meant deliverance from the spell of bad books.
Many a city and home needs a book-burning. Besides in this instance it was a voluntary book-burning,
not oppression.

Paul is drawing his work in Asia to a close and his
thoughts are reaching out to the other cities in the
empire. His original plan had been to go direct from
Ephesus to Corinth, thence to Macedonia, returning
again by Corinth on his way to Judea (II Cor. 1 : 16).
But this plan was abandoned when he wrote the first
Epistle to Corinth, for he there (I Cor. 16 : 5 f.) expresses an unwillingness to come "by the way." He
wishes, if possible, to spend the next winter with them
(it is now spring, I Cor. 16 : 8). He hopes that they
will speed him on his journey after that "whitherso-
ever I go." This programme agrees exactly with the
one outlined in Acts 19 : 21 as actually carried out.
Why Paul had sent Timothy to Corinth (I Cor. 4 : 17)
and then the Epistle instead of going himself, thus giving
color to the charge of fickleness (I Cor. 4 : 18 f.; II Cor.

---

[1] "Prolegomena," p. 80. Cf. Robertson, "Short Grammar of
the Greek New Testament," p. 23.

1 : 17 ff.), is a matter that belongs to the discussion of the troubles at Corinth which will be taken up directly. It is clear from Acts 19 : 22 that Timothy had come back from Corinth before Paul left Ephesus since he had sent him and Erastus on to Macedonia ahead of him, unless, indeed, he went to Corinth that way and returned (II Cor. 1 : 1), which is not likely. He is later in Macedonia with Paul. Paul's plans at Ephesus include Macedonia, Achaia, Jerusalem, Rome (Acts 19 : 21), and soon Spain comes into that programme (Rom. 15 : 24–28).

He was, indeed, hurried away from Ephesus rather sooner than he had expected. It is possible, though not certain, that I Corinthians was written from Ephesus about the passover time (I Cor. 5 : 7). He did not remain till Pentecost (I Cor. 16 : 8) in spite of "a great door and effectual" which was opened unto him. The "many adversaries" at last proved too much for him. It had already come to be like fighting wild beasts to go on at Ephesus (I Cor. 15 : 32). He was in daily peril of his life. He had held his ground at Ephesus longer even than at Corinth. But finally a condition arose that drove him away, a consolation perhaps to many a pastor who has had to leave the scene of former triumphs for Christ. The story does not differ greatly in principle from the greed of the masters of the poor girl in Philippi and the jealousy of the rabbis in Thessalonica. Demetrius carried on a "god-factory" in Ephesus. He claimed to manufacture the best type of silver shrines of Diana on the market. The preaching of Paul had not only had a bad effect on evil books. It had run down the demand for the wares of the house of Demetrius. His craft and Paul were in direct opposition. Paul had touched the rights of invested capital. Luke has drawn the picture with a master's hand. Demetrius gathered together all the craftsmen of the company and laid before them the danger to their pockets and their piety, and in this order (Acts 19 : 27). Their shout took up the appeal to the dignity of Diana as a matter of course. The rest took care of itself. As in Thessalonica, so here they fail to get hold of Paul himself, but do seize two Macedonian friends of Paul, Aristarchus and Gaius. The scene in the vast theatre is that of the typical mob. Paul was bent on facing these "wild beasts," but he was restrained by the disciples and the Asiarchs. It is interesting to note the friendly attitude of these Asiarchs toward Paul. Ramsay[1] calls these "High Priests of Asia" heads of the worship of Rome and the emperors in the province. He argues therefrom that imperial policy was not yet hostile to Christianity and that the educated Greeks in Ephesus did not share the superstitious hatred of the vulgar toward Paul. A mob is not very discriminating. They had started out against Paul as a Christian, but he was also a Jew. Now Jews hated idols as did Paul, and somehow their rage got started toward the Jews. These put forward Alexander, one

[1] "St. Paul the Traveller," p. 281.

of their number, to explain the difference between the Christians and the Jews. But the fact that Alexander showed his Jewish face was enough for the mob. They had been all confusion till now they became unanimous in their shout for Diana against the Jews. After two hours the town clerk quieted the crowd and demanded that Demetrius take his complaint against Paul to the courts of the proconsul. There is also the regular assembly. He rightly called the mob a riot. His speech shows the true insight into the whole business and that it was mock-patriotism or mock-piety that started it, piety for revenue, in truth. It is plain from Acts 20 : 1 that Paul did not tarry long in Ephesus now. It was useless.

4. *The Trouble at Corinth: 1 Corinthians.*—It has seemed best to present the work at Ephesus as a whole. We must now, however, bring up that side of his life at Ephesus which concerned Corinth and then discuss briefly the first Epistle to the Corinthians. So far as one can tell, the troubles broke out at Corinth after Apollos came. An Apollos party, a Paul party, a Cephas party and a Christ party soon resulted (I Cor. 1 : 12 ff.). It is not at all probable that this divisive spirit grew merely out of likes and dislikes of various disciples in Corinth for Apollos or Paul. That element was present beyond a doubt (I Cor. 3 : 4 f.). The two men differed greatly in style and training. Paul had more weight and intellectual grasp, Apollos more oratorical display in his speech. The two

types of preachers always exist and have their following. But Apollos would not be a party to such rivalry, and so he left. He came back to Ephesus. Paul besought him much to return to Corinth, but he stoutly refused (I Cor. 16 : 12). One can but respect the feelings and conduct of Apollos in the matter.

But this was not all. There is no evidence that Peter had ever been in Corinth, though that is barely possible. The partisan use of Peter's name by the Judaizers, who did come to Corinth, does not prove that Peter had come. His conduct at Antioch had given them all the handle that they needed to pit Peter against Paul. They were quick to take advantage of the split over Apollos and Paul to drive another wedge into this Pauline Church. The name of Cephas (I Cor. 3 : 22) was used as the chief Apostle. Indeed, it was alleged by the Judaizers that all the real Apostles opposed Paul's Gentile programme. The Pharisaic party among the Jewish Christians in Corinth would respond to this so that Paul will have to insist to the church at Corinth, where of all places in the world it ought to have been unnecessary to do so, that he was "in nothing behind the very chiefest Apostles" (II Cor. 12 : 11). The Judaizers gained a strong following here. It is probably this Judaizing party that will stand out against Paul the longest (cf. II Cor. 10–13) after the Apollos and the Christ party have surrendered. When Paul writes II Corinthians there are probably only two parties, the Pauline and the Judaizing.[1] The first Epistle won over to Paul the Apollos and the Christ party.

The Christ party is rather nebulous after all. Paul drops the term in I Cor. 3 : 22. Perhaps it was a party of reaction against the other three. Away with Apollos, Paul, Peter, they urged. Let us use only the name of Christ. It was more a contention for the name than a protest against Paul's teachings and easily melted back into the Pauline position.

But before Paul wrote the Epistle that we term I Corinthians he had probably written another letter about the dreadful peril of immorality in that worst of Greek cities (I Cor. 5 : 9, 11). Some of the disciples had been swept back into the vortex. The household of Chloe (I Cor. 1 : 11) had come to Ephesus and told Paul of the dissensions in the Corinthian Church. He had himself thought of going (1 Cor. 4 : 18–21), but instead had sent Timothy (4 : 17), whom he warmly commends to them (16 : 10). He will surely come soon, but does not wish to come with the rod (4 : 21). It is held by some scholars that Paul did himself make a hurried visit to Corinth and came back to Ephesus. This is, indeed, a possible interpretation of "the third time" in II Cor. 12 : 14; 13 : 1. But the language may as well refer to his plans to come three times, though as yet he has only gone once. In either view he has not yet gone the third time. Observe also "a second benefit" in II Cor. 1 : 15. He put off his pro-

[1] Sabatier, "The Apostle Paul," p. 159.

posed visit out of consideration for them (II Cor. 1 : 23). He wished to spare them. It is argued, on the other hand, that "come again with sorrow" (II Cor. 2 : 1; cf. 12 : 21) means that he had already had one sorrowful visit, but that is not a necessary interpretation. It may mean a second which would be a sorrowful visit.

In the meantime the Church had sent a formal deputation to Paul at Ephesus (Stephanas, Fortunatus, Achaicus, I Cor. 16 : 17). They had refreshed Paul's spirit. A letter from the church had also come which made specific request that Paul help them with other problems also, such as marriage (I Cor. 7 : 1), meats offered to idols (8 : 1), spiritual gifts (12 : 1), and probably the doctrine of the resurrection (15 : 1). This demand offered him the occasion to group together a discussion of the main problems in the church at Corinth.

The Epistle called I Corinthians is that discussion. It was written probably in the spring of 57 (or 56), though Ramsay[1] thinks that it dates in the autumn of 55. This great document is all ablaze with passion and power. It is vital with the real difficulties that confronted the church in Corinth. Apparently it is a pamphlet to meet an emergency rather than a formal theological treatise. But it is just here that its tremendous value for modern life lies. Paul had to meet the live issues of a mission church in a great and wicked city. These issues vary greatly in value.

[1] "St. Paul the Traveller," p. 275.

They range from petty prejudices about preachers to the great doctrine of the resurrection, from serious moral lapses to the eating of meats offered to idols, from the problem of marriage to the collection for the poor, from going to law before the heathen to misuse of the spiritual gifts. There is no one central doctrine advanced in the Epistle. The various topics are treated in successive groups: the divisions in 1–4, the moral questions in 5 and 6, marriage in 7, meats offered to idols in 8–10, abuses in church worship 11–14, the doctrine of the resurrection in 15, the collection and sundry personal items in 16. There is a kind of unity and progress in the whole. Each part is treated with force and enthusiasm. But the remarkable thing about it all is that in the treatment of casuistical questions Paul does not use mere dialectical skill. He seeks the Christian principle that will guide one aright.[1] In doing this he marked the way for Christians in all similar matters. Some, indeed most, of these problems in casuistry have long since passed away, but others have arisen like them. Hence I Corinthians is the most modern of all Paul's writings. Some of the same problems survive with us in a somewhat altered form. But in any case Paul's Christian insight helps every honest-hearted man to-day who longs to walk in the footsteps of Jesus.

But let no one think that a controversial document written in the heat of passion has no literary quality.

[1] Sabatier, "The Apostle Paul," p. 161.

The noblest passage in literature on love is I Cor. 13. The classic on the doctrine of the resurrection is I Cor. 15. These are enough to distinguish any work and testify to the genius of Paul. But his whole tone, besides specific remarks, shows that he is conscious of divine guidance in the message which he sends. He ploughs his way through the maze of theological quibbles and the bog of immorality to the clear light of truth in Christ.

The emphasis laid on the collection for the poor at Jerusalem is noteworthy, for Paul is pushing this offering from Gentiles to Jews on a large scale at the very time that the Judaizers are seeking to make Paul out an enemy of Moses and an apostate Jew. All the varied gifts of the great missionary statesman come into play. The very existence of spiritual Christianity is at stake. The battle between Paul and the ceremonialists is now world-wide. Paul is almost omnipresent. He deals them a heavy blow in I Corinthians, one that tells mightily as we shall soon see.

We have seen (I Cor. 4 : 17; 16 : 10) that it was a little uncertain how Timothy would be received in Corinth. We do not know whether he came back to Corinth or met Paul in Macedonia. He is with him when he writes II Corinthians (1 : 1). Findlay[1] follows Beyschlag and Pfleiderer in thinking that Timothy was mistreated in Corinth by some one who took it as

[1] Art. Paul in Hastings' "D. B."

an insult that Paul had sent another instead of coming himself. According to this view Paul has this matter in mind in II Cor. 2 : 5–11, not merely the case of the incestuous man in I Cor. 5, a matter easily disposed of. Paul may, indeed, have written another letter to Corinth demanding an apology from this insolent brother and his following, the writing of which caused Paul anguish of heart, though it was necessary to do it (II Cor. 2 : 1–4; 7 : 5–16). The majority stood with Paul on this point, though a minority were still obstinate. A part of this theory is that Titus[1] was the bearer of this lost letter sent also from Ephesus. One cannot be dogmatic here, for the data are somewhat conflicting. It is, however, a possible interpretation of a difficult stage in Paul's career.

Another point coupled with this theory is that in II Cor. 1 : 9; 6 : 9 Paul alludes to a well-nigh fatal illness which overtook him in Asia. The revolt in Galatia and Corinth added to his illness made this the darkest hour of Paul's life so far.[2] We are indebted to this experience for Paul's interpretation of death in II Cor. 4 and 5.

But, whether or not Titus was sent to Corinth with another Epistle now lost to us, he was sent there. Paul was not wholly satisfied with the effect of I Corinthians, or new problems arose (if Timothy so reported).

---

[1] Ramsay, "St. Paul the Traveller," p. 284, thinks that Titus was the bearer of 1 Cor. rather than the brethren in 1 Cor. 16 : 17.
[2] Findlay, Art. Paul in Hastings' "D. B."

Then he sends Titus. It does not appear that Titus was with Paul during the second missionary tour. Ramsay,[1] with his usual brilliant acumen, suggests that possibly the Judaizers had interpreted Paul's dropping Titus after the Jerusalem conference for Timothy, who was circumcised, as a back-down on Paul's part. So Paul replied by taking Titus with him on this third tour. After Timothy returned from Corinth, he sent Titus there to confront the Judaizers themselves.

It is, indeed, curious that Luke nowhere in Acts alludes to Titus. Ramsay[2] thinks that this was due to the fact that Titus was kin to Luke, who does not mention his own name. This hint has been carried further by Prof. Alexander Souter,[3] who proposes the idea that Titus was Luke's own brother. He agrees with Ramsay that Luke was one of the two other envoys besides Titus sent by Paul from Macedonia to Corinth (II Cor. 8 : 16–24). He takes "the brother" in II Cor. 8 : 18) to be Titus' brother (Luke). This is possible. However, we know that both Timothy and Erastus had been sent to Macedonia (Acts 19 : 22). If these were still in Macedonia with Luke, the two would come naturally out of these three.

So then, besides the riot in Ephesus that forced Paul out of Ephesus, we may have to think of possible

---

[1] "St. Paul the Traveller," p. 285.
[2] "St. Paul the Traveller," p. 390.
[3] *The Expository Times*, 1907, and Luke, Hastings, "D. C. G."

illness as combining therewith. Indeed, his illness may have been the reason that the craftsmen of Demetrius did not get him. If so, his weak condition would greatly enhance his peril from the mob.

5. *The Suspense in Troas.*—It had been his hope to meet Titus at Troas (II Cor. 2 : 12) on his return from Corinth *via* Macedonia. But the rather sudden departure from Ephesus had brought Paul to Troas ahead of time. None the less, he is restless in spirit because he does not find Titus. His bodily weakness would make the disappointment harder to bear. He had expected to preach the Gospel at Troas, where little had apparently been accomplished when he was here before. The door of opportunity was now wide open (II Cor. 2 : 12), but he was not able to enter it. It is often true of ministers that an overwrought physical condition closes the door that has opened for them. With a sad heart Paul moves on from Troas toward Macedonia, hoping to see Titus. Corinth fills his heart now. Is the work at Corinth to be ruined? If that may happen, his work everywhere may go to pieces. The world looks dark for the great Apostle who journeys alone from Troas. He is "pressed on every side," "perplexed," "pursued," "smitten down," "always delivered unto death for Jesus' sake" (II Cor. 4 : 8–11). Is it worth while after all?

6. *The Rebound in Macedonia: II Corinthians.*— It is a remarkable transition that Paul makes in II Cor. 2 : 14. He breaks forth into a pæan of praise

to God for the glory and dignity of the Christian ministry without any apparent cause. The despondency at Troas is suddenly replaced by the spirit of triumph in Macedonia. It is not till 7 : 5 that he resumes the thread of the narrative in 2 : 13. He comes back to the historical situation in Macedonia in 7 : 5–16 where the explanation of the passionate outburst in 2 : 14–7 : 4 is found. "For even when we were come into Macedonia our flesh had no relief, but we were afflicted on every side; without were fightings, within were fears." God "comforted us by the coming of Titus."

That was joy of itself to see Titus again, but his story gave yet more joy. He "told us your longing, your mourning, your zeal for me." Titus then had accomplished what Timothy failed to do. If Timothy had been mistreated by the incestuous person or by one who had resented Paul's assertions of apostolic authority (I Cor. 5 : 4 f.), he had not written primarily for their sakes, but for the good of the whole church (II Cor. 7 : 12). He had written sharply and with bitter tears (II Cor. 2 : 4) and anguish of heart. We are here assuming a lost letter between I Corinthians and II Corinthians, to which he is referring. He had put the church to the test in the matter (II Cor. 2 : 9). He had, in fact, regretted the writing of the letter after Titus had gone with it (7 : 8). He disliked so to give pain. But now he regrets it no more. He is even glad that they were made sorry (7 : 8), since it had resulted in repentance. Mere sorrow is not repentance. Their sorrow was a godly sort that had led to repentance. Hence, he is glad that he wrote, since he sees the revolution wrought in the church (7 : 11). He is comforted since Titus was comforted by them (7 : 13). He had dared to glory of them to Titus, and now he knows that it is the truth.

One can but regret the loss of this third Epistle. It went to the heart of the controversy between Paul and his enemies in Corinth. Hausrath[1] has suggested that we possess that letter in II Cor. 10–13 which has somehow come to be joined on to the fourth Epistle, our II Cor. 1–9. This view has found some support in spite of Klöpper's refutations in 1874, as from Dr. J. H. Kennedy, The Second and Third Epistles to the Corinthians (1900).[2] But Dr. Dawson Walker[3] presents very strong arguments against the partition of II Corinthians. We treat the Epistle as a unit.

If so, what is the explanation of the great difference in tone between chapters 1–7 and 10–13? An adequate reason is not difficult to find. Indeed, it is clear from II Cor. 2 : 5 that only "in part" had sorrow come to the Corinthians. True (verse 6), it was the majority ("the many") who took Paul's side and inflicted the needed punishment whether on the incestuous person or an insolent offender against Paul's

---

[1] "Der Viercapitel Brief des Paulus an die Corinther."
[2] Dr. Dawson Walker (Review and Expositor, Jan., 1907) quotes Adeney, Bacon, König, McGiffert, Plummer, Schmiedel for it.   [3] Ibid.

authority in the person of Timothy. Paul wished "obedience in all things" (verse 9). It was the gracious acquiescence of the majority of the church that led Paul to write in the exultant strain of 2 : 14–7 : 16. In 1 : 3–2 : 13 Paul had explained the sorrowful train of circumstances that led up to his depression of mind when Titus came. He attributes his recovery of heart to the loyal friends in Corinth. But Titus had told Paul the whole story. The Judaizing emissaries still had a following (II Cor. 3 : 1; 11 : 22 f.; 12 : 11). There are now only two parties in the church at Corinth, the Pauline and the Judaizing or Anti-Pauline. The repeated efforts of Paul to compel submission and to overcome the Judaizing faction had brought matters to a high state of tension. Thus it will appear that the tone of Paul in II Cor. 10–13 towards the recalcitrant minority really suits the situation better after the return of Titus than before.

Paul really had, it seems, three motives in writing this very remarkable Epistle, which reveals his inner consciousness better than any of his writings.[1] In the Thessalonian Epistles the conflict of Christianity with the Man of Sin (the Kingdom of God *vs*. the Kingdom of Rome) showed that eschatological problems held a prominent place in Paul's thoughts. But recently Paul has looked death in the face and he has passed through "a crisis in his soul"[2] which is reflected

[1] Sabatier, "The Apostle Paul," p. 165.
[2] Sabatier, "The Apostle Paul," p. 179.

in II Cor. 4 and 5. It is an intensely personal Epistle and wonderfully exemplifies the trials and consolations of a minister of Christ. The three motives for writing again and at once were to express his gratitude to the majority with an explanation of his conduct toward them (1–7), the pushing on of the collection for the poor saints at Jerusalem (8 and 9) and the rebuke of the stubborn minority (10–13). Each of these sections of the Epistle stands to itself in a sense, yet all three concur and harmonize with the actual situation.

We do not know who carried the Epistle. Ramsay[1] considers very improbable the usual notion that the envoys mentioned in II Cor. 8 : 16–24 conveyed it. But Findlay[2] follows the old view that Paul exhorts the church at Corinth to show proper respect to these three "messengers of the churches" "in the face of the churches" as the bearers of the Epistle as well as agents for the collection. The charge may have a reference to their previous mistreatment of Timothy. If this view is correct, Timothy was not one of the three, since he sends his salutation with Paul to the church (1 : 1). The committee would then probably be Titus, Luke, Erastus. We are grateful for this discussion of the great collection. It shows how Paul enlisted the churches in the enterprise, what difficulties he met, what success he attained. The comity of the churches is also manifest. Paul is anxious to stir Achaia on

---

[1] "St. Paul the Traveller," p. 286.
[2] Art. Paul in Hastings' "D. B."

this subject. They had been kept so busy by the Judaizers in regulating Paul's theology that they had overlooked the matter of the collection.

If the closing chapters (10–13) seem harsh and bitter, one must recall Acts 15, Gal. 2, and I Cor. 1–4, besides the many hints in II Cor. 1–7. Paul has reached the point where endurance ceases to be a virtue. The Judaizers turn every overture for peace into weakness. They ridicule his forbearance and his threats. They malign him, they pervert all that he says and does. They do not wish to be satisfied. They only wish new occasions for injuring Paul. Personal controversy is always to be regretted. It is sorrowful to reflect how easily theological controversy lapses into personalities. But Paul will not surrender to this insolent minority. He will expose them. He does it with the skill of a master. One is reminded of Matt. 23, where Jesus' invective against the Pharisees in the temple is recorded. Paul uses here irony, ridicule, sarcasm, denunciation, threat. He is holding the rod in his hand as he writes. He will wield it when he comes if necessary. One must remember that Paul here is using the authority of the Apostle which the Lord gave him (12 : 12; 13 : 10). Ordinary ministers may well hesitate before they assume exactly this tone even under some provocation. But the time does come even now when there is nothing left for the true preacher to do but to lift up his voice and spare not (II Cor. 13 : 2).

7. *The Triumph in Corinth.*—Paul distinctly implied that he would not come at once to Corinth (II Cor. 12 : 20; 13 : 1, 5, 10). It would be only wise to give this powerful Epistle time to have its effect before he went himself. Luke says (Acts 20 : 2) that Paul gave "much exhortation" in "those parts." We may suppose, therefore, that Paul and Timothy went on through Macedonia and "round about unto Illyricum" (Rom. 15 : 19), since after reaching Corinth Paul will write to Rome about that ministry when he "fully preached the Gospel of Christ." He here, as always, made it his ambition to preach Christ where he had not yet been proclaimed so as not to build on another's foundation (Rom. 15 : 20). We have no record of this ministry as indeed we have none of Paul's labors in Arabia, Judea, Cilicia, Crete, Spain, if he did go there.

One could wish for some account of the reception of II Corinthians on the part of the Judaizing faction. But Luke expressly tells us that Paul came to Greece and spent three months there (Acts 20 : 2 f.). At last, therefore, he came and he staid. This simple story gives eloquent testimony to the efficacy of the Epistle. Doubtless the Judaizing emissaries disappeared before Paul came. The opposition dwindled away. When Paul actually arrived, all is at peace once more. He is loved and honored as he ought to have been all the time.

8. *The Appeal to the Deserting Galatians.*—Paul had saved the day at Corinth after a terrific struggle. But

the cause has nearly been lost in Galatia. I do not raise again the question whether the Epistle to the Galatians was addressed to the Roman province as a whole, or to the Lycaonian and Phrygian disciples alone (South Galatia), or to the real Celts (North Galatia). That is an interesting historical inquiry, but, apart from a few incidental references, the interpretation of the Epistle is not materially changed whichever theory one adopts.

The Epistle throws practically no light on the time and place of its composition. In this respect it is quite unlike the Thessalonian and Corinthian letters. As to place, in fact, there is absolutely nothing to help one form an intelligent opinion. We know a little about the relation of the date to Paul's first visit to the readers of the Epistle. He had preached the gospel to them rather by accident "because of an infirmity of the flesh" (Gal. 4 : 13) "the former time" (or "first"). Does that mean that he had preached to them on two separate visits before he wrote? That is possible, but not necessary. If he is not writing to the Celts of North Galatia, two visits would include the first and second tours. If he is addressing the Celts, the date would come after Paul had passed through "the upper country to Ephesus" (Acts 19 : 1) on the third tour. In that case the letter would be written either from Ephesus or from Corinth. On the other hand, if Paul does not mean that he had been twice among the Galatians and is writing only to South Galatia, the

date could come soon after the first tour and not far
from the time of the Jerusalem Conference. The
place could be Antioch.

Where there are so many alternatives one welcomes
everything that will help. In Gal. 1 : 6 Paul marvels
"that ye are so quickly removing from him that called
you in the grace of Christ unto a different gospel."
But here again we do not know Paul's standard of
comparison for "so quickly" nor the visit which forms
the starting-point. All that we really know is that in
a few years from his last visit the Galatians are deserting
Paul and his gospel of grace for the weak and beggarly
elements of the world (4 : 9). In lieu of any decisive
external evidence, I follow Lightfoot's plan[1] in placing
this Epistle just before Romans. In these two Epistles
we have the same general theme. In Romans Paul
gives a more orderly, impersonal and dispassionate
discussion of justification by faith. In Galatians the
subject is at white heat. He is all aglow with fire
and indignation. It would seem, therefore, that
Galatians was written before, but not long before,
Romans. We know that Romans was written while
he was at Corinth, just before he started on his last
journey to Jerusalem with a view of going to Rome
and Spain (Rom. 15 : 22–31). The doctrinal atmosphere of the two Epistles is the same. Indeed, it is
not difficult to hear the echo of II Corinthians in

[1] "Comm. on Galatians." But cf. Ramsay, "Historical
Comm. on Galatians."

Galatians. The heavy blows that did such good execution in Corinth are now turned upon Galatia. Paul had heat on the subject of the Judaizing controversy about the time of the Jerusalem Conference, but it is hard to think that the situation in Galatia had developed so far as we find it in the Epistle. With some hesitation, therefore, I put Galatians toward the beginning of Paul's "three months" in Greece. Romans came at the close. In the fall of 57 (or 56) A.D., therefore, when Paul reached Corinth, we may suppose that messengers had come over from Galatia to tell the story of the desertion of the Galatians.

The situation was really very bad. They had been bewitched by some wizard among the Judaizers (Gal. 3 : 1). One could wish to know who this man was. The Galatians at first had treated Paul like an angel (4 : 14), had even been ready to pluck out their eyes and give them to him (when he had eye trouble?). But now they look upon him as an enemy because he tells them the truth. They have wandered after a false gospel which is no gospel (1 : 7) at all. They have fallen away from grace and gone back under the bondage of the law (5 : 3 f.). They had been running well till this hinderer came. Now the Galatians have largely gone over to Judaism in the observance of Jewish days and feasts. Paul is afraid that his labor is all in vain (4 : 11). These Judaizers do not themselves keep the law which they have laid upon the necks of the Gentiles (6 : 13).

Paul pronounces an anathema on these perverters of the gospel (1 : 8 f.). He cares nothing for the favor of men in a matter of this kind, this Apostle who was all things to all men if so be he could save some. It is, indeed, a fierce indictment which the Apostle has drawn and vividly portrays the success of the Judaizers since Paul was there. It shows well also what would have been the fate of Corinth if Paul had not put his whole soul into the struggle there. The desertion of the Galatians, however, astonished Paul beyond measure (4 : 9). They were Gentiles and had tasted freedom in Christ.

Paul changes his tone from invective to passionate pleading (4 : 19 f.). He is keenly alive to the bondage of Pharisaism since he once wore that yoke. He calls the Galatians "my little children" and wishes that he could see them once more, for then he would change his tone. He is in travail again over them. Meanwhile, he pleads with them to stand fast in the freedom which Christ gave them and not to be entangled in the yoke of bondage (5 : 1). He does not mean license, but liberty (5 : 13). He even takes the pen in his own hand and gives a closing summary in large letters (6 : 11). Did he have eye trouble still? He closes with a demand that no one trouble him more. He has the right to that respect by reason of "the marks of Jesus," "branded" on his body (6 : 17) in perils oft for Christ. It is a powerful plea, and must have had an immediate effect. One may suppose that, as the Judaizers were driven out of Corinth, so they were expelled out of Galatia by this tremendous polemic.

As an apologetic for spiritual Christianity the Epistle to the Galatians has never been surpassed. The sparks fly hot from the anvil. The book met a great crisis and solved it. Luther used it with telling effect also in the Reformation, in his call to justification by faith, not by works. The manifest genuineness of the Epistle has made it a bulwark of the faith to-day. The heart of the gospel is in the Epistle. It is a permanent exposition of the spiritual life as against mere ceremonialism on the one hand and license in morals on the other. The note of reality is the dominant one here, the note of a live faith, a faith that shows work as proof of the faith. The Apostle has to vindicate his right to speak to the Galatians with authority (1 and 2). He then expounds his gospel to them (3 and 4) and pleads with them to be true to this gospel of freedom and life (5 and 6).

9. *Paul's Gospel: The Epistle to the Romans.*—It is probable that the Epistle to the Romans was not written till shortly before Paul's departure from Corinth. He is expecting to come to them soon (Rom. 1 : 10; 15 : 22–25). He must first go by Jerusalem (15 : 26–28), but it is manifest that he expects to start for Jerusalem promptly (15 : 25). We find him in Philippi during the passover feast (Acts 20 : 6) of this year on the way to Jerusalem. We may assume,

therefore, that the Epistle to the Romans was written from Corinth toward the close of winter in A.D. 57 (or 58). The bearer of the letter was "Phœbe our sister, who is a servant of the church that is at Cenchreæ" (Rom. 16 : 1). Her going to Rome gave Paul the occasion for writing to the church there.

This is the first of Paul's epistles to a church that was not established by him. He recognizes that this point will be observed and justifies it on the broad ground of his apostleship to the Gentiles (15 : 15 f.). He acknowledges his debt to all the Gentiles, both Greeks and Barbarians (1 : 14). He feels hopeful that they may be mutually helpful and confesses to a desire to some fruit among them as well as among the rest of the Gentiles (1 : 12 f.). In writing to them he does not wish to infringe upon the work of others (15 : 20). He had always avoided that. We do not know, indeed, who established the church at Rome. The numerous friends of Paul and former fellow-workers in various parts of the empire now in Rome (Rom. 16) explain to some extent the growth of the church there. Some of these names are Greek, some Latin, some Jewish. Doubtless, the member-ship as a whole consisted of all three elements with a predominance of the Gentile element, since it is on that ground that Paul justifies his writing to the church. But Paul writes to the church as a whole without con-sidering now one section, now the other![1] Whether

[1] Sabatier, "The Apostle Paul," p. 190 f.

the church arose under Jewish or Gentile auspices we cannot tell. The influx of the large body of Christian workers mentioned in Rom. 16 (for I take this chapter as a genuine part of the Epistle) was enough of itself to explain the rise and growth of the church in the imperial city. The tide of travel and life was toward Rome and drew many Christians along.

It is evident that Paul had already much influence in Rome. The names of his followers and friends given in Rom. 16 prove that the church already, before he wrote, had a positive Pauline influence. The names of Prisca and Aquila, already so closely linked with that of Paul in Corinth and Ephesus, greet us first on the list. Paul bears testimony to their devotion to him at the risk of their lives (Rom. 16 : 4), perhaps at Ephesus, and also to the gratitude of "all the churches of the Gentiles." It is possible, according to Hort,[1] that Prisca was connected with one of the important families (Priscus was a great Roman name) and was not a Jewess. Luke only calls Aquila a Jew of Pontus. At any rate, they are both here and have opened their house for a meeting of a portion or all of the church at Rome (16 : 5). Epænetus is from Asia (16 : 5). Paul knows of the great labors of Mary at Rome (16 : 6). Andronicus and Junias Paul calls his kinsmen and fellow-prisoners. They have a reputation among the Apostles and have been Chris-

[1] "Prolegomena to St. Paul's Epistles to the Romans and to Ephesians," p. 14 f. Cf. also Sanday and Headlam on "Romans."

tians longer than Paul (16 : 7). All the names called
are dear to Paul for one reason or another. Nor does
he name all whom he knows in Rome (16 : 14 f.).
From the personal side Paul has ample justification
for writing to the church at Rome.

The Epistle gives us a glimpse of Paul's life in Corinth
during the three months there. Gaius is his host,
and of the whole church in truth (16 : 23). Paul
had baptized him (I Cor. 1 : 14) and he was evidently
a man of importance. He may or may not have been
the recipient of the third Epistle of John. Erastus,
who has been with Paul in Ephesus and Macedonia
(Acts 19 : 22) is the treasurer of the city of Corinth.
Not many mighty were called there, but some were.
Some of Paul's kinsmen are with him here and Timothy
(16 : 21). We know the name of the scribe to whom
Paul dictated the Epistle, Tertius, who puts in a
sentence of his own (16 : 22). We are grateful for all
these personal items.

But Paul had a larger and stronger reason for writing
to the church at Rome than these. It is no less than
the first step of his plan of campaign in the west. He
is now at the zenith of his work. He has established
powerful churches in Cilicia and Syria, Galatia and
Asia, Macedonia and Achaia. He looks to the great
west and longs to win it to Christ. Rome is on the
way to Spain and must be the base of operations for
the work in Spain. He wishes, therefore, to prepare
their minds for this great campaign (15 : 24. 28).

It is no sudden impulse with him. He has long had the desire to come to Rome itself (15 : 23) and had oftentimes purposed to come. (1 : 13). He had been planning for this journey for some time (Acts 19 : 21). From Rome he could reach not only Spain, but also Gaul, Germany, North-western Africa, and even Britain. The church at Rome is the key to the work in the western half of the empire![1] Hence Paul wishes to get in definite touch with them before he comes to carry out his plans. We now see in outline Paul's statesmanlike grasp of the situation in the empire which he purposes to take for Christ.

The purpose of the Epistle was not, therefore, primarily polemical[2] as was true of Galatians. Most likely some Judaizers had gone on to Rome in pursuit of their plan to graft Judaism on to Gentile Christianity. They have definitely failed in the east, outside of Jerusalem, and Paul is going there. They are in Rome when Paul is there (Phil. 1 : 15 f.). It is entirely possible that a few of them had gone on to Rome. But, if so, they have made little headway as yet. Paul does indeed discuss the Judaizing controversy which has so largely consumed his energies of late, but he does so in a much calmer spirit and more indirectly. The treatment of meats offered to idols and the observance of Jewish days in Rom. 14 and 15 indicate that the Jewish problem was a real one in the church

---

[1] Sabatier, "The Apostle Paul," p. 188 f.
[2] Hort, "Romans and Ephesians," p. 5 f.

as it naturally would be in a church where both Jews and Gentiles mingled. The position taken is that held by Paul in I Cor. 8–10, though the discussion is briefer and with less heat. The Jerusalem agreement is not alluded to in either instance, and had long ago been abrogated by the Judaizers, though Paul, for a while at least, kept this part of the settlement. There was, to be sure, no reason to refer to it, now that the Judaizers had renewed the strife and were violating the decision. The rather, Paul presents fundamental considerations growing out of the Christian principles of love and forbearance.

But one word more is to be said. Probably most of the Roman disciples knew of the world-wide conflict between Paul and the Judaizers. They had heard the perversion of Paul's gospel. It was only proper that Paul should give them, since he could not come to them at once, a more formal exposition of what his gospel really was. He is fully conscious of possessing a definite message which he calls his gospel (Rom. 2 : 16; 16 : 25). It was not that of the Judaizers. He is not ashamed to preach his gospel in Rome also (1 : 15). If it was good enough for Corinth, it was good enough for Rome. He wishes them to be established according to his gospel (16 : 25) which he is sure is the mind of Christ (1 : 1, cf. Gal. 1 : 6–10). This Epistle is not a treatise nor a mere book of systematic theology. It is not a sermon. It is at bottom, while in the form of an Epistle, a careful exposition of the fundamental principles of Paul's message to the Gentiles which he considers to be the gospel of God (Rom. 15 : 16) He does not mean to imply that they are heretics or ignorant (15 : 14 f.). He will confine himself to what God has wrought through him (15 : 18). His gospel is the gospel of experience. It is well to remember, therefore, that in this most abstract of Paul's Epistles he himself grounds his doctrines in God's dealing with him. He will, therefore, attempt to expound the gospel to them in Rome. He is not ashamed of that gospel anywhere (1 : 16).

Findlay[1] well suggests that "fronting the imperial city, Paul rises to a higher stature and assumes a loftier accent. The added stateliness of diction and amplitude of treatment betray an imagination, and a statesmanlike sense, touched by the majesty of Rome." The Epistle is planned upon a grander scale with more artistic and literary skill than the preceding ones. He states this theme in 1 : 17 to be the revelation of God's righteousness by faith. Around this central idea he developes what is an apologetic for his whole career, a polemic against the Judaizers, a fundamental and philosophical discussion of the plan of redemption in its bearing on Gentile and Jew. In the rest of chapter 1, Paul proceeds to show how the Gentiles are lost without the gospel. But the Jew is not a whit better off because he does not live up to his increase of light (chapter 2 and 3 : 1–20). In 2 : 21–31 Paul expounds

[1] Art. Paul in Hastings' "D. B."

his theory of the plan of salvation. He then shows how at bottom it is in harmony with the covenant of grace as shown in the case of Abraham (ch. 4). He points out the great advantages of justification by faith in practice and in theoretical comparison between Christ and Adam (chapter 5). Paul answers the objection of a carping Jew who might urge that salvation by grace was really an invitation to license. Instead of that it is an appeal to life in Christ since one has died to sin (ch. 6 and 7 : 1–6). But the consecrated life is not an easy one (7 : 7–25) and is possible only by the help of the Holy Spirit who makes the triumphant outcome beyond doubt (ch. 8). Here we reach the conclusion of Paul's theology as applied to justification and sanctification. He feels called upon, however, to relate the elective purpose of God to the salvation of both Jews and Gentiles since so largely the Jews are turning away from Christ (9–11). The whole argument is magnificent and is unsurpassed for profundity, analysis, and power. He makes a great appeal for consecration to Christ and mutual helpfulness (12–15). He has, in reality, given us his philosophy of history and his hope of the ultimate triumph of the gospel over Jew as well as Gentile. When Paul began his work it was doubtful what the Gentiles would do. Now the Jew is the problem. We can only be grateful for this grand exposition of the mature theology of Paul at the climax of his career written with deliberation and care.

10. *The Gathering Storm at Jerusalem.*—The horizon
has brightened all round save at Jerusalem. This
city has continued to be the home of the Judaizers.
We are not at liberty to say that any of the Apostles
sympathized with them. It way be assumed that the
Apostles remained firm in their compact with Paul
(Gal. 2 : 9). James, the chief Jerusalem elder, has
continued to be Paul's friend, as will appear on Paul's
arrival there. But the Jerusalem church was very
large and the Judaizers very active. It would be easy
in the long absence of Paul to misrepresent his real
position. The noise of the conflict between Paul and
the Judaizers would reach Jerusalem. The Judaizing
missionaries would return to report, and so the Jerusalem
church would have the full benefit of the Judaizing
side of the controversy.

Paul was not unaware of the situation in Jerusalem.
While at Ephesus he was planning to go to Jerusalem
(Acts 19 : 21), though when he wrote I Corinthians he
was thinking of sending the collection by messengers of
the churches with letters to Jerusalem (I Cor. 16 : 3 f.)
and to go himself only if it seemed meet. But before he leaves Corinth it is clear that he must go himself because of the disobedient in Judea (Rom. 15 : 31).
He had used the utmost prudence in the collection
to be above suspicion in the eyes of men (II Cor. 8 : 21;
12 : 17). The collection has been going on quite a
while and is now complete. Galatia, Asia, Macedonia,
and Achaia (I Cor. 16 : 1; Rom. 15 : 26) have contributed

toward it.   Agents of the churches from each province accompanied Paul to Jerusalem (Acts 20 : 4 f.).   Some mss. add "as far as Asia," but this is probably a gloss. Luke goes from Philippi with him to Jerusalem (Acts 20 : 6).   Trophimus of Asia is expressly mentioned in Jerusalem (Acts 21 : 29).   Paul had taken a contribution there before with Barnabas from the Gentile church at Antioch to Jerusalem (Acts 11 : 30), and it had a good effect.   Besides, he had promised the Apostles at the Jerusalem Conference to do this thing (Gal. 2 : 10).   It is now supremely important that something be done to conciliate the Jerusalem Christians who have had their minds poisoned against Paul and his work. Paul feels that it is only just for the Gentiles thus to acknowledge this debt to Jerusalem (Rom. 15 : 27). He is not certain of the outcome and asks for the prayers of the Roman disciples as he faces his adversaries again in their home.   He did that once and was victorious.   But that was some seven or eight years ago.   Many changes have come meanwhile.

The Judaizers seem to have vanished from Corinth when Paul came, but not so the Jews.   They are as hostile as ever, though more cautious.   They do not repeat their inglorious experiment before Gallio, but resort to a secret plot to kill him as he was about to sail for Syria, possibly on a pilgrim ship carrying Achaian and Asian Jews to the passover.[1]   Fortunately

Ramsay, "St. Paul the Traveller," p. 287.

Paul discovered the scheme in time and changed his route by Philippi. God overrules all things. One of the blessings of this change of plan was that Paul picked up Luke again in Philippi (Acts 20 : 6), who goes with him to Rome and is with him when he writes his last letter. Luke might, indeed, have gone on to Jerusalem with Paul anyhow, meeting him at Ephesus, but the sudden change in Paul's plans indicates the contrary. Luke passes over Paul's week in Philippi with a verse only. One could wish to hear again of Lydia. We may be sure of Paul's welcome here, for this church was loyal and actively helpful. Perhaps Luke and Lydia explain much of their zeal for Paul and his work. The rest of the party had gone on to Troas ahead of Paul, and Luke also came after the passover in a voyage that took five days (Acts 20 : 6).

The stay at Troas gave Paul opportunity to do some work that he had not been able to do when he was last here. They are meeting on the first day of the week (Acts 20 : 7), after the fashion that was soon to become universal among the Christians in the breaking of bread. Luke the physician was interested in the death and recovery of Eutychus (Acts 20 : 9–12), who slept and fell out of the window while Paul preached. It was a long sermon, and Paul resumed it after bringing life back to the young man.

We may not tarry long with Paul and his party on their way to Jerusalem. Paul walked alone from Troas to Assos where he again took ship with his com-

panions. In the beautiful spring-time they sail slowly
through the Grecian Archipelago, stopping at Mitylene,
passing by Chios, touching at Samos, and on to Miletus.
Paul did not wish to stop at Ephesus, since he was anxious to reach Jerusalem by Pentecost (Acts 20 : 16).
Besides, he had probably not yet forgotten the manner
of his departure just a year before. But he had time
at Miletus to send for the elders of the church at
Ephesus, who came. Luke probably heard[1] the address of Paul to this body of preachers (Acts 20 : 17–35).
Possibly he took notes at the time. At any rate, he
has preserved it with wonderful sympathy and tenderness. Here we see Paul talking as a preacher to preachers (cf. Jesus in John 14–17). He speaks about his
own pastoral problems at Ephesus and how he met
them. He urges them to fidelity to themselves and to
the flock, to feed the church of God, to guard the flock
against "grievous wolves" who will come among
them. As for himself, he is going bound in the spirit
from a stern sense of duty to Jerusalem, not knowing
what his fate there will be except that the Holy Spirit
has repeatedly told him that bonds and afflictions
await him (Acts 20 : 22 f.). But he does not care for
that, if only he may really accomplish his course and
his ministry. His life is not dear to himself apart from
that. He may never see them again (20 : 25), as he
now feels. It was a pathetic scene as he knelt on the
sea-shore, prayed, and wept with these devoted min-

[1] Cf. Ramsay, "Luke the Physician," p. 23.

isters. They went with him down to the ship and saw
it sail out of sight. Did they ever see Paul again?

Luke hurries his narrative on by Cos, Rhodes, to
Patara, where a new ship was found, one going to
Phœnicia (21 : 2). They come in sight of Cyprus,
going to the south of it. Did not Paul think of Barnabas, of Mark, of Sergius Paulus? At Tyre they landed
and the same warning came from the Holy Spirit about
his fate at Jerusalem. Paul evidently took it all as
information, not as prohibition (Acts 21 : 4). But
another pathetic parting occurred on the shore. There
was a stop at Ptolemais, and now they come to Cæsarea,
the port for Jerusalem. Here Paul meets Philip the
evangelist (21 : 8), the former deacon (Acts 6) and
friend of Stephen. Like Stephen, he had become a
powerful preacher (Acts 8). His four virgin daughters
have the gift of prophecy. One can but wonder if
the subject of Stephen came up between Paul and
Philip. Paul, as has often been said, was the real successor of Stephen. But Agabus, a prophet from Judea,
comes and gives Paul a most dramatic warning as to
the fate that awaited him in Jerusalem (21 : 11). This
was more than enough both for Paul's party and his
friends in Cæsarea. Their pleading did come near
breaking Paul's heart, but did not change his adherence to his sense of duty. Bonds and death for
the name of Jesus had no terrors for Paul (21 : 12–14).
The brethren acquiesced in the will of the Lord when
they failed to have their own way (verse 14).

This almost tragic narrative of Luke will enable us to understand the gravity of the situation at Jerusalem as Paul saw it. He was not willing to go on to Rome and the west and leave a cankering sore at Jerusalem right in the heart of Christendom. Under God he had won the east for Christ and saved it from the Judaizers. He would win the west. But, if he left the great church at Jerusalem practically at outs with him, the trouble might break out again in Syria, Galatia, Asia, Macedonia, Achaia. And if he should be able to hold his following again there would be a schism in the Christian body. There was already a Judaic type of Christianity of a harmless sort represented by James and Peter. In principle this conception of Christianity did not differ from the Gentile type represented by Paul. But the Judaizers were driving the thing to the extreme. They were not content for the Judaic type and the Pauline type to exist side by side. They aimed to destroy the Pauline type and compel Peter and James to come over to their view. If they failed in this, the next step would be an open split. They could organize a denomination composed only of loyal Pharisaic Christians. No uncircumcised Gentiles would be admitted. Paul saw this peril as he came toward Jerusalem. Once the cloud was no bigger than a man's hand. Now it covers the face of the heavens. But he will not run in the face of danger. He is willing to die if he can save the cause of freedom for the Gentile Christians and overthrow the power of the Judaizers who have intrenched themselves in Jerusalem.

He will then go on, come what may. Paul's party falls in with Mnason, of Cyprus, one of the early disciples. Possibly he knew Paul at Antioch or during the first tour in Cyprus. He has a home in Jerusalem, it seems, whither he is now going probably for the feast of Pentecost. Some of the disciples from Cæsarea went on also. So it is a goodly company, but one with the shadow of a grave portent overhanging them. Perhaps they have something of the courage of Thomas who proposed that the disciples go to Jerusalem with Jesus to die with him (John 11 : 16). There are, indeed, many points of similarity between Paul's last trip to Jerusalem and the situation of Jesus as he faced his death. Paul comes to Jerusalem conscious of approaching disaster. Jesus foresaw clearly the death that was coming. Paul was largely in the dark save that he knew that he was beset by his enemies here. The time that Paul was at the conference here the church was on his side in the controversy. How is it now? How will the believers receive him? He knows only too well what the Jews will do if they get a chance.

CHAPTER X

PAUL AT BAY

"If, then, I am a wrong-doer, and have committed anything worthy of death, I refuse not to die; but if none of these things is true whereof these accuse me, no man can give me up unto them. I appeal unto Cæsar" (Acts 25 : 11).

1. *The Charge of the Judaizers.*—Paul had come to Jerusalem to face this charge. His fame had filled all the Jewish world. Jerusalem had long been all agog with it. The Jews thus hated him with more intensity than ever and indorsed the hostile attacks made upon him by their brethren in various parts of the world. In the later accusations against Paul he will be described as a general disturber of the peace all over the world.

Paul's reception by the leading disciples in Jerusalem was all that he could wish. The brethren "received him gladly," and on the next day Paul and his company paid a formal visit to James and all the elders who had met at the house of James (Acts 21 : 17 f.). They listened to Paul's story with the same enthusiasm that they had shown when he first recited his account of the work during the first missionary tour. He took his time, for he had much to tell, and "rehearsed one by one the things which God had wrought through his ministry." They "glorified God" now as before. So far all was well. Paul was assured of the loyalty of James and the elders. They had not believed the perversions of the Judaizers.

But the elders felt obliged to tell Paul that Jerusalem was full of rumors about him, diligently circulated by the Judaizers (Acts 21 : 21), to the effect that Paul was opposed to the observance of the Mosaic ceremonial law by the Jewish Christians; in fact, that he taught the Jews of the Dispersion to forsake Moses and the customs of the fathers. It is easy to see what a serious situation this new charge created. At the time of the Jerusalem Conference Paul contended for freedom for the Gentile Christians from the Mosaic regulations and won his point. No issue was raised about the Jewish Christians. It was simply assumed that they would keep up the customs of the fathers.

It is easy to see why this new charge was trumped up against Paul. They had failed to carry their contention for the bondage of the Gentile Christians to the Mosaic ritual. Their resentment against Paul led them to manufacture this charge in order to ruin him. It was this charge that caused Stephen's death (Acts 6 : 11). The charge against Stephen was false and was supported by hired witnesses, as was that against Jesus about the destruction of the temple. In reality the Pharisees had opposed Jesus mainly because they considered him hostile to their traditions. So Paul is in the goodly succession of Jesus and Stephen. In all probability it occurred to Paul that now at last he himself was to face the very charge that cost Stephen his life. That story Paul knew only too well. In Paul's case, however, the perversion of his position came from the Judaizers, fellow-Christians, alas!

The saddest part about the matter was that the charge of the Judaizers was credited by the many thousands among the Jews in Jerusalem who had believed (Acts 21 : 20), or at any rate they were disposed to credit it. It was the old story of readiness to believe evil of a good man. They probably argued that, as Paul had gone so far about the Gentiles, it was only a step further to make the Jews also throw off the yoke of Moses.

It is hardly necessary to state Paul's real position about the Jewish Christians and the Mosaic ceremonial law. He has nowhere said that it was wrong for Jewish Christians to observe it. His battle had been for the Gentiles and had been successful. The case with the Jews was very different. As Jews they felt the insufficiency of the law and became Christians in order to be saved as Peter had so well said at the Jerusalem Conference (Acts 15 : 10 f.). Christianity was the complement of Judaism, not Judaism the complement of Christianity. Both Jew and Gentile were under sin (Rom. 3 : 20) and needed to be redeemed by the grace of Christ. That done, there was no need to

impose Greek philosophy on the Jew nor Jewish law
on the Greek. It might, indeed, be needless for the
Jewish Christian to keep up the ceremonial law.
Neither circumcision nor uncircumcision availeth
anything. But it was not wrong nor had Paul so
taught.

2. *The Plan for Answering the Charge.*—The
brethren in Jerusalem had evidently decided on what
to do before Paul came. They put the matter to him
gently (Acts 21 : 20). In truth, Paul is *persona non
grata* to the saints as a whole in Jerusalem. It will
not be possible to conceal his presence in town (21 : 22).
The thing for Paul to do is to be seen in the temple offering sacrifices for himself and four men who have a vow.
Thus "all shall know that there is no truth in the things
whereof they have been informed concerning thee"
(21 : 24). Clearly the falsehood of the Judaizers will
be completely answered and all will see "that thou thy-
self also walkest orderly, keeping the law." It is plain
that James and the elders are greatly troubled over the
situation. It is time for action, not mere talk.

In itself the thing that they ask Paul to do is not at
all inconsistent with this general position. Indeed,
he had been anxious to come to the Jewish Pentecost
which was probably now going on. He had urged the
Galatians as Gentiles not to observe the Jewish feast
(Gal. 4 : 10), but for the Jews such matters were
subjects for individual freedom (Rom. 14 : 4–8). At
Cenchreæ Paul may have completed a vow similar to

the one now upon these four men (Acts 18 : 18). He had had Timothy circumcised. Hence with apparent alacrity Paul acquiesced in the proposal and on the next day purified himself with the men and entered the temple. An offering was made for every one of them, and the service was to continue for seven days (21 : 26 f.). Paul, of course, did not consider the sacrifice as of real efficacy in itself, but merely as part of the shadow that found its realization in the real sacrifice of Jesus our Passover (I Cor. 5 : 7).

The brethren make it plain to Paul that his conduct is not to be interpreted as a reversal of the agreement made before concerning the freedom of the Gentiles. They only wish that the Gentiles continue to respect Jewish prejudices concerning things sacrificed to idols, blood, things strangled, and fornication (21 : 25). This pointed reference to the Jerusalem letter to the Gentile Christians is interesting since it is alluded to only once after the return to Antioch (Acts 16 : 4). Evidently the brethren at Jerusalem continue to regard it as still an agreement that is binding in spite of the conduct of the Judaizers. Paul himself, as we know from I Corinthians and Romans, had gone into the subject of meats offered to idols more exhaustively, though his advice is in accord with the decision of the conference.

So far as one could judge beforehand, the advice of the brethren to Paul seemed wise. He had all to gain and nothing to lose by such a course. Suppose that Paul had refused to do what was asked of him. It would have been instantly construed as proof of the charge against him. To be seen obeying the law as a pious Jew in the temple would do more with the common people than any amount of explanation or argument.

3. *The Jews from Asia Upset the Plan.*—In all probability the conduct of Paul did dispel the prejudices against him in the minds of the disciples at Jerusalem who had been misled by the Judaizers. The leaders among the Judaizers do not themselves appear in the present situation. So far as is known the Christian Jews of Jerusalem, who noticed what he did, were satisfied. The thing seemed a master-stroke of wisdom.

But Paul had enemies of many kinds. He had labored in various parts of the world and had left behind him many rankling animosities. The feast of Pentecost had brought many Jews to Jerusalem from the Dispersion. "The Jews from Asia" here at the feast knew Paul of old in Ephesus. They were hardened against the Way long ago (Acts 19:9) and joined in the clamor against Paul's friends in the theatre at Ephesus (19:33). They well knew the power of uproar with a mob as they saw it on that occasion. It so happened that Paul had brought Trophimus, one of his Greek converts from Ephesus, with him to Jerusalem as one of the bearers of the collection. One day they saw Paul and Trophimus walking together in the city (21:29). Another day they saw Paul in the temple (21:27). That was enough for them.

They "supposed" that Paul had brought Trophimus into the temple also as he walked with him on the street. They felt that he was none too good to do so anyhow. The definite charge that Paul brought Greeks (Trophimus has now been multiplied) into the temple and so defiled this holy place is merely the local coloring to their previous hatred (21:28). The first charge was more general: "This is the man that teacheth all men everywhere against the people, and the law, and this place." They claimed to know how he had done at Ephesus. It was once more the charge against Stephen (Acts 6:13). Paul had heard the cries of the mob after Stephen's blood as he held his garments. Now he hears the yelping wolves as they gnash their teeth at him.

It matters not that Paul at this very moment was engaged in an act of worship in accordance with the Mosaic ritual. It was a small consideration that Paul did not have any Greeks with him then. The Jews from Asia did not say where the Greeks were nor when the act of defilement occurred. They had raised the cry of "fire," so to speak. Then they vanish out of sight. It will be probably five years before Paul will be set free from the consequences of this malicious falsehood. He had faced many perils before this. Mobs had raged round him at Lystra, Thessalonica, Berœa, Corinth, and at Ephesus he had to fight with veritable wild beasts in human form. But this is a Jewish mob, a religious mob, a fanatical rabble like those that clamored for the blood of Christ and of Stephen. It is not difficult to start a senseless mob (all mobs are senseless) after an innocent man. Only touch a sensitive spot and the mischief is done. In Ephesus the Temple of Diana was the cry. In Jerusalem the Temple of Jehovah. The whole city was soon in a stir. Paul was literally dragged out of the temple and the doors shut to keep him and his imaginary Greeks out. The next thing was to kill him. Probably the masses of them knew little of Paul of late years save that they heard of him as a renegade Jew. But enough knew of his great work for Christ to give edge to the movement against him.

The Roman power saves Paul from death. The sight of the Roman military tribune with soldiers stopped the murderous act. The mob left off beating Paul (21 : 32). But the captain thought that he must be a dreadful man to be the victim of such a mob's hate. He would take no chances and so bound Paul with two chains. He got little information from the crowd as to who he was and what he had done. Probably some did not even know who Paul was. Few knew what the charge of the Jews from Asia was. All who had ever heard anything bad about Paul spoke it out. The captain was only puzzled by the uproar. The soldiers actually had to lift Paul upon the stairs of the tower of Antonia from the violence of the crowd. Paul heard them yell "Away with him" (21 : 36). Jesus had heard that same cry a generation ago.

The captain was at his wits' end, like Pilate before him. Inside the castles, in astonishment that he knew Greek (21 : 37 f.), he asks Paul if he is not the dreadful Egyptian Assassin. Paul is proud to claim his Jewish ancestry and his citizenship in Tarsus. He was, indeed, a civilized man! That was reassuring to the captain. But what was the trouble all about? The Jews were curious people surely.

4. *Paul's Defence to the Mob.*—A moment like this calls for all of one's resources. It was worth something if he could get this hostile rabble to listen at all. They had already prejudged his case. They did not wish to pause for a speech. They longed for his blood. Not even the presence of the Roman soldiery had kept them quiet.

The captain gave Paul leave to speak with probably much doubt as to the outcome. It was one of the queerest cases that had ever come under his care. It was a magnificent spectacle to see Paul stand on the stairs and lift up his hand unto this people whom he so much loved (Rom. 9 : 1-5) and who so hated him. He spoke to the captain in Greek (Acts 21 : 37), but to the Jews in Hebrew (Aramaic, 21 : 40). That very fact gave him a better hearing. They would probably, nearly all of them, have understood the Greek, but there was a greater silence when he spoke in the tongue of the people (20 : 2). He had won that much. He had their attention. He even called this rough crowd "brethren and fathers." Members

of the Sanhedrin had come into the crowd (22 : 5).
He put himself *en rapport* with his hearers as far as it
was possible.   One is reminded of a like behavior on
Paul's part on Mars Hill.

Paul pleaded for a respectful hearing on the ground
of his Hebrew birth and training (22 : 3–5).   It is a
familiar story to all of them who cared to know,
especially to the members of the Sanhedrin with whom
he had once had such intimate relations.   He had been
educated here in the school of Gamaliel and had once
looked upon Christ as they still do.   He knew what it
was to lust for blood with the persecutor's hunger.
Their passion towards him he had once shared towards
others.

He explains that his conversion was due to the direct
intervention of God and hence should command their
attention (22 : 6–16).   It was the last thing that he
had ever expected to happen to him.   The change
in him was of God's doing, and no one should charge
him with being a turncoat or renegade Jew.   The details that Paul gives all prove that his conversion was
due to the direct interposition of Jesus himself.   Could
any one blame him for surrendering to Jesus, then?
Would they have done differently?

This is not the first time that he has told his story in
Jerusalem (22 : 17–21).   When his preaching, a long
time ago, met with opposition in Jerusalem, Jesus told
him in a trance to get out of Jerusalem quickly because
the Jews would not hear his testimony.   He had that

trance as he prayed in this very temple where he was
just now worshipping.   He had reminded the Lord
Jesus that all people in Jerusalem would know that his
change was sincere since he had been so public in his
opposition to Stephen and the rest.   But even so the
Lord Jesus bade him depart for there was no work for
him in Jerusalem.   As it was then, so it clearly is
now.   He did not choose to go to the Gentiles of his
own accord. He would have been glad to have preached
at Jerusalem if that were possible.   It was the Lord's
will that he go to the Gentiles.

Paul probably had much more to say, as at Athens.
He had laid the foundations for a skilful apologetic
for his ministry to the Gentiles, and he could now put
in its true light exactly what he had preached to the
Gentiles, why he had come to Jerusalem, what he was
doing in the temple at the very moment when the
Jews from Asia started the hue and cry about him.
But the mob would have none of it.   Paul had used
one word too many, the word "Gentiles" (22:21 f.).
The charge against him had been that he had brought
Greeks into the temple.   They instantly react to that
and all of Paul's fine diplomacy has come to naught.
A mob is fickle at best or worst.   The psychology of a
crowd, the mob mind, is a curious reality.   The excitement once started again was more virulent than
ever.   Garments, dust, yells, all filled the air.

The poor captain was now sorry that he had let
Paul speak.   The speech had been in Aramaic and he

had probably not understood a word of it. As a result, he is more mystified than ever. But he is now out of patience also. If no one can tell him what all this business means, he will examine Paul by scourging, that he may know "for what cause they so shouted against him" (22:24). He is tired of being in the dark. Luke gives much detail. When Paul was tied with thongs, he dropped a remark that positively frightened the centurion. It was unlawful to scourge a Roman at all. It was unlawful to scourge anybody uncondemned. It was a narrow escape, and the chief captain eagerly asked if Paul was really a Roman (22:27 f.). Paul was proud to say: "I am a Roman born." It was the one magic word in all the world. The examination was postponed indefinitely. He had been too rash with Paul and had bound him severely for scourging. One need not wonder that Paul here appealed to his rights as a Roman citizen. It was plain that he could not get justice from the Jewish mob nor even from the Roman officials without doing so. But instantly a new turn comes to the affairs of Paul. The Roman captain sees that Paul cannot be mistreated bodily, nor must any official irregularities be allowed. The forms of legal usage must be observed else he will have to answer for his failure.

5. *Paul before the Sanhedrin.*—The chief captain had failed utterly to unravel this Jewish snarl. He did not have the wit nor the courage of Gallio to cut the Gordian knot of thin peccadillos and punctilios.

Besides, though Paul was a Roman citizen, his offence seemed to concern the Jews somehow. So he called a meeting of the Sanhedrin to clear up the matter for him. Surely Paul was guilty of something or other. These grave judges could determine what his crime was.

It is a familiar experience for Paul to meet with this body of distinguished Jewish officials. If he had not been a member himself, which was entirely possible, he, at any rate, had been the official agent of the body and had often had conferences with them. Many of them were known to him by face. But it was a new experience for him to be on trial before the Sanhedrin. Here again he was following in the footsteps of Stephen.

But Paul has a very brief word to add to what he had said on the steps of the tower the day before: "Brethren, I have lived before God in all good conscience until this day" (Acts 23 : 1). It was a simple enough thing to say; it contradicted all the charges made by the mob against Paul and evidently indorsed by the Sanhedrin. They had long wished to have him in their power, and now by a turn in the wheel of fortune that time had come. It was an insult to the body for Paul to assert that all he had done against Judaism, as they conceived it, was done in good conscience. If anything, it only made the matter worse.

This point of view explains the conduct of the high priest who so hotly resented Paul's brief defence. It also throws light on Paul's indignant response to the high priest's command. It is not merely to be noted that Paul did not turn the other cheek. Jesus did not do that, but firmly protested against such treatment. What is more noticeable is that Paul pronounced a bitter curse on the high priest, calling him a "whited wall," a vivid way of terming him a hypocrite (23 : 3). A good many explanations have been offered for Paul's remark that he did not know that it was the high priest (23 : 5): such as his weak eyes, the change of dress in the high priest, etc. It seems to me that the most natural view is that Paul was so angry that he was not at the moment considering the fact that it was the high priest to whom he was speaking. His denunciation of the high priest was a sudden explosion, not a deliberate reviling.

But clearly Paul's outburst had not helped his chances for acquittal by the Sanhedrin or recommendation to the captain for release. It was plain that the body as a whole was already hostile to him.

Paul's perception (23 : 6) that one part were Sadducees and the other Pharisees was, of course, nothing new to him. It was merely that he then saw how he could turn that fact to his advantage. These two sects were still bitterly hostile on many points. Paul knew all about their controversies. One may here recall how Gamaliel had declined to help the Sadducees persecute the Apostles on the issue of the resurrection of Jesus from the dead. On that issue alone, apart from the claims of Jesus to be the Messiah, the Pharisees

had no fight with Christianity. Paul probably knew
all about the conduct of Gamaliel on that occasion.
On this point, as opposed to the Sadducees, he was still
a Pharisee (23:6). It was also true that at bottom
the charge against him involved the question of the
resurrection of the dead in the case of Jesus. That
was the point that turned the scales with him when he
became a Christian as he had explained to the mob on
yesterday. He brushed aside the superficial charges
made by the Asian Jews yesterday and which nobody
remembered clearly enough to tell the chief captain.
Those charges had not come before the Sanhedrin.
As a matter of fact Paul felt himself to be on trial for
his whole Christian career, not for any special act in
that career. Hence he was entirely justified in his
statement of the case. He had not said all that was
true of himself. He did not, of course, mean that he
was merely a Pharisee. They knew full well that he
was also a Christian. What he means for the Sanhedrin
to understand is that, although a Christian, as he had
explained on yesterday, he was still a Pharisee on the essential doctrine of the resurrection, and that this
doctrine was really at stake in the case against him.

A great deal depends on the way a thing is put.
Paul had purposely and shrewdly stated the matter
so as to array the two parties against each other.
Surely no one can fairly say that Paul had no right to
save his own life by a skilful manœuvre like this.
What he did was in no sense immoral. He divided

to conquer as any able general will do. It was war in which Paul was now engaged. He was in the hands of men who were bent on his ruin. He told no untruth nor acted one. Yet he so completely outgeneraled his enemies that the grave and dignified judges lost control of themselves in a theological scramble and lost all sight of Paul (23 : 9 f.). This incident throws a curious sidelight on the intensity of the feeling between the two great Jewish parties since they could not control themselves when in court. Probably such discussions were common, as Paul knew. The jury was now hopelessly hung. In the heat of debate the Pharisees had actually become the champions of Paul and openly proclaimed his innocence, while the Sadducees as stoutly maintained his guilt (23 : 9 f.). The division among the judges was strictly according to party lines as is often the case to-day when a number of judges act on a partisan issue.

Indeed, so fierce had become the furor between the two parties that the chief captain actually had to rescue Paul by force to keep him from being torn to pieces in their attacks on each other. He was safe in the castle from the Sanhedrin as yesterday when he had been rescued from the mob. Still the mystery remained to the chief captain. What was the matter with Paul? What had he done? The Sanhedrin had behaved as badly as the mob.

Ramsay[1] discusses at some length why Luke has

[1] "St. Paul the Traveller," p. 307 f.

gone into the series of trials at Jerusalem and Cæsarea
in such detail.   It is due, he thinks, to Luke's idea that
this experience in Paul's life marked an epoch in the
history of early Christianity.   He thinks that some
light may be thrown on the matter by reason of the
fact that this contact with Roman provincial and finally
imperial law set an example or precedent for Christians
afterward.   He is sure that Luke contemplated a
third book to take up Paul's career after his acquittal.
That may be true, but one cannot prove it from Luke's
use of "first" ($\pi\rho\hat{\omega}\tau o\nu$, Acts 1 : 1), a usage common
in the Koine vernacular,[1] as in modern English, where
only two subjects are under consideration.   One may
add that, after all, the space given by Luke to this period
of five years when he was with Paul is not greatly out
of proportion to the space devoted in Acts to the five
years before.   This close grapple with the Jewish
people, the Sanhedrin, Roman provincial governors
and finally the Emperor himself did vitally concern
not only Paul's own career, but the development and
progress of Christianity unhindered by Jew and Roman.
Heretofore the Roman, save at Philippi under a misapprehension, had not been really hostile.   But now
at last Paul has to get a better adjustment with Roman
law than the temporary permission resulting from
Gallio's indulgence.   The matter, of course, was
pressed against Paul on the ground of his personal
shortcomings, not that of Christianity *per se*.   But,

[1] Moulton, "Prolegomena to N. T. Greek Grammar," p. 79.

as a matter of fact, it was the great success of Paul that had concentrated Jewish hate on him.

Paul had never needed the help of Jesus more than now. James and the elders were not very prominent just now. We know very well where their sympathies were. But their advice had all turned out wrong somehow. It was vain to give mere advice, and they had naught else but prayer. Paul's life had been saved twice, once from the mob, once from the Sanhedrin. No hope lay in further appeal in either direction. The Roman captain seemed kindly, in a way, but he was afraid to be too friendly to Paul for fear the Jews would complain to Felix, the Governor at Cæsarea. The road began to seem long to Paul. That night Jesus stood by him as he had appeared to him once before in Jerusalem when the Jews were hostile to him. Then Jesus bade him leave Jerusalem for work among the Gentiles. Then he fled to escape trouble. Now he cannot escape. He is caught in the toils. His enemies howl about him on every side. But Jesus has a cheering word even now (23 : 11). It is that after all he shall go to Rome. He will not then die at once. His life will be spared, but Jesus had no word about freedom. He will testify in Rome as in Jerusalem. At Jerusalem his testimony had borne little fruit save a harvest of trouble. What has Rome in store for him?

6. *Paul's Rescue from the Conspirators.*—Paul needed the comfort of this reassurance on that very day, for

at dawn the Jews banded together under a curse neither to eat nor drink till they had killed Paul (Acts 23 : 12). The riot had failed, the Sanhedrin had failed, the Roman captain was uncertain. A plot was the only sure thing. One recalls the plot against Paul by the Jews of Corinth on his departure.

It was a formidable conspiracy of forty Jewish zealots. It was essential to the plan to tell the Sanhedrin and let them be partners in the crime. The Sanhedrin had a technical ground on which to request another hearing of Paul's case, since the matter had not come to a clear issue before and the captain had himself taken Paul from them. The Sanhedrin could easily use this pretext, "as though ye would judge of his case more exactly" (23 : 15). They were brutally told the whole plot: "And we, before he comes near, are ready to slay him." Luke plainly implies that the Sanhedrin agreed to this murderous plot, and they were the ecclesiastical lights of Judaism.

But Jesus had not deserted Paul. "Paul's sister's son heard of their lying in wait." You can count on a boy to learn what is on foot. So many people knew the scheme that some were overheard talking of it. This boy was worthy of his uncle and went and told Paul. The rest was easily managed. Soon the boy goes with a centurion to the chief captain. Note the centurion's point of view about "Paul the prisoner" (23 : 18), just one of the many prisoners on hand! He little knew that he was dealing with the greatest

man alive at that time, one of the greatest of all time.
The chief captain was a man of skill. He took the
boy aside and held his hand as he told his story. He
told it simply and begged the chief captain not to let
Paul fall into the trap set for him.

Put it to the credit of Claudius Lysias that he had
courage enough to thwart this plot. He naturally enjoined silence on the boy, and sped Paul out of Jerusalem
at nine o'clock that night (the third hour) under the
protection of four hundred and seventy soldiers. Paul
was a Roman citizen and Lysias was determined that he
should not be murdered. This desire explains the size
of the guard and the three kinds of soldiers sent (legionary soldiers, horsemen, and spearmen). In order to
guarantee speed, "beasts" were provided for Paul.
Lysias was doubtless glad of a way out of a troublesome
situation. He was perfectly willing to pass Paul on to
Felix, with his compliments, just as Pilate had tried to get
Herod Antipas to decide the case of Jesus. His letter
was therefore very courteous. He now, for the first time,
betrays some knowledge of the charges against Paul.
They were merely "questions of their law" (23 : 29)
He even expressed the opinion, as Pilate did about
Jesus, that he had "nothing laid to his charge worthy
of death." But all the same he made no recommendation in the case, though he implied that he ought to be
set free. He explains that he had already brought him
before the Jewish Council to learn what the charges
were about. He did not get any definite information,

but only that they disagreed among themselves about Paul. So he has sent Paul the prisoner down to Cæsarea with the charge to his accusers to come before Felix also. This he did because of a plot. Thus far the letter is in accord with Luke's story of the facts. But he puts too favorable a color on his arrest of Paul. He had, indeed, rescued Paul from the mob, but not until he learned that he was a Roman! He thus covers up his peril of scourging a Roman citizen, and turns his conduct into a defence of the rights of the Roman citizen. He is now rid of Paul and has cleared his skirts of any possible harm from the case.

The soldiers only accompanied Paul as far as Antipatris, but the seventy horsemen, after a night's rest there, went on with him to Cæsarea. Lysias had told Paul's accusers, it seems (23:30), that he would be sent to Cæsarea, but evidently had not revealed his plan for doing so. Hence he succeeded in delivering Paul to Felix with the letter. The usual Roman procedure is manifest in the question of Felix about Paul's province (Cilicia). It was only proper for him to wait till the accusers came, and he was kept in Herod's palace (prætorium) in Cæsarea. Felix promised Paul a full investigation.

7. *Paul before Felix.*—As explained in a previous chapter, one could wish that he knew exactly the date of Felix's recall. It was after he had kept Paul two years (Acts 24:27). The matter cannot be discussed here. It may be assumed to be either 60 or 59 A.D.

Hence Paul appears before Felix first in the spring of
58 or 57.   Felix was a representative of the worst type
of Roman provincial governor.   He is a fit successor
of Pilate, a man guilty of every vice.   Tacitus[1] bluntly
said of him that "in the practice of every kind of lust
and cruelty he exercised the power of a king with the
temper of a slave."   How much Paul knew of Felix
we do not know.   But the Jewish rulers knew his
vulnerable points as they did about Pilate and will not
nesitate to make charges to the Emperor about Felix
as they threatened to Pilate to do.   Felix is open to all
that is worst in Roman provincial administration—
to graft, bribery, indifference, selfish advantage.   It
is not a hopeful outlook for Paul.   Relentless Jewish
hatred will press the case against him before a governor
who has no scruples about abstract justice nor particular
interest in a troublesome Jewish rabbi who happens to
have also Roman citizenship.

The case of the Sanhedrin is ably presented.   The
high priest Ananias took five days to get the charges
against Paul properly prepared.   He comes with
"certain elders, and with an orator, one Tertullus"
(24 : 1).   They seem to have laid their side before
Felix before the trial.   Tertullus has a Roman name
and is clearly a Roman lawyer who knows how to plead
before a governor like Felix from the point of view of
Roman provincial law.   His speech could have been

<hr />

[1] Hist., V. 9.   Cf. Conybeare and Howson, Scribner's ed.,
Vol. II, p. 275.

in Latin, but was probably in Greek since it was assented to by the Jews (24 : 9). He was an adept in flattery and adroitness. He actually praises Felix as a reformer! He fawns before the corrupt Governor to carry his point. His smooth sentences roll along till he comes to Paul, whom he damns by a phrase—"this pestilent fellow." Paul the prisoner is now Paul the pest, a common nuisance! He repeats as a fact the supposition of the Jews from Asia in the temple that he had "assayed to profane the temple" (24 : 6). But the keen Roman lawyer has added two other points to get a case that will stand in Roman law. He charges Paul with being "a mover of insurrections among all the Jews throughout the world," a rather vague charge, and yet one for which they could get a specious form of proof from what had occurred in Antioch, Iconium, Thessalonica, Corinth, Ephesus. He would know how to twist the facts like an unscrupulous pleader. The other charge is that of heresy, and consists in his being "a ringleader of the sect of the Nazarenes." Here it is assumed that this new sect is different from Judaism, is, in fact, a *religio nova et illicita*, and has no standing in Roman law. Hence to be a ringleader in this unlawful sect was itself a crime. The decision of Gallio in Achaia, of course, had no weight in Palestine. Eventually the matter must be passed on by the Emperor himself. Was it a crime to be a Christian if Christianity was different from Judaism? Technically, Tertullus had scored a legal point against Paul and had thrown suspicion on him by the other two charges. One charge was true, for he was a Nazarene (note the term). Another charge was true only in a perverted sense, for the disturbances were raised against Paul; he did not cause them himself. The other and the original one was flatly untrue; he had not profaned the temple nor tried to do so. This, then, is the line of attack of Paul's Jewish enemies.

He had escaped the mob, the Sanhedrin, the conspiracy. What will be his fate before Roman law? The provincial courts were proverbially slow and the governors willing to use prisoners for private gain. Paul has no advocate to plead his cause. He has no witnesses to substantiate his statements. He is in much the same position as Jesus before Pilate. What can he say that will make a legal defence against the legal quibbles of Tertullus? Paul is courteous, but no fawning sycophant. He says all that he can consistently with truth in praise of Felix, which is very little (24 : 10). One thing is plain, Felix can learn the facts, if he wishes to do so (24 : 11), about the charge of defiling the temple. Witnesses could be gotten to prove Paul's conduct since he arrived in Palestine twelve days ago. The charge of insurrection is equally groundless and cannot be proved. But he will not deny being a Nazarene, a term which he does not use (recall Nathanael's slur against Nazareth). He follows the Way which the Jews call a sect, a departure

from Judaism, but which he considers the real fruition
of the true Judaism of the law and the Prophets.   The
Prophets, like Paul, hoped for a resurrection of both
just and unjust.   He has walked in this Way with good
conscience toward God and men and done his duty.
In reality, therefore, Paul has found a legal shelter
for Christianity in the Roman indulgence of Judaism.
So far from profaning the temple recently, he was at
the very moment of the mob's attack engaged in the
act of purifying himself in the temple "with no crowd,
nor yet with tumult" (24 : 18).   Indeed, he had come
to the city to bring alms to his own people.   The trouble
in Jerusalem all arose from some Jews from Asia, who
are not here as they ought to be.   Let these members
of the Sanhedrin tell what charge they found against
me when I stood before them except it be the doctrine
of the resurrection which all Pharisees hold.

It was a masterly defence and completely disposed
of the charge of profaning the temple, and put the
Jews on the defensive about the charge of insurrection.
The only point left was the legal standing of Christianity, the doctrine which Paul confessed, but which
he claimed to be the true Judaism which Roman law
allowed.   Felix reserved the right to pass judgment
on this point till he could learn more about the tenets
of "the Way" and see what Lysias had to say about
Paul's statement of the recent facts.   Meanwhile,
Paul was to have indulgence and to see his friends.
Luke, we know, was with him in Cæsarea at the close

of his story (27 : 1) and was probably there most of the two years. So far Felix had acted circumspectly with Paul.

It seems that Felix did not wait long to hear more exactly from Paul "concerning the faith in Christ Jesus" (24 : 24). It was on this point that Felix claimed to have most trouble, since Paul had confessed his guilt, if crime it was in Roman law. One would suppose that Paul would be disposed to give a presentation of Christianity that would give it, if possible, a legal standing. But Paul shows complete indifference to that phase of the subject beyond what he had already said. If Roman jurisprudence branded that a crime, let it be done. Indeed, Paul seems on this occasion to forget that he is a prisoner. He preaches a sermon that exposed the sinfulness of Felix and the infamous Drusilla instead of giving an abstract discussion about the relation between Christianity and Roman provincial law. The power of the sermon was shown in the terror of Felix (24 : 25). But a vicious demagogue like Felix was not to be won by one sermon. He had a conflict of emotions. He loved money and hoped to get a bribe from Paul for his freedom and the legal standing of Christianity. His love of gold led him to frequent communion with Paul (24 : 26). One may wonder how he expected to get money out of Paul. Probably Luke and others of Paul's friends had come. He had spoken of taking alms up to Jerusalem. Paul's standing as a Roman citizen of Tarsus showed that he was not a pauper. Ramsay[1] thinks that Paul was now able to draw on his father's fortune for the expenses of his trial. He does not mean that Paul bribed Felix. Far from it. The very fact that he left Paul bound for two years proves that he received no money from him. But the long-drawn-out trial would require a deal of money in many ways that were legitimate, especially in the matter of the appeal to Cæsar which came later.

When Felix failed to get money from Paul, he lost interest also in the legal status of Christianity. He was unable to restrain uprisings in Palestine, indeed in Cæsarea itself. On his recall for failure to manage the affairs of his province, he left Paul in prison as a sop to Jewish hatred, hoping to lessen their charges against him in Rome. It is some comfort to reflect that Pilate and Felix gained nothing by their paltering servility to the Jews against innocent men. Felix knew perfectly well that Paul was innocent of any crime against Roman law as Lysias had written him. He knew already enough about Christianity to know that it was no crime for a Jew to be a Christian, if we take the language literally (Acts 24 : 22).

8. *Paul before Festus.*—One may well imagine that Paul shed no tears over the departure of Felix. Two years he had let an innocent man remain a prisoner. Festus might be better. He does, indeed, bear a somewhat better reputation. Some of the books are dis-

---

[1] "St. Paul the Traveller," pp. 310 ff

posed to credit him with candor and a disposition to befriend Paul. But I am not able to see in his treatment of Paul anything more than the perfunctory routine of the ordinary politician who seeks to curry favor with the people at the expense of an innocent man, a governor who aims to keep up the show of fairness, but who lacks the courage to do the right thing when it is not the popular thing.

The hatred of the Jewish leaders against Paul has not disappeared during these two years (Acts 25 : 2). It is, in fact, the main thing in their interview with the new Governor when he appears ceremoniously in Jerusalem. They make a specious request that Paul be brought to Jerusalem. But it is to the credit of Festus that he was not caught in this net of Jewish chicanery. They planned to kill him on his way to Jerusalem, a revival in another form of the former plot that vividly pictures the relentless wrath in Jerusalem against Paul. They seemed to think that if they could only kill Paul, Christianity would disappear. It was Christianity that they so despised. But Festus had not yet taken his bearings, and Paul's case was new to him. He was soon going to Cæsarea anyhow. They would therefore come down and make their charges in regular form.

No Roman lawyer is mentioned in the presentation of the "many and grievous charges" (25 : 7) against Paul. The Jews from Jerusalem stood around in solemn line and made their accusations. The number seems to have grown with the years. Perhaps they did not present them in clear-cut legal form, but they could not prove them any better than before.

Paul's defence this time is very short, but very clear. He denies sinning against the Jewish law, the Jewish temple or the Roman Cæsar (25 : 8). He deserved to be set free at once. Nothing is here said about the crime of being a Nazarene. Perhaps Felix had told them that there was nothing in that.

Curiously enough, Festus now proposes that Paul agree to go up to Jerusalem to be tried there before him (25 : 9). The suggestion is self-explanatory and convicts Festus of hollow insincerity. Luke pointedly accuses him of wishing to curry favor with the Jews. He will later himself confess that Paul, in his opinion, had done nothing worthy of death or even of bonds (25 : 25). He should have set Paul free. Festus' later excuse, (25 : 18 f.) that he wished to take him up to Jerusalem to clear up these Jewish questions, is quite beside the mark, for the trial in Jerusalem was to be before Festus (25 : 9), not before the Sanhedrin. He had found Paul a troublesome prisoner and recalled the suggestion of the Jews in Jerusalem which he had rejected. It was a mere trick on the part of Festus. In Jerusalem he would probably have found some pretext to throw the case over to the Sanhedrin as Pilate tried to do with Jesus. Festus is derelict in his duty here as was Felix, as was Pilate.

Paul quickly and clearly saw through the whole

scheme of Festus (25 : 10). He was standing at Cæsar's judgment seat as a Roman citizen. He was not willing to go back into the jaws of death in Jerusalem. Paul pointedly tells Festus that he himself knows his innocence of any crime against the Jews, though unwilling to decide according to his knowledge. He has tried the Jews and refuses to go back to them. "No man can give me up to them. I appeal to Cæsar." These are brave words and bold words. Were they also wise words? It is easy to retort that they led to three more years of imprisonment. But, if he had gone to Jerusalem, death was his fate. If he remained in Cæsarea, he had the example of Felix to go by, and Festus was starting the same dilatory tactics. Wisdom was in the line of Paul's decision. Sooner or later Christianity must be passed on by the imperial government. Paul was a Roman citizen and had the right of appeal. Ramsay[1] argues that only a serious case would be entertained when an appeal was demanded. But, after all, Festus was probably more than glad to be well rid of a case that promised trouble for him with the Jewish leaders with whom he had to get on somehow and which had given Felix such annoyance. He had conferences with the assessors (council), but quickly announced his decision that Paul was to go to Cæsar (25 : 12). So he was to go to Rome after all.

9. *Paul before Agrippa.*—Paul is no more a matter of serious concern to Festus except on one point.

[1] "St. Paul the Traveller," p. 310.

He must present in legal form the charge against Paul and some adequate explanation of his continued imprisonment. It is while Festus is in this frame of mind that Agrippa and Bernice came to Cæsarea by way of salutation to Festus (Acts 25 : 13). One may imagine the languid air of the palace when the conversation flagged and Festus, for lack of other topics and because his guests were Jews, "laid Paul's case before the King." He relates the story (finely preserved by Luke) with the air of nonchalance and a tone of superiority to Paul and Jesus natural to this Roman Governor of easy manners and morals. He stands for his adherence to Roman usage in the matter of the request at Jerusalem (25 : 16), and expresses his surprise at the pettiness of the Jewish charges against Paul, merely "certain questions against him of their own religion, and of one Jesus, who was dead, whom Paul affirmed to be alive" (25 : 19). Put yourself in the place of Festus and use his eyes as you look upon the career of Jesus and Paul's relation to him, and you will duplicate the attitude of some modern savants who with supercilious scorn write down Jesus and Paul.[1] Festus actually counted it a merit in himself that he offered

[1] "And the root mistake of much of what is called religious-historical exegesis is that it is guilty of *a new kind of isolation*—an isolation which, in its results, proves much more serious than the old. And the first essential for a true exegesis of the Pauline writings—and of the Biblical in general—is a sympathetic understanding and realization of the new experience which is determinative of this content." Rev. J. M. Shaw, *The Expository Times*, March, 1909, p. 253.

to take Paul up to Jerusalem to clear up these Jewish details! He almost implies that he might have set him free if he had not appealed to Cæsar!

The interest of Agrippa was aroused.. It was evidently an interesting case. He should hear him to-morrow. Hear him for what? Mainly for the entertainment of Agrippa and the court, and partly to see if Agrippa can elicit from Paul any charge which Festus may send to the Emperor (25 : 26). Festus actually jokes about his absurd predicament in having to send a man to Rome with no legal charge against him! It did not occur to him that thereby he condemned himself for not setting Paul free.

Festus makes a sort of court function of the affair (25 : 23). They all knew Paul's ability at any rate. Paul takes the matter seriously, though well knowing that nothing could come of it for himself save the opportunity to put his cause in its true light before Agrippa and these people of prominence. One may suppose that Luke was present. This is the second formal defence of Paul's career that we have in Acts. The one on the stairs of the tower of Antonia was obviously delivered under very different circumstances. He is still defending himself against a charge of which he is not guilty. The circumstances and the character of the address of Paul render his defence before Agrippa one of the really great orations of history.

He has a graceful introduction (26 : 2 f.). Whatever were the limitations of Felix and Festus in their failure to understand Paul's case, here at last was a man who was "expert in all customs and questions which are among the Jews." Hence he asks for a patient hearing. The Sanhedrin at Jerusalem were disqualified by their hatred. Agrippa is competent, and it is the first time that Paul has had this good fortune.

Paul recounts the story of his early life to show that he is not prejudiced against Judaism (26 : 4 f.). This is a matter of common knowledge among the Jews. Indeed, he had been the strictest sort of a Pharisee.

As a matter of fact, the real charge against him now, that of being a Christian, grows out of his belief that Jesus rose from the dead, a fact in perfect harmony with one of the leading tenets of Pharisaism (26 : 6–11). Pharisees were the last people in the world to scout the resurrection from the dead. He once felt just as the Jews do now toward him. But he became a Christian in response to a direct manifestation of Jesus himself. A new light came to him which he could not ignore (26 : 12–18). It was a wonderful experience that on the road to Damascus. It was the Lord's doing.

Who then can blame him if he was not disobedient unto the heavenly vision? (26 : 19–23). He had preached repentance and good works worthy of repentance to both Jews and Gentiles. Indeed, he was engaged in a good work in the temple when the Jews seized him, but they seized him because he had preached to the Gentiles. It was race prejudice in truth. God is still with him, and after all his message is in perfect harmony with what Moses and the Prophets foretold, that the Messiah must suffer, must rise again and be proclaimed to both Jew and Gentile.

Agrippa had listened intently, but it was Festus who was carried away with excitement as Paul rose in power toward the close. Festus, indeed, looked upon Paul as a learned fanatic. It was all beyond his depth, and he thought that Paul was losing his mind with his philosophical subtleties. He showed his excitement by his loud voice.

But Paul calms Festus and turns with a pointed appeal to Agrippa about his knowledge of the Prophets. If he admitted his knowledge of the Prophets, he either had to agree with Paul's interpretation of them or oppose it. He did not care to do either and so accused Paul of trying to entrap him (26 : 28). His answer ἐν ὀλίγῳ cannot mean "almost" but it is not certain whether he meant with little persuasion, in a little time or to some extent. Either interpretation is possible and suits the context. At any rate, Agrippa was too much of a Jew to be caught on a syllogism. But Paul makes a noble prayer for him with a delicate exception of "these bonds."

But Agrippa showed his freedom from prejudice by plainly saying to Festus that Paul was innocent of any wrong from the Jewish point of view and could have been set free if he had not appealed to Cæsar (26 : 32). Festus knew that before. Did he learn what charge to make against Paul? It would seem not.

10. *Going to Rome at Last.*—Jesus had said so at Jerusalem over two years ago. Paul had planned it a number of years before. In a true sense the journey to Rome had become the goal of his ministry. But it was not just to go to Rome. He wished to make Rome the spring-board, in a way, for going on to the farther west. He has not given up that hope in spite of the reverses of the last two years. His forebodings about what was in store for him at Jerusalem had more than come true. The cloud of Jewish hate had burst upon his head with terrific force. And yet he was not sorry that he had come on to Jerusalem. He had brought the collection for the poor saints. He had put himself right with the great body of disciples in Jerusalem who had been led astray by the Judaizers. He had a host of real friends now in Jerusalem. There was no longer any real peril of a schism in Christianity over the Gentile problem. Hence the real objects of his visit to Jerusalem had been accomplished. The leaders among the Judaizers will no more be able to stir the masses of the Jerusalem disciples against Paul. Hence they will have no real base of operations. Their future movements will be insignificant in consequence. At last the Judaizing controversy may be considered over.

It would be interesting to know how Paul occupied himself during the two years at Cæsarea. If Luke wrote his Gospel during this period, as is possible, one may think that Paul was in touch with him.

The Gospel of Luke is often called Pauline in tone. Luke gives abundant evidence in his Gospel to justify his claim to real historical research for the facts and skill in the use of his materials (Luke 1 : 1–4). He was near the sources of information and manifestly made abundant use of his opportunity whether he actually wrote the Gospel at this time or later. But Paul was too active in mind to be entirely inert all this time. It is almost tragic, however, to think of five years of the prime of Paul's life being hindered thus. What could he not have done in the west during these years?

Ramsay,[1] who is so fruitful in original hints as well as fresh facts about Paul, suggests that Luke (of Philippi) and Aristarchus (of Thessalonica) could only accompany Paul as his slaves. They had to pass on the voyage as Paul's slaves, and this circumstance would give Paul added importance and dignity. Clearly "Julius treated Paul kindly" (Acts 27 : 3) in the matter of seeing his friends at Sidon, though it might not follow that he would allow two friends to go with him all the way to Rome. Luke, perhaps, might have claimed the right to go as Paul's physician if Julius had that much of the spirit of indulgence. But, at any rate, it is certain that Paul enjoyed more distinction and consideration as a prisoner of importance than the "certain other prisoners" who may have been merely already condemned to death and just more "human victims

[1] "St. Paul the Traveller," p. 316.

to amuse the populace by their death in the arena" at Rome.[1] The Augustan band or "troop of the Emperor" may have been one of the auxiliary cohort under a legionary centurion detached for service in the provinces.[2]

One had to take advantage of what ships he could get to go to Rome. Julius took Paul under his care along with his band of soldiers and the other prisoners, but he could not start from Cæsarea directly for Rome. This particular ship was bound for Adramyttium (27 : 2), probably a coasting vessel now on its way home.[3] Such a ship would naturally go by the province of Asia (27 : 2). The reason for following so close in shore by Sidon, under the lee of Cyprus (Paul's ship, 21 : 1, to Jerusalem had gone west of Cyprus), off Cilicia and Pamphylia, grows out of the prevailing westerly winds at this season (summer) in the Mediterranean.[4] At Myra, in Lycia (27 : 5), a change in ships was made by Julius. The first stage in the voyage, therefore, is in the Adramyttium coasting vessel from Cæsarea to Myra (27 : 1–5).

The next stage is from Myra to Fair Havens in "a ship of Alexandria sailing for Italy" (27 : 6–8). This was an Alexandrian grain ship (27 : 38). With a steady western wind a sailing ship of the ancients could not safely go directly from Alexandria to Crete.

---

[1] St. Paul the Traveller, p. 314.   [2] Ramsay, *Ibid.*, p. 315.
[3] Smith, "The Voyage and Shipwreck of St. Paul," p. 62 f.; Conybeare and Howson, Scribner's ed., Vol. II, p. 310 f.
[4] *Ibid.*, p. 67 f.

But it would be easy to sail straight for Myra, which "was one of the great harbors of the Egyptian service."[1] This was probably the usual course for this time of year. The voyage was very slow in the face of a contrary westerly or north-westerly wind. It would be necessary to tack in and out along the coast, and even so it was "with difficulty" that they came "over against Cnidus, the wind not further suffering us." Smith[2] shows that the wind was what would in popular language be termed north-west. Up to Cnidus the ship could work along under the lee of the shore ("weather shore"). But here a halt had to be made for beyond was the open sea. It would be useless to go on up the coast of Asia. Only two courses were open, one to wait at Cnidus for better winds, the other to make to the south-west and get under the lee of Crete where the ship would be protected from the north-west wind and would have made some progress toward Rome. The lateness of the season argued for going to Fair Havens on the south of Crete. This course was possible with a north-west wind, and Salmone (the eastern promontory) was reached without much apparent trouble. But now the course had to be more directly westward so as not to get away from the protection of Crete, and at once fresh difficulty was found. But they coasted along till Fair Havens was reached.

Luke (27 : 9) explains that much time was spent

---

[1] Ramsay, "St. Paul the Traveller," p. 319.
[2] "Voyage and Shipwreck of St. Paul," p. 76.

here until after "the Fast was now already gone by."
This "Fast" was on the tenth of Tisri, and was usually
about the last of September or the first of October.
Ramsay[1] thinks that it is in 59 that the voyage was
made instead of 60, and so finds the Fast that year
October 5th. He argues that the party sailed from
Cæsarea about August 17th. At any rate, it is perfectly plain that the time of the year has come, before
the north-west wind ceases, when it is dangerous to
put out into the open sea.[2] One must remember that the
ancients had no chart, no compass and were unable to
sail with safety during the autumnal and winter storms.

A council was called by the centurion to decide
what to do. He seemed to be in supreme control.
The captain and the sailing-master were in the conference along with Paul. It was a tribute to Paul
that, though a prisoner, he was treated as a man of
experience and resource in an emergency like this.
According to Ramsay,[3] the centurion outranked the
captain of the ship and so had the final decision of
the course to be pursued. The point at issue was not
whether to go on to Rome or not. That was obviously out of the question. It was merely whether
to winter at Fair Havens or to put to sea in the endeavor to reach Phœnix, a better haven of Crete, and
not very far away. This harbor probably corresponds

[1] "St. Paul the Traveller," p. 322.
[2] Smith, "Voyage and Shipwreck of St. Paul," p. 84.
[3] "St. Paul the Traveller," p. 325.

to the modern Lutro, the only secure harbor on the south of Crete. The interpretation of Smith[1] is that Luke follows Herodotus in speaking of the harbor from the landward view of the harbor, which really faces north-east and south-east and thus was protected from the north-west and south-west wind. It is not strange that Paul's advice was not taken by the centurion since the captain and the sailing-master were willing to try the voyage to Phœnix (27 : 11). It was the old contrast between a mere preacher and a business man, a man of common sense. Paul made his plea upon rational grounds ("I perceive," 27 : 10) and foretold disaster and loss of life as the outcome. The risk was too great. It seems, moreover, from the expression "the more part" that Paul was not alone in his advice against taking such chances (27: 12).

But when the wind changed to a gentle zephyr from the south they had Paul at a hopeless disadvantage and the start was made. But he laughs best who laughs last. The wind that had changed once could change again. This new sudden "tempestuous wind" (typhonic) was called Euraquilo (27 : 14). Smith[2] shows that this wind blew close from E.N.E. The change came after they had passed Cape Mataler and were out in the open sea. The language of Luke is very vivid. The wind "beat down from" Crete on the

[1] "Voyage and Shipwreck," etc., p. 87 f. But Ramsay, "St. Paul the Traveller," p. 326, opposes this idea.
[2] "Voyage and Shipwreck," etc., p. 100.

ship. The Cretan mountains rose seven thousand feet high.[1] The ship was headed toward Phœnix and was fairly caught "and could not face the wind" and survive. There was only one thing to do, and that was to give way to the wind and be driven by it. But that meant ultimately to strike the Syrtis or quicksands of North Africa. It was no longer a question as to who was right or wrong. The lives of all were in peril. The one chance for escape came as the ship, scudding before the wind, came under the lee of the little island of Cauda or Clauda. What was done must be done quickly. Three things were accomplished. The little boat was hoisted on board to secure it. The ship itself was undergirded with ropes that it might the better stand the terrific strain of wind and wave. They lowered the gear. Full sail would mean ruin in such a storm. Only enough was left up "to keep the ship's head to the wind."[2] The ship itself was on the starboard tack with her head to the north so as to avoid the Syrtis.[3] With the sail down, and under the lee of Cauda, the ship was brought as close to the wind as it would stand. The ship could sail within seven points of the wind and would have six points for leeway, a total angle of thirteen points.[4] However, if the

[1] Ramsay, "St. Paul the Traveller," p. 327
[2] Ramsay, "St. Paul the Traveller," p. 329.
[3] Smith, "Voyage and Shipwreck," etc., p. 122.
[4] Smith, "Voyage and Shipwreck," etc., p. 125 f. This position of Smith has been recently challenged, but on insufficient grounds.

wind was E.N.E. the course of the vessel would be
W. by N.[1] When this was done there was nothing
to do but to wait. They would escape the Syrtis.
What was before them? They were drifting.

They labored exceedingly with the storm (27:18).
After one day they began to throw the freight over-
board. On the next day the tackling or furniture of
the ship was cast out. Then for many days there was
the dreadful monotony of no sun and no stars. The
tempest raged upon the ship till "all hope that we
should be saved was now taken away." They had
lost their appetites and their hope. Then it was that
Paul spoke (27:21). He had not said "I told you
so" before. He would not have done it now merely
for that thankless task. But he had a message of cheer,
and they needed it sorely. They will lose the ship,
but will save their lives. He knows that, for "an
angel of the God whose I am" has told him. It was
not because they deserved it. God meant for Paul to
stand before Cæsar (27 24) as the ambassador of
Christ and had given him the lives of all. Paul believes
God and urges all to be of good cheer even in the face of
certain shipwreck. It might be worse. It was one
gleam of light in the black darkness. The centurion
and the captain are silent.

They drifted on till the fourteenth night came
(27:27). They had come to the Sea of Adria. It
was once supposed that Luke meant what is now

[1] Conybeare and Howson, Scribner's ed., Vol. II, p. 331.

termed the Adriatic Sea between Italy and the mainland. Like many geographical terms in popular usage, it was extended (cf. Asia) to include the sea between Malta, Italy, Greece, Crete. Luke's usage, like Strabo's, was that of "conversation, not of literature." [1] This point is pertinent, for it is plain from the course of the vessel, W. by N., that it could not have gone into the Sea of Adria in the technical literary sense. It is obvious both from the direction, distance and time that the island on which the vessel was stranded, Melita, is the modern Malta.[2] The distance between Cauda and Malta is less than 480 miles. Thirteen days at 36 miles a day would be 468 miles. It was a little over thirteen days, and the direction is that of Malta.

The sea became choppy ("driven to and fro") as they neared land, and the sailors at midnight suspected the truth. The soundings confirmed it. The peril now was that they would be hurled upon the rocks in the night. The four anchors from the stern are easily understood as the wind was still E.N.E. To have put out the anchors only in front might have snapped them or broken the ship as it swung round before wind and wave. If not, it would be hard to handle the ship so as to beach her. The end would come with day if the anchors held. Paul comes to the front again at this crisis, for the sailors with cold selfishness were seeking to save themselves under cover of

---

[1] Ramsay, "St. Paul the Traveller," p. 334.
[2] Smith, "Voyage and Shipwreck," etc., p. 126.

the darkness by means of the boat that had been preserved. With sailors and boat both gone the rest would be in poor plight. The sailors professed that they were going to swing out anchors from the foreship also (27 : 30). Paul had plainly promised that the lives of all would be spared. But he now as pointedly told the centurion and the soldiers that they would lose their lives if they let the sailors go. The soldiers were quick to see the point, and settled the matter by cutting the rope and setting the boat adrift before the sailors got into it.

Paul is now master of ceremonies. "He speaks as the prophet, not the anxious passenger."[1] Ramsay rightly sees no objection to Paul's rise to this point of view in the crisis. The fasting had not been voluntary, indeed. No one had taste for food at such a time. But it had gone on too long. Desperate work was ahead of them and they needed food. Paul begged them to eat with the assurance that not one should lose a hair of his head (27 : 34). This was not mere optimism; it was faith in God. He said grace for this unusual breakfast in the early dawn. It was a goodly company of 276 souls in all. They lightened the ship by throwing the wheat into the sea so that they could run the ship as far up on the pebbly beach as possible. St. Paul's Bay, in Malta, with its little island, creek, and two seas meeting, fulfils all the conditions of Luke's narrative.

[1] Ramsay, "St. Paul the Traveller," p. 337.

When the ship was run aground it was not long before the stern began to break in pieces before the waves. Now the soldiers fail, as the sailors did before, to rise to any nobility of conduct. They actually propose to kill all the prisoners for fear some of them may escape (27 : 42). Once again Paul's promise of no loss of life came near to failure. But the centurion Julius had evidently recognized his obligations to Paul, who was no ordinary prisoner and a Roman citizen besides. He desired to save Paul and hence refused to let the soldiers have their way. It is a vivid picture of the rescue of all, some on planks, some on plunder from the ship, some by swimming. They were safe on shore as Paul had said.

Luke appears wonderfully well as an historian in chap. 27. He is here on a par with Thucydides in grasp and power. Indeed, this chapter furnishes more information about ancient seafaring than any other source. Smith's "Voyage and Shipwreck of St. Paul" is the great monograph on this chapter.

Luke is particularly proud of his hero for his conduct during this voyage. Even "the barbarians" of Melita (28 : 1 f.) could be uncommonly kind. The term with Luke means only non-Greek, not uncivilized. Luke here writes from the Greek point of view. It is a pathetic picture, the cold, the rain, the bedraggled condition of the whole company. Paul was not a mere spectator, and his zeal was responsible for his not perceiving the viper which came out by reason of the heat and fastened on his hand. There are said to be now no vipers on the island, but that proves nothing about this time. The snake may or may not have been poisonous; but the people thought it so. Popular interpretation of such incidents is well illustrated here. One moment Paul is a murderer, the next a god. At Lystra it was first a god, and then one fit only for death. Paul's stay of three months in the island was not without good results. Publius was the ruler of the island whose title was "first" according to inscriptional support. As at Cyprus, Thessalonica and elsewhere, Luke is found to be minutely accurate. Paul appears here as the healer of diseases (along with Luke?), after the manner enjoined in James 5 : 14 f. He had the example of Jesus also.

In the early spring or late winter (February) "a ship of Alexandria which had wintered in the island" (28 : 11) with the sign of *The Twin Brothers* set sail for Italy. They had probably been caught here just as Paul's second ship had been at Fair Havens, but had followed wise counsel and waited for spring. One can imagine Paul's eagerness to get on to Rome, and Luke greatly abbreviates the narrative here. They do spend three days at Syracuse, famous seat of Greek culture. At Rhegium they wait a day for a south wind which blows them safely to Puteoli. Here Paul and his party land. Nothing is said about Julius and his soldiers and other prisoners. It is simply assumed

that they go along too. It is noteworthy that Paul
found brethren at Puteoli. It was, indeed, a great
harbor and shows that Christianity was spreading
from Rome over Italy (cf. Heb. 13 : 24).

11. *The Reception at Rome.*—Ramsay[1] explains the
double mention of coming to Rome (28 : 14, 16) by
the two senses of the word Rome as city-state in Greek.
Paul first came to the district of Rome, then to the
walls of Rome. He had spent seven days at Puteoli,
and that gave time for the brethren there to send word
on to Rome that the great Apostle was approaching
the city. They had received his Epistle nearly three
years before this. It is possible that they had been
notified of his trials in Judea. At any rate, they send
a delegation out to greet Paul at the Market of Appius
and The Three Taverns. He was travelling the famous
Appian Way, portions of which are still in use and
testify to the greatness of the Roman roads. Paul
was not insensible to the great historic scenes all
around him as he neared the mighty city. But at this
moment his chief joy was in seeing the brethren, perhaps some of those whom he already knew and loved
(cf. Rom. 16). He had had enough to discourage
the stoutest heart. But now "he thanked God and
took courage." Jesus had kept his word. He had
brought him to Rome. True, he had not expected
to come in this manner. The brethren must excuse
the soldier and the chain (28 : 16).

[1] "St. Paul the Traveller," p. 347.

It used to be said that Paul was delivered over to one of the Prætorian Prefects, who at that time was the noble Burrus. But Ramsay[1] argues plausibly, following Mommsen, that the *Stratopedarch* in some mss. of Acts 27 : 16 (absent from the oldest) means *Princeps Peregrinorum*, the commanding officer of the "soldiers from abroad" who were used to conduct prisoners to Rome and had a camp on the Cœlian Hill called *Castra Peregrinorum*. It was to this *Stratopedarch*, not to the Prætorian Prefect, that Julius delivered his famous prisoner. It may be replied that Paul in Phil. 1 : 13 and 4 : 22 shows somewhat close relations with the Prætorian Camp. But still he did not live in either camp, but in his own hired house (Acts 28 : 30). If he was under the control of the *Stratopedarch*, he might still occasionally preach to the Prætorian Guard.

Paul's first joy was with the brethren whom he knew in Rome. They probably brought others to see him so that he soon had new friends in Rome. It was an unspeakable joy for him to have this spiritual fellowship. He is established in his own house, but he does not know how long he will have to wait for his trial. He must have known by this time how slow Roman legal procedure could be. Certain forms had to be observed. The charge against him had to arrive, if by this time Festus knew what to do about the matter. The witnesses had to be gathered together. Other reasons

[1] "St. Paul the Traveller," p. 348.

will occur later. These were present at the first and made it plain that an immediate trial was out of the question.

12. *The Effort to Win the Jews.*—Paul waited only three days to get together the chief men of the Jews (28 : 17). It was important to have their sympathy if possible. Besides, Paul was anxious to win these Jewish leaders to the service of Christ. Poppœa, the infamous wife of Nero, was a Jewess. If his case came before Nero himself, she might be reached by the hostile Jews. So Paul gives them a brief account of the history of his case. He was innocent of any wrong to the Jewish people or customs; yet the Jews had delivered him up to the Romans who had desired to set him at liberty but for the Jews who were so bitter against him. Hence he had appealed to Cæsar. But he is not here to make any accusations against his people. In fact, he is bound with this chain because of the hope of Israel. It was a skilful plea, but the Jews were wary. They had received no letters about his case nor had any of the Jews from Palestine now in Rome said aught against Paul. But they would like to hear his views, for, they must confess, "his sect" was everywhere spoken against by the Jews. He had that much against him. He was a Christian. It was not a very hopeful beginning, though they were willing to listen.

So, on a stated day, Paul endeavors to win the great crowd of Roman Jews that came. He gave them his interpretation of the kingdom of God and sought to

prove that Moses and the Prophets foretold Jesus as
tne Messiah. It was an all-day meeting. He had
some success also, but a number disbelieved. Paul's
"one word" to this part who resisted is in accord with
Rom. 9–11. He reminds them of the curse of Isaiah
on them (6: 9 f.), a curse often on the lips of Jesus.
But the Gentiles in Rome will hear, if the Jews do not
(Acts 28 : 28).

13. *The Delay of Paul's Trial.*—Luke passes over
two whole years of Paul's life in Rome with no record
save what is contained in two verses (28 : 30 f.). He
lived in his own hired dwelling, had free intercourse
with his friends in spite of his chain and the soldier,
had perfect freedom in preaching the kingdom to all
who came and in teaching the things concerning the
Lord Jesus Christ, and he did this with boldness.
This, therefore, is Luke's picture of Paul's life in Rome
for two years. We are grateful for this much information, but cannot help wondering why we do not have
more, especially as Luke was with Paul nearly all of
this time.

If Luke wrote the Acts a good while afterward,
it may be explained that his object in the Acts was
merely to take Paul to Rome. That was the climax
of his career. With that goal Luke was satisfied and
may have meant to write another volume carrying on
Paul's career to the end. That is a possible interpretation, though it leaves unexplained why Luke should
have mentioned the item about the "two years" if he

only meant to take him to Rome.   In reality he takes
him almost up to the time of his release.

If, on the other hand, we suppose that Luke finished the Acts at the point where he stops the book,
we have the "two years" explained and also the reason
why he went no further in this volume.   The question
of a third volume is not raised.   Luke used the leisure
of the years in Rome to write the book with Paul to
draw on for much information for his career.   We
should still have left the perplexity why Luke gave
so little space to the two years in Rome.   But, after
all, they may have been rather uneventful years.
There were friends of Paul coming and going.   He
wrote great Epistles to distant churches.   But the
life itself in Rome before the trial may not have been
marked by unusual incident.   On the whole, I incline
to this interpretation of the situation.

The trial itself must wait on the whim of Nero or
of one of the two Prætorian Prefects.   We do not know
before whom Paul actually appeared.   We know how
dilatory Tiberius was in such cases, and Nero was
proverbially averse to real business.   He was the
victim of caprice and impulse.   Ramsay[1] suggests
that his opponents may have wished also to put the
trial off as long as possible, knowing that they could
not make a real case against Paul (cf. the dilemma of
Festus).   He thinks also that the Imperial Office may
have been making investigation.   He adds: "The whole

[1] St. Paul the Traveller," p. 356.

question of free teaching of an Oriental religion by
a Roman citizen must have been opened up by the case;
and it is quite possible that Paul's previous proceedings
were inquired into."

As we look back upon the Rome of the early 60's
the three men who stand out most prominently from
our point of view are Paul, Nero and Seneca. But
at that time it would have seemed ridiculous to the
world at large to put Paul in the same class with Nero
and Seneca. Paul in reality rose so far above them
both in all the real elements of character and manhood that one now feels like apologizing for mentioning them in connection with Paul. It is a striking
instance of the superiority of the spiritual forces of
life over the material. Pomp, station, power were with
Nero and his brilliant but servile and inconsistent
minister of state, Seneca. Paul was only a Jewish
Christian preacher, a prisoner with ugly charges
against him from the Jews themselves, at best a fanatic
out of touch with the real life of the time. Pilate,
Caiaphas, and Jesus met one day in Jerusalem. We
do not know that Nero, Seneca and Paul ever met
in Rome. They meet in our ideas of the Rome of the
time. Paul had appealed to Nero, the incarnation
of unbridled lust and whimsical power. Seneca was
the brilliant Stoic philosopher who turned out aphorisms
and sententious sayings for the benefit of other people
who had himself little real moral fibre and force. It
has been thought by some that Seneca and Paul met

and had influence, the one on the other. But Lightfoot[1] is followed by Ramsay[2] in the view that what bond of contact may exist was not personal nor direct, but indirect. Paul knew the Stoic tenets of the day. He had lived in Tarsus, the home of Athenodorus, a leading Stoic philosopher who had afterward come to Rome. Seneca shows evident use of Athenodorus. There is no real evidence for thinking that Seneca was a disciple of Paul nor that Cæsar himself was a believer because the gospel took root in some members of his numerous household (Phil. 4 : 22). But Paul, Nero and Seneca represent the great forces of the time. Nero was the acme of Roman absolutism. Seneca was the refinement of Roman Stoicism putting a good interpretation upon the evil life of the time under cover of half-hearted protest. Paul was the uncompromising exponent of the supremacy of the spirit over the flesh, the gospel that was to brush aside Stoicism and to subdue the civil power to Christ. But that will only come after ages of conflict. Victory will ultimately be on Paul's side in spite of his lowly estate and partly because of what he here undergoes. And Paul never gave way in Rome to the obsession of circumstance. He was always the ambassador of Christ even if in chains (Eph. 6 : 20).

14. *The Love of the Philippians for Paul: The Epistle to the Philippians.*—Paul did not lose interest

---

[1] "Commentary on Philippians."
[2] "St. Paul the Traveller," p. 354.

in the problems of the East by reason of his imprisonment in Rome. It could have been easy for some men to become out of humor with everybody and everything when checked and hedged in as Paul now was. So far from that Paul is the comforter and inspirer, not only of the many friends in Rome, but also of the churches back in the East where he had so long labored. He retains his world outlook and world sympathy and his environment does not change his buoyant optimism nor slacken his energy of thought and action.

Communication between Rome and distant parts of the empire was easy and constant, thanks to the fine system of Roman roads and postal service. Paul was not long without expressions of sympathy from the East, as friends of his would be going from Rome or coming to Rome. The going of some of these friends gave him the opportunity to send messages to several of the churches that are of priceless value to the modern world. New problems had arisen in some parts of the East since Paul was there that furnish the occasion for a discussion of the person of Christ and the dignity of the Christian life upon a loftier plane than Paul had reached before. It is not that his theology has changed, but that it is enriched in his grapple with the new issues. He here sounds depths and reaches heights beyond what he did even in the Epistle to the Romans.

The order of this third group of Paul's Epistles is a matter of dispute. There is no doubt at all that three of them were sent at the same time (Philemon, Colos-

sians, Ephesians). Onesimus was the bearer of the
letter to Philemon (10) and along with Tychicus of
that to the Colossians (4 : 7–9). Tychicus was also the
bearer of the letter called that to the Ephesians (6 : 21).
The only matter of dispute is whether the Epistle to
the Philippians was written before or after this group
of three. Unfortunately there is no absolutely conclusive evidence on this point and the scholars disagree.[1]
Timothy is with Paul when all are written (Phil.
1 : 1; Philem. 1). Aristarchus (Col. 4 : 10) and Luke
(Col. 4 : 14) are with Paul when the group of three are
sent, besides a number of others (Col. 4 : 10–14). It
seems as if neither Aristarchus nor Luke is present
when Paul writes to the Philippians (2 : 19–21). But
there are several ways of explaining this fact. In both
Philippians (1 : 25; 2 : 24) and Philemon (22) Paul
expects to be set free, a little more confidently, indeed,
in Philemon, except that he uses "shortly" in Phil. 2 :24.
He wishes prayers for his release (Col. 4 : 18). In the
absence of decisive evidence either way I fall back upon
Lightfoot's use of the doctrinal situation. In Colossians
and Ephesians there is no echo of the Judaizing controversy, but in Phil. 3 we do have something of the
same point of view found in the great doctrinal Epistles.
Then again in chapter 2 of Phil. the person of Christ
comes to the fore as it does more prominently still in
Colossians and Ephesians. As a matter of fact it is not
necessary for any great length of time to exist between

[1] Hort, "Judaistic Christianity," p. 114, puts Philippians first.

Philippians and the rest. They may all come in the last year of Paul's first imprisonment in Rome, Philippians at the beginning of that year.

Paul has been long enough in Rome for some positive work for Christ to have been done. The gospel has made progress in Rome by reason of his imprisonment even in the Prætorian Guard (Phil. 1 : 12–14). His courage, though he is in bonds, has been contagious. True, he has found enemies even in Rome, who seem to correspond with the old Judaizers in the East (1 : 15 ff.). These rejoice in Paul's troubles and enjoy annoying him by preaching in Rome, right where Paul is, a perverted gospel. But Paul finds joy in the fact that even so men can learn something of Christ though mixed with error. There are enemies of the cross of Christ in Rome as there were in Philippi, as Paul used to tell them, and it causes him to weep to say so now (3 : 18). The gospel has gone not simply to the Prætorian Guard, but even to Cæsar's household (4 : 22). We are grateful for these glimpses of Paul's life and work in Rome.

In the Epistle Paul describes beautifully and delicately the love of the Philippians for himself and his appreciation of their affection. The saints at Philippi had been the first to contribute to Paul's support and for a while the only church to do so (4 : 15). He would not allow the mission church where he labored to pay him for fear of being considered a man seeking their money, though he was entitled to it (I Cor. 9 : 7–18).

The Philippians had helped Paul repeatedly (Phil. 4 : 16) from the first until now (1 : 5). They had the fellowship in the mission cause that comes from giving to its advancement. He would not allow the Corinthian church to do anything for him even after he left, though by this time other churches had followed the example of the Philippian church (II Cor. 11 : 7 f.; 12 : 13 f.). He appreciates more than he can tell their spirit and this present gift (Phil. 4 : 18), and he is rich indeed. Not that he cares so much for the gift, but the love behind it (4 : 17). He has learned by bitter experience the secret of contentment, how to be filled and to be hungry (4 : 11–13). But God will bless them for their gift (4 : 19).

Paul is grieved over the misfortunes that befell Epaphroditus after his arrival in Rome. He was sick nigh unto death (2 : 30). Did he come in the summer and catch the Roman fever? After Epaphroditus recovered, he learned that the Philippians had heard of his illness and this knowledge added to his grief. Hence he is going back to Philippi with Paul's letter and love (2 : 25 f.). Good thus came out of evil for the Philippians and for us.

The Epistle itself is full of love and joy. The very noblest side of Paul's nature is uppermost in this message of hope from his state of imprisonment. He had with Silas even sung praises in the jail at Philippi. The key-note of the letter to the Philippians is joy. The letter is not keyed to the discussion of a great doctrine. It is rather discursive after the manner of I Thessalonians and I Timothy. But in chapter 2 : 1–11 we have the classic passage about the humiliation of Christ, while in 3 : 1–16 we have not only the contrast between Paul's ideals as a Pharisee and as a Christian (cf. Rom. 7), but also the matchless passion of his striving for the goal of Christ-likeness. This singleness of aim (3 : 13 f.) and identity of spirit with Christ (1 : 21) is enough to distinguish any epistle. Put beside this also the motto for high thinking and high doing (4 : 8 f.).

One would like to know the name of the "true yoke-fellow" addressed in 4 : 3, since the Epistle as a whole is directed to the saints, bishops, and deacons (the entire church) at Philippi (1 : 1). But Paul had many fellow-workers in Philippi besides Clement, and the two sisters who did not have the same mind (4 : 2 f.).

It is not necessary to think that Paul had suffered undue depression about the delay in his trial because of the balance that he strikes between life and death (1 : 21–24). For several years surely he has looked death in the face. In his last letter to Corinth (II Cor. 5 : 1–10) he expressed the same preference for death that we see here. It is not the melancholia of a hypochondriac, but the spiritual aspiration of one who is longing for the end of the road where he can get out of the harness and rest with Christ (1 : 23). But meanwhile he will work gladly, knowing that the Lord is near him (4 : 5).

15. *A Specimen of Paul's Work in Rome: The Epistle to Philemon.*—The Epistle to the Philippians makes it clear, besides Luke's closing comment in Acts, that Paul was not idle in Rome. He is still the central moving force in Gentile Christianity. His heart goes out to all the world, and he fights his battles with his pen and his prayers. These Epistles breathe, indeed, the atmosphere of his surroundings, but they have caught also the breath of Heaven. Paul moves on the holy heights of spiritual vision. But now we have a sample of Paul's work in Rome itself.

All sorts of people came to Rome. Runaway slaves came among others. Slaves were not necessarily degraded persons. They were often captives taken in war and might be superior in culture to their masters. In Rome itself the Greek slaves were often the schoolteachers in the family. It is clear that Onesimus had run away from his master Philemon at Colossæ (Philem. 12) and it is implied that he had taken something as he left (18 f.). Paul had labored successfully with those in high station, but he was not above winning a slave to Christ and calling him a brother in Christ (16), his child in the gospel (10).

It was, indeed, a very delicate situation with so many slaves in the Roman Empire. It is now Paul the aged and the prisoner of Christ (9) who sends back the converted runaway slave to his Christian master (12). The law will be observed, but he is not to come back just as he was. He is to be loved and treated as Paul

would be (17), and Paul hints that Philemon will set
him free (21).   He gave a new conception of love for
a slave that has set all slaves free in Christendom and
will ultimately shake off all shackles everywhere.

This is a purely personal letter, but it is rich in the
spirit of Christ.   Besides Philemon it is addressed to
Archippus and Apphia.   Was the church that met
in the house of Philemon at Colossæ (2) the same as
the one that meets in the house of Nymphas (Col.
4 : 15)?   Were they separate organizations or different
meeting-places for the same body?   Besides Aristarchus, Luke and Timothy, Paul has with him Demas,
Epaphras and Mark (Philem. 1, 23 f.), who has now
regained the favor of Paul.   Like Onesimus, who was
once unprofitable to Philemon (11), Mark has become
useful to Paul.

16. *The New Peril of Gnosticism: The Epistle to
the Colossians.*—It was the coming of Epaphras from
Colossæ to Rome (Col. 1 : 7; 4 : 12) with news of the
new heresy in the Lycus Valley that stirred Paul to
action in the matter.   Paul had not preached at Colossæ, but Epaphras had established this work.   He
had labored also much at Hierapolis and Laodicea
(4 : 13), also in the same valley in the province of Asia.
We have here indications of the spread of the Gospel
in a province already mentioned by Luke (Acts 19 : 10).
Paul had apparently seen signs of the new heresy
when at Miletus (Acts 20 : 29 f.).   Paul is so much
aroused about the situation in the valley of the Lycus

that he sends Tychicus and Onesimus now to comfort their hearts (Col. 4 : 8 f.), and hopes to send Mark later (4 : 10). Indeed, he had already communicated with them about Mark, whether personally through Barnabas, Mark's cousin, or by letter, we do not know. But this is not all. Paul sends also along with this Epistle one to the Laodiceans. He urges that each church make an exchange of Epistles (4 : 16), a hint as to the custom with Paul's other Epistles. It is generally supposed that this Laodicean Epistle is the one known to us as the Epistle to the Ephesians.[1]

It is evident, therefore, that Paul has the situation well in mind before he writes the Epistle to the Colossians. Although Mark was the cousin of Barnabas, he is grouped by Paul with Aristarchus and Justus as belonging to the party of the circumcision (4 : 10 f.). Mark had been working with Simon Peter also, or, at any rate, soon will be with him (1 Pet. 5 : 13). Paul cherishes no bitterness towards Jewish Christians as such. These men were not Judaizers, but were following the ministry alluded to in Gal. 2 : 9. It is in this Epistle (Col. 4 : 14) that Paul gives Luke the praise of "the beloved physician." That was probably not merely Paul's own love, but the common feeling among the Roman Christians toward this noble servant of Christ. There are few more beautiful relations in life than that between the preacher and the Christian physician. In concluding Paul

[1] Cf. Rutherford, "Epistles to Colossæ and Laodicea" (1908).

calls attention to the signature with his own hand
(4:18).

What was the new heresy in the Lycus Valley?
It is difficult to explain Paul's language in this Epistle
without thinking of an incipient Gnosticism that had
been blended with Jewish Essenism. There is no
doubt about the existence of Gnosticism of an advanced type in this part of Asia in the second century.
The case of Simon Magus in Acts 8 is a forecast also
of what was coming. Hort,[1] indeed, fails to see any
evidence of either Essenic or Gnostic influence in
Colossians. He sees merely Jewish speculation with
some Greek influence as at Corinth. This is a justi-
fiable reaction against the extreme opinion that the
Gnosticism of the second century is found at Colossæ
in A.D. 62-3. Still, I can but think that Lightfoot, in
his masterly essay on the Colossian Heresy,[2] has laid
down the lines of truth on this subject. There was
in Colossæ a cult that was a mixture of Greek philosophy and Essenic teaching. The Essenic doctrine had
already incorporated some Persian and Greek ideas.
It was a time of philosophic syncretism. The Essenes,
of course, had their home in the wilderness of Judea,
but their influence went beyond that region. Some
travelling Jewish teachers had probably picked up
these mystic ideas about God, matter, angels, morals,
before they came to Colossæ. Here they fell under the

[1] "Judaistic Christianity," pp. 116-129.
[2] "Commentary on Colossians."

spell of Christian teaching.   What they did was to in-
corporate the chief Christian doctrines into their philosophy and seek to propagate the result as the true
philosophical gospel.   The peril of that situation
Paul was quick to see.   Hence this eager and powerful
Epistle to open the eyes of the Colossian Christians
to the subtle danger confronting them.

The main outlines of this incipient Gnostic philosophy can be drawn from Paul's condemnation of it in
the Epistle and from the well-known later develop-
ments.   Similar forms of teaching are condemned in the
Pastoral Epistles of Paul and in the Epistles of John
and possibly also in the Apocalypse.   The new teachers had a theory of the universe which considered
matter essentially evil while God is good.   Their philosophical problem was how the good God could have
created evil matter without responsibility and contamination.   Hence they imagined a series of inter-
mediate agencies called æons that came in between
God and the creation of matter.   Each one in the
series was further away from God till the last one was
far enough from God to cause no contamination to
the deity and yet near enough to God to have power
to create matter.   This curious theory of the origin
of matter and evil satisfied some minds.   One may
remark in passing that no one has yet presented an
adequate explanation of the origin of evil.   But certainly this theory of the essentially evil character of
matter is wrong.   Hence the Gnostic Christians at

once had trouble with the person of Christ. Where
did he come in? Was he above these æons or merely
one of them? They seem to have put him at the bottom of the list. So Paul is contradicting this theory
when he insists on the primacy of Christ in his relation
to God whose very image he is (Col. 1 : 15–17). "He
is before all things," æons included, if there are any.

In the practical working out of the theory about
the nature of Christ the Gnostics fell into two wings.
One view was that Jesus only seemed to be a man.
In reality he had no human body (cf. modern theosoph-
ical theories popular in some quarters). These were
called Docetic Gnostics, as Ignatius makes clear.
Hence Paul speaks of the "blood of his cross" (1 : 20),
"body of his flesh" (1 : 22), and remarks that "in
him dwelleth all the fulness of the Godhead bodily"
(2 : 9). The other type of Gnostics, called later
Cerinthian Gnostics from Cerinthus, held that Jesus
was a mere man, but that the divine Christ (æon) came
upon him at his baptism in the form of a dove and left
him on the cross when Jesus felt himself deserted.
Paul seems to have this view in mind when he insists
on "Christ Jesus the Lord" (2 : 6) as the one whom
they received and in whom they are to walk.

Paul sums up "all the fulness of the Godhead" in
Jesus Christ (1 : 19: 2 : 9). It was not distributed
in a series of æons. "Fulness" was one of the favorite Gnostic terms. Jesus was head over the physical
universe (1 : 15–17) and the spiritual body or church

general (1 : 18), "that in all things he might have the preëminence." Hence he is to be "the Head" (2 : 19) for all believers. So angels are not to be worshipped (2 : 18). No false philosophy can take the place of "the mystery of God, even Christ, in whom are all the treasures of wisdom and knowledge hidden" (2 : 2 f.). In answer, therefore, to the Gnostic debasement of Jesus, Paul expounds the dignity and glory of the person of Jesus. He does not here use the term God, but he describes him in language which leaves no other alternative possible as to his real meaning. Just as the Judaizing controversy developed clearly and fully Paul's position about faith and works, so the Gnostic controversy was the occasion for the richer exposition of the person of Christ. It is easy to see how the deity of Christ is no new idea with Paul. The roots of it go back to the vision of Jesus on the road to Damascus, and he shows it at many points previous to this Epistle. But here the cross of Christ stands out, not against Pharisaic legalism as in the four great doctrinal Epistles, but against the bondage of false philosophy (2 : 13–16.)

In practical life also the Gnostics divided. Some took the ascetic turn. Since matter was evil, they would separate themselves from life around them by external renunciation and self-imposed regulations for the abuse of the body (2 : 20–23). But this plan was a failure. Mere asceticism is of no avail against the indulgence of the flesh. The other party went to the extreme of license and argued that evil could not be kept from the body, which was itself evil. The soul, however, could be kept pure in spite of the sinful indulgences of the body. The soul alone was worth while. Let the body have license in its indulgences. Against this low view of life Paul sets the ideal of life in Christ and urges a fight to the death on the sins of the body, putting off the old man with his doings and putting on the new man with the new heart and the new life (3:1–17). It is a noble appeal that Paul makes, and he applies it to the various classes of the time. He sees the social side of Christian endeavor and carefully explains how each section of society may meet its specific difficulty in the spirit of Christ.

17. *A General Appeal to the Churches of Asia: The Epistle to the Ephesians.*—Paul seemed to feel so strongly the importance of vigorous treatment of the new heresy that he sent another letter along at the same time which he wished passed around among the churches (Col. 4:16). A natural inquiry is raised as to the fate of this Epistle to the Laodiceans. Curiously enough the words "at Ephesus" (Eph. 1 : 1) are wanting in the oldest Greek mss. Marcion actually calls the Epistle known to us as that to the Ephesians the Epistle to the Laodiceans. There are no personal greetings as one would expect (cf. Col. 4:10–17) in a letter to Ephesus, where Paul labored three years. The whole tone of the Epistle is that of a circular letter. The term church throughout has the general, not the local, sense and is synonymous here with "body" (1:22 f.),

"one new man" both Jew and Gentile (2 : 15), "one body" of both (2 : 16), "commonwealth of Israel" (2 : 12, 19), "household of God" (2 : 19), "a holy temple in the Lord" (2 : 21), the bride of Christ (5 : 23). He seems to have in mind the Christians of Asia as a whole, both Jew and Greek (cf. 1 Peter 1 : 1; 2 : 4). One may suppose either that several copies were made with a blank left for the name of this church or that, as the one copy was passed around from church to church, other copies were made. One came to Ephesus, the capital city of the province of Asia, and that copy naturally is the one preserved to us.[1]

This general appeal of Paul against the Gnostic heresy well illustrates his interest in the Kingdom of God. He is still the ecclesiastical statesman, though a prisoner at Rome. He is as yet debarred from going to Spain, but he is eager to conserve the cause in the East. These two Epistles (Colossians and Ephesians) challenge comparison at once. They were sent at the same time, but obviously Colossians was composed before Ephesians as the one that directly called forth the discussion of the Colossian heresy. As has often been pointed out, there is much the same relation in manner of treatment between Colossians and Ephesians that we see between Galatians and Romans. The specific treatment precedes the general discussion. Hence in Ephesians there is less warmth than in Co-

[1] Two new commentaries on Ephesians are worth mentioning: Westcott (posthumous) in 1906, and Robinson in 1907.

lossians. The subject is handled with less passion, but with more intellectual grasp. The heights and depths of the spiritual interpretation of life are touched in Eph. 1–3, the most profound passage in all Christian literature.

In Colossians Paul was anxious to exalt Christ to his true position of dignity and power. In Ephesians he rather assumes that place for Christ and unfolds the corresponding dignity of the body of Christ, the church, his bride. Here the doctrine of election is treated (1 : 3–14), not as needing defence by reason of the failure of the Jews to respond to the gospel message (Rom. 9–11), but rather as an exhibition of the love of God to both Jew and Greek. Two great prayers glorify this Epistle (1 : 15–23; 3 : 14–21) that sound the depths of profound emotion and scale the heavenly places in noble aspiration.[1] Chapter 2 is Paul's best exposition of the breaking down by Christ of the middle wall of partition between Jew and Gentile. He is here not defending the right of the Gentile to equal terms with the Jew in Christianity (Galatians and Romans). He is the rather reminding the Gentiles of their glorious privilege, made possible by Christ, and urging them to be worthy of membership in the body of which Christ is Head. He is jealous that Gentiles shall prove worthy of their new position.

The fuller discussion of the Christian life in its private and social aspects in Ephesians grows naturally

[1] Cf. Stalker, "The Life of St. Paul," p. 103.

out of this broad and exalted conception of the Christian's connection with Christ. The exalted Head calls for an exalted body. This intimate relation between the redeemed and Christ reaches the height of nobility in the discussion in 5 : 22–33. One cannot forbear remarking how pertinent is the detailed discussion of the Roman armor in 6 : 10–20. Paul surely had ample opportunity to become familiar with every piece of that armor as he watched the soldier to whom he was chained.

If Paul's prison life in Rome had done nothing for the world save give it the Epistles to the Colossians and Ephesians it would have been more than worth while. The heat and burden of a busy life are now behind him. The sun has turned toward the west with him. He is an old man, but not a broken man. If there is less fire than in the four great Epistles, as they are called, there is equal light here, if not more. Clearly, Paul is now more serene, more restful in spirit, more tender, more spiritual in his insight. It is a normal development to which he has come. He will never go back to the stormy time of I Corinthians, II Corinthians, and Galatians. "The greatness of the Church and the divine glory of Christ fill Paul's prison meditations."[1] He has not merely rounded out his doctrine. He has finished the pyramid. Jesus Christ is all and in all with Paul (Col. 3 : 11). Christ is for all men and all men are for Christ. There is a greater Kingdom in the world

[1] Findlay, Art. Paul in Hastings' "D. B."

than that of Rome. Even in Rome, indeed partly
because in Rome, Paul sees the splendor and glory
of that Kingdom, the true *imperium*, that shall gather
into its sweep men of the whole earth. In fact, that in
one sense had already come true (Col. 1 : 6). Paul is
loved everywhere and his authority is acknowledged
everywhere. No church now resists his word or will.
He is now, in reality, the Apostle of the whole world.
He has no apology to make for his chains, but he is
humble and asks the prayers of all Christians that he
may be a better preacher of the mystery of the Gospel
(6 : 19 f.). He is anxious for other doors for the word
(Col. 4 : 3). "As Nero's prisoner at Rome and Christ's
bondsman for the Gentiles, St. Paul rose to the full
unassailable height of his doctrine and his vocation."[1]
He speaks with the power of Isaiah and the sweetness
of David. Love for the whole world lights up his eyes.
His face shines like that of Moses coming down the
Mount. He has been often looking at the face of
Christ.

[1] Findlay, Art. Paul in Hastings' "D. B."

CHAPTER XI

PAUL FREE AGAIN

"I exhort, therefore, first of all, that supplication, prayers, intercessions, thanksgivings, be made for all men; for kings and all that are in high place; that we may lead a quiet and tranquil life in all godliness and gravity" (1 Tim. 2 : 1 f).

1. *The Outcome of the Trial.*—One is at liberty to suppose that Agrippa and Festus may have made on the whole a favorable report to Rome concerning Paul. Julius may have recommended consideration also.[1] But, while Paul waited the humor of the fickle Nero, the years drew on. We miss the master hand of Luke in the description of this trial before Nero (or the Prætorian Prefect) as we have it in the trials at Jerusalem and Cæsarea. To me this very absence argues for dating the conclusion of Acts before the trial came off. The presumption in Acts points to Paul's acquittal since neither Felix nor Festus had been able to find a charge against him that would stand in Roman law. Besides, Paul himself confidently expects to be set free (Phil. 1 : 25; Philem. 22). It is more than doubtful if any capital charge was presented

[1] Stalker, "The Life of St. Paul," p. 157.

against him. But we cannot assume that he was simply set free without investigation or trial. As before in Cæsarea, Paul probably made his own plea. Did his enemies repeat the same charges made to Felix and Festus? If so, they failed as before in spite of the influence of Poppæa who would be open to the appeal of the Jews against Paul. There were already believers and friends of Paul both in the Prætorian Guard and in Cæsar's household. Hence he was not without some friends on the inside of court circles. Perhaps Paul's enemies and their Roman lawyer bungled their case or may have displeased Nero by some accident. Seneca, indeed, may have taken a momentary interest in the matter on the side of justice. Paul would have little difficulty in showing that he had kept within the Roman law concerning Judaism as a *religio licita*. He could cite the position of Gallio at Corinth. As the brother of Seneca, that decision would be pertinent and timely. His religion was the true Judaism. At any rate, he was set free.

There is a considerable amount of evidence among early Christian writers indicating that Paul was set free. We do not have space for that phase of the discussion here. Scholars are not agreed upon it, but the balance of probability distinctly favors his release.[1] There is no evidence of real worth against the positive witness for Paul's release. The Pastoral

---

[1] See Ellicott, "Pastoral Epistles"; Conybeare and Howson, Scribner's ed., Vol. II, pp. 436 ff.; Spitta, "Urchristentum," Bd. I.

Epistles come into the scale. If they are genuine, as
I think, they settle what doubt may remain. They cannot be fitted into Paul's career up to the close of Acts.
We have no right to assume that his life and work closed
with the end of Acts. The very tone and temper of
these Epistles call for a somewhat later time. They
fit in exactly with a probable picture of Paul's closing
days. For the present, therefore, they may be used
as conclusive argument for Paul's release from the
first Roman imprisonment and as material for the
construction of the closing period of his ministry.
Sometime during A.D. 63, therefore, we may imagine
Paul as free from chain and soldier. Some five years it
had taken him to allay the storm raised that day in
the temple at Jerusalem.

2. *The Visit to the East.*—Before Paul went to Rome
he was eager to go on to Spain. But now, after five
years, new problems have arisen in the East. He is
anxious to visit Philippi and Colossæ. It is all speculation, to be sure, and one must not be dogmatic, but
it is at least possible to think that Paul carried out this
last purpose. He was needed in the East, and it would
cheer him to revisit the scenes of his former labors.
Refreshment of heart would come to him after the
long years of suffering and separation. But we have
absolutely no details of this visit. How long he remained in the East we have no means of knowing.

3. *The Visit to Spain.*—Clement of Rome (cf.
Phil. 4:3), writing to Corinth from Rome (ch. 5),

expressly says that Paul "had gone to the limit of the West" before his martyrdom. That could only mean Spain from the Roman point of view. In the Canon of Muratori it is stated that Paul went to Spain. In the spring or early summer of A.D. 64 we may imagine Paul at last in Spain. He had reached the goal of his ambition after much tribulation. He had some fruit in the West also. One may pass by as without foundation the late tradition that Paul went on to Britain. He was probably in Spain when the awful catastrophe befell Rome, July 19, A.D. 64.

4. *The Burning of Rome.*—It is difficult to think that Paul would have escaped if he had been in Rome after this dreadful event. Indeed, some scholars think that both Paul and Peter fell victims in A.D. 64 to the fury of Nero against the Christians. But I am not able to see the facts in that light. The whole world knows the story of this "mad freak of the malicious monster who then wore the imperial purple."[1] He chose to lay the blame of his deed upon the Christians, perhaps brought to his attention by the trial of Paul, in order to shield himself from popular wrath. The heart grows sick at the thought of the horrible details of Nero's persecution of Christians in Rome. Oil was poured over their clothing and they were tied to posts or trees and lighted at night like street lamps, while Nero rode furiously around in his chariot. But the point about this charnel house of crime that bears

[1] Stalker, "The Life of St. Paul," p. 164.

directly on Paul is that henceforth he would be a marked man, as indeed all prominent Christians were. Paul's release had virtually given Christianity a legal standing in Roman law as a form of Judaism. But now Nero had made a sharp distinction between Christians and Jews. Christianity was now *religio illicita.* To be a Christian was crime enough to deserve death (I Peter 4 : 16). The fashion of persecuting Christians had the sanction of the imperial example and command. It was now no mere popular outburst in a distant province against a man who interfered with established custom or business interests. Subservient flatterers and hirelings of Nero would seek to curry his favor, while this spell was on him, by informing against important Christians or delivering them up to his wrath. Henceforth there was no safe spot for Paul on earth nor for Peter either. John did, for the present, seem to escape this storm of persecution. But with Paul it is merely a question of time when his Roman enemies will get hold of him. He had escaped the vengeance of Greek and Jewish mobs, of Judaizers, of the Sanhedrin. Where can he turn now to make a stand against the rage of Nero, the madcap Emperor of Rome?

5. *The Return East for the Last Time.*—One is certain that Paul would not go by Rome when he left Spain. He may, indeed, have remained in Spain till 66 when the first fury of the Roman wild beast had subsided. He came by Crete with Titus and left

him there (Tit. 1 : 5). He had probably had his interest in the island aroused at the time of the voyage to Rome when he could not tarry. He came also to Miletus and probably did not go to Ephesus if one may judge by the directions given to Timothy (I Tim. 1 : 3). Paul seems to have left Timothy at Miletus,[1] where he left Trophimus sick (II Tim. 4 : 20). Timothy, therefore, is in charge at Ephesus, but Paul later sends Tychicus there also who had returned to Rome (II Tim. 4 : 12). Paul touched also at Troas on his way (II Tim. 4 : 13). He had possibly expected to come back here and so left his cloak and books with Carpus. He was on his way to Macedonia (I Tim. 1 : 3). The Jewish War had begun in A.D. 66. Paul would be hated by the Romans not merely as a Christian, but as a Jew.

6. *Paul's Concern for Timothy and the Work in Ephesus: I Timothy.*—Paul is apparently in Macedonia, and it is probably the late summer or early autumn of A.D. 67. The three Pastoral Epistles seem to come fairly close together. I shall not enter into a formal defence of these letters as Pauline. They do differ in style from the other groups of his Epistles. Indeed, all four groups have differences of style. Within bounds this is only natural. Style is not merely the mark of the man, though that is true. It is equally the function of the subject and ought to vary with the theme. Moreover, each man's style changes with the

[1] Cf. Findlay, in Sabatier's "The Apostle Paul," p. 366 f.

shifting periods of his life. Milton and Shakespeare, not to say Tennyson, are good illustrations of this variation in style. The severe critics of the Pastoral Epistles admit Pauline elements in them. The Pauline strain is manifest and strong. The real point to be faced is whether the facts given in these letters can be put into an intelligible scheme of Paul's life and whether the style is appropriate to him at the close of his career in the discussion of the themes embraced in the letters. The use of the new facts here brought out is perfectly admissible, as already shown. The style is, indeed, more chastened, less vigorous, more discursive, even less orderly than that of Paul in his earlier Epistles. But if one thinks of an old soldier of the cross, whose fire has somewhat died down, who is counselling young ministers concerning the problems that confront them, he will not be ready to say that the reflective, contemplative, personal character of these letters is not natural.

Paul tells why he wrote to Timothy. It is to impress further the exhortation given concerning his remaining awhile at Ephesus (I Tim. 1 : 3). Timothy seemed to have been at this time a travelling evangelist (II Tim. 4 : 5), but special reasons demanded his staying a season at Ephesus. We can form some adequate conception of Timothy's career so far. He was with Paul most of the time during the second and third missionary journeys, went with him to Jerusalem with the great collection, and rejoined him in Rome. He was one of the most faithful of all of

Paul's helpers and gave him much satisfaction. He seems not to have had robust health. The church at Ephesus had a body of elders, as we know, but Timothy was sent here as Paul's special representative as Tychicus was later (II Tim. 4:12). The conditions which Paul foresaw when at Miletus years before (Acts 20:29 ff.), and which he sought to rectify in the Epistles to the Colossians and the Ephesians, still demanded attention. "Certain men" at Ephesus (I Tim. 1:3) were preaching a "different doctrine," one devoted to "fables and endless genealogies," the same mixture of Jewish Gnosticism. The result was simply dispute, empty talk, violent affirmation. Paul was anxious that Timothy should seek to rescue the church from the influence of this barren philosophizing. It was a formidable task for a young preacher like Timothy who had once been unsuccessful in the troubles at Corinth. "Let no man despise thy youth" (I Tim. 4:12), Paul exhorts him. He will need wisdom and firmness.

Paul writes in a tone of sympathy with the young preacher and his problems. He himself had little of that in the beginning of his ministry save the fellowship of Barnabas. Paul is reminded vividly of Christ's goodness to him in putting him into that ministry which Timothy now adorns. Paul now looks back over a long and checkered life of service for Christ. He has been at the chariot wheel of Christ in his triumphal procession both as captive and as incense-bearer. He has had prisons oft and once for five years, but he simply and frankly thanks Christ Jesus his Lord for calling him to this high and holy work, unworthy though he was (I Tim. 1 : 12–17). That spirit in the old preacher is one of the ways of securing more young men for the ministry. One may thank God for the old preacher, full of years and of wisdom, who is able to enrich the lives of younger men. Paul is ripe with experience and grace and mellow with tender love as he warns and exhorts Timothy. He is, indeed, conservative now, as old men normally are, but he is not excessively so. His interest in the young preachers about him is one of the ways of keeping young himself.

Paul shows a keen desire that Timothy shall fulfil the promise of his youth (1 : 18), for others, alas, had made shipwreck, as Hymeneus and Alexander. He must be an example in upright living (4 : 12), a constant student (4 : 13), for here many fall short, diligent in the use of his gift, consecrated so as not to fritter away his energies, watchful about his health and his piety, that his progress may be manifest to all (4 : 14 f.). One can endure much in a young preacher if he is steadily growing in knowledge and power. He will have many temptations to follow after money and pleasure (6 : 11). Paul concludes with a passionate plea for Timothy to guard the deposit which he has received, to be faithful to his trust (6 : 20).

But there is more than this intensely interesting

personal strain in the Epistle. Though directed to Timothy the letter was evidently intended for public use also. It deals with church problems very largely, such as the qualifications of the bishop and the deacon, the treatment of a class of aged widows, the conduct of the rich, of servants. Social problems are prominent in the church life of the time. It is a rather more advanced type of church life that confronts us here than we meet in the Corinthian Epistles, but not more developed than one need expect by A.D. 67 in Ephesus.

The Apostle is anxious about the future of Christianity. He sees signs of heresy, of strife, of apostasy. But prayer and faithful preaching will meet the situation. It is interesting to note Paul's generous attitude toward the state (2 : 1 ff.) as in Rom. 13 : 1-7. He cherishes no harsh feelings. He sees the relation between good government and the welfare of the Kingdom of God. He asks prayers for kings. Not yet has the state everywhere been willing to allow Christians to "lead a tranquil and quiet life." Paul had felt the heavy hand of an oppressive state upon him. The shadows were gathering fast around him now.

7. *The Cause in Crete: The Epistle to Titus.*— Titus came into fellowship with Paul earlier than Timothy. He appeared at Jerusalem with him at the conference about A.D. 50 (Gal. 2 : 1, 3). He was Paul's mainstay in the Corinthian troubles (II Cor.

7 : 13 f.). He had been with Paul on his last visit to Crete (Tit. 1:5). He will be with him again at Rome before leaving for Dalmatia (II Tim. 4:10). Like Timothy (I Tim. 1:2) he was Paul's own true child in the faith (Tit. 1:4). Paul was clearly proud of these two young ministers who had so well justified his hopes about them.

Paul is apparently still in Macedonia and expects to spend the winter in Nicopolis (Tit. 3:12). It is probably near winter (A.D. 67). Zenas, the lawyer, and Apollos are possibly the bearers of the letter (3:13). Here is another glimpse of Apollos, whose friendship with Paul is unshaken. The lawyer, like Luke the physician, is a Gentile, it seems. Paul is hoping to send either Artemas or Tychicus to Titus later (3:12). Thus we see how Paul keeps in touch with the work all over the world. He has friends in Crete who love him (3:15). Not the least element of power in Paul is his vital touch with men. He makes friends and keeps them.

Paul shows real knowledge of the local conditions and difficulties of the work in Crete. They seem to have been specially susceptible to the "vain talkers and deceivers," especially to them of the circumcision (1:10). Here we seem to have an echo of the old Judaizing controversy. The Pharisaic party died hard, evidently, and finally drifted into a definite sect called Ebionites. But Paul is positive that their "mouths must be stopped" for they "overthrow whole houses," teaching "for filthy lucre's sake." Surely they were the lowest type of religious demagogues. But they had success in Crete. Paul is not surprised at this since one[1] of their own prophets (poets) had said:

"Cretans are always liars, evil beasts, idle gluttons."

It was severe, but Paul indorsed it. Prof. J. Rendal Harris[2] has shown that the reputation of the Cretans as liars began with the fact that they claimed that Zeus was dead and was buried on their island. The recent discoveries of Evans[3] at Knossos have shed a flood of light on the ancient civilization that flourished here far back in the Mycenæan age and even before that time. The type of heresy here was Jewish (1 : 10, 14), but may have had Gnostic elements (1 : 16) mingled with Pharisaism. Paul urges sharpness (1 : 13) if need be.

There are fewer personal exhortations in the Epistle and one wonders if Titus were not rather older than Timothy as well as more vigorous. He is in particular to avoid wrangling and disputes with factious men who fight about the law (3 : 9 f.). The directions about church officers and social problems do not differ greatly from those given to Timothy. He has in mind "rulers" (3 : 1) also, and is as anxious for uprightness of life as for orthodoxy of belief (3 : 8). In general

[1] Epimenides, sixth cent. B.C., an oracular (prophetic) poet.
[2] Cf. *Expositor* for 1907.
[3] Cf. excellent summary in Burrows, "The Discoveries in Crete" (1907).

the position of Titus in Crete seems to be the same as
that of Timothy in Asia, a sort of general evangelist.
Neither of these Epistles discusses a great doctrine at
length, though Paul's favorite teachings recur.

CHAPTER XII

PAUL FACES DEATH

"For I am already being offered, and the time of my departure is come. I have fought the good fight, I have finished the course, I have kept the faith; henceforth there is laid up for me the crown of righteousness which the Lord, the righteous judge, shall give me at that day" (2 Tim. 4:6 ff.).

1. *The Arrest.*—The winter came on, the winter of 67 and 68. Paul had left Erastus at Corinth on the way to Nicopolis (II Tim. 4:20). We have not Luke's graphic pen to describe the occasion and the circumstances of this second arrest. Probably while at Nicopolis during the winter or early spring, Paul suddenly finds himself under arrest as the result of the work of some informer anxious to ingratiate himself into the good graces of Nero and his favorites whose pastime was now the persecution of the Christians. They had grown weary of mere gladiatorial shows. The tortures of Christians, men and maidens, added novelty to the *blasé* life of Rome. His very nearness to Italy invited the attack of professional informers. Nicopolis, monument of the victory of Octavius at Actium, was a good place for such men to gather.

2. *The New Charges.*—We are justified in saying this much. The trouble in Jerusalem had arisen from the Jews as a protest against Paul's work in its bearing on Judaism. His Jewish enemies had tried to give an imperial turn to these charges, but had failed both in Cæsarea and Rome (before both provincial and imperial courts). But Christians could not now find shelter under the privileges granted to Judaism by Roman law. The Christian leader was now assumed to be, *ipso facto*, guilty of dark and dubious practices. The Jews themselves were not in good standing at Rome now that the war in Judea was raging. It may be inferred logically, therefore, that the newly invented charges against Paul had to do with the Roman state and in particular with the burning of Rome. That accusation was still doing duty whenever it was needed against a Christian. It was a matter of public knowledge that Paul had been in Rome not long before the burning of Rome. It would be easy to charge that his departure was only temporary, that he had returned, that he was resentful because of his long imprisonment, that he was in truth a ringleader of the whole affair, that he had since been hiding in distant parts of the empire. It would be easy also to add to this accusation charges of disloyalty against the Emperor because of his language about Jesus as King as at Thessalonica (Acts 17:7). The pathos of the situation lies partly in the fact that he was at this very time urging prayer for kings and all in au-

thority (I Tim. 2 : 1), and urging obedience and orderly
behavior on the part of all Christians (Tit. 3 : 1).
It was just as it had been in his worship in the temple
at Jerusalem when arrested before. Paul must now
confront not a mob, either Greek or Jewish. He had
learned how to escape them by the help of God. He
was not to confront the Jewish Sanhedrin whose re-
finements in theology he well knew. He was not to
appear before cowardly provincial governors who did
not dare do what they knew was right. He was not,
indeed, to face Roman law at all in its free exercise.
He would not probably appear before Nero in person,
but before the City Prefect, who would merely register
the known desire of Nero about Christians. Certain
forms of law would be observed, but the wheels of the
law would grind out condemnation.

3. *The Close Confinement.*—The freedom enjoyed
during the first imprisonment is all gone. He is
probably thrown into the Mamertine Prison or, at
any rate, is under close military custody (II Tim.
1 : 16). One is reminded of the condition of John the
Baptist in the prison at Machærus and Paul's own fate
in the inner prison at Philippi (Acts 16 : 24). So he
is back in Rome again, the new Rome of Nero's mad
revels under the tutelage of Tigellinus. Seneca wrote
philosophy while Nero gave full rein to his passions.
There is no relief to the dark picture save what comes
from the inward light of the spirit. It was, indeed,
"the irony of human life," for Paul to be in the hands

of a man who was "nothing but a compound of mud
and blood."[1]

4. *The Desertion of Paul's Friends.*—Not many
Christians remained in Rome at a time like this.
Many had suffered the martyr's death for Jesus.
Others had left the city and probably did wisely in
doing so. Crescens had gone to Galatia, perhaps,
with a message from Paul, and likewise Titus to
Dalmatia (II Tim. 4 : 10), showing that his work in
Crete was of a temporary nature. So Paul had sent
Tychicus to Ephesus (II Tim. 4 : 12). Prisca and
Aquila are absent in the East with Timothy (II Tim.
4 : 19) as well as the house of Onesiphorus. Paul is
grateful to Onesiphorus, "for he oft refreshed me and
was not ashamed of my chain; but, when he was in
Rome, he sought me diligently and found me" (II Tim.
1 : 16 f.). These simple words tell volumes about the
difficulty of finding Paul now and the danger of being
known as his friend. In his former imprisonment
his visitors were many and they came and went "unhindered." It was an honor among Christians to be
in the list of Paul's friends. But now one had to
consider whether he was willing to lose his life for the
sake of seeing the Apostle to the Gentiles. He could
not be rescued. He might be comforted, but at a very
high price. Onesiphorus did not count the cost. He
had his reward in comforting the lonely Apostle.
Most Christians who had to be in Rome made it con-

[1] Stalker, "The Life of St. Paul," p. 166.

venient, so it seems, to be ignorant of Paul's where-
abouts and to make no inquiries. Some remained
and were loyal to Paul (though not constantly with
him), like Eubulus, Pudens, Linus, Claudia and "all
the brethren" in Rome who were still spared by Nero
(II Tim. 4 : 21). But Demas forsook Paul, "having
loved this present world, and went to Thessalonica"
(II Tim. 4 : 10). He suddenly found a pressing demand
for his services there and Paul felt the desertion keenly.

5. *The First Stage of the Trial.*—This has already
passed when he writes his last Epistle, our only source
of information for this closing period of Paul's life.
The less serious charge apparently came first. What
it was we do not know. It may have been that Christianity was a *religio nova et illicita*. This matter was
involved in his former appearance at the bar of Nero.
It had fallen through then and may have failed now.
We know the name of one of the accusers at this first
stage of Paul's last trial. "Alexander the coppersmith
did me much evil" (4 : 14). He may have been the
same Alexander who at Ephesus (Acts 19 : 33) sought
to clear the Jews of any connection with Paul and his
denunciation of Diana and her temple. The name
is a common one. But if he is the same man, he was
doubtless glad of his chance to settle his account with
Paul since the multitude would not hear him that day.
His resentment was of long standing and his repre-
sentations told heavily against Paul. Paul warns
Timothy to beware of him if he ever comes his way,

"for he greatly withstood our words" (II Tim. 4 : 15). He seems to have been the chief spokesman among the accusers.

It seems that a considerable audience was present at this stage of the trial (4 : 17). Paul was the most famous Christian in the world. Common as the condemnation of Christians had come to be, fresh interest would be aroused by this case. When Paul came to Rome the first time, he was met by a delegation of brethren whose coming gave him courage. Now he looked around in vain for any one to take his part (4 : 16). "All forsook me." Had Luke failed to be present on that day? Paul cannot help thinking of all the peril that he has risked for other Christians. It does seem a little hard now to be left alone in the mouth of the lion. "May it not be laid to their account."

But he had help. It was his last opportunity to speak the message of eternal life to all the Gentiles present. "The Lord stood by me and strengthened me" (4 : 17). Was it a vision? Jesus had come to his side at Jerusalem after his conversion, when the Jews refused to hear him, at Corinth when they rejected his message, at Jerusalem again when they clamored for his blood. Paul had turned away from all his former friends to follow Jesus. Now all his Christian friends leave him. But Jesus does not leave Paul. With Jesus at his side he cares not for Nero, worse than a Numidian lion, whose hungry mouth

was ready for him (4 : 17).   Paul may mean that as a
Roman citizen he could not be thrown to the wild
beasts. He was acquitted, therefore, on this first charge.
But it was only a matter of time till the end came.

6. *The Loneliness of Paul.*—It was in the spring
when Paul was writing, the spring of 68. He has
passed through part of the winter or early spring in
the dreary Roman prison. He has missed his warm
cloak which he left at Troas with Carpus (4 : 13) on
his way to Macedonia to winter at Nicopolis. He does
not know how long the trial will be drawn out. It
may last till the next winter, and so he urges Timothy
to be sure to come to Rome before winter (4 : 21). It
makes him shudder to think of another winter without
that cloak.

But that is not the worst of it. He is lonely. "Only
Luke is with me" (4 : 11). Thank God for the faithful
physician who will risk all for his patient and friend.
There is no complaint of Luke, but both of them
hunger for the fellowship of others. Paul makes a
direct appeal to Timothy to come to him. We do not
know where Timothy was when he received this Second
Epistle. The mention of Ephesus (1 : 18; 4 : 12) can
be argued either way. He may have left Ephesus by
now as Titus had left Crete. The presence of the
house of Onesiphorus and of Prisca and Aquila with
Timothy may argue still for Ephesus as his abode.
But, wherever he was, we may be sure that he made
all "diligence to come shortly" to Paul (4 : 9). There

was no doubt of the devotion of Timothy to the grand old hero of the cross in the Roman prison. Timothy would risk his life for Paul. It seems from Heb. 13 : 23 that Timothy did come and was put into prison. When the Epistle to the Hebrews was written (probably A.D. 69, just before the destruction of Jerusalem and after Paul's death) Timothy has been set free. Whether he came before Paul's death or not is very uncertain, since the end came long before the oncoming winter.

It is a pleasant circumstance to note that Paul singles out Mark (II Tim. 4 : 11) as a young minister who can be counted on to be true in this time of trial. He has already been useful to Paul for ministering and has gotten bravely over the Perga experience. It is a good thing to reflect that a young man who makes a mistake may recover his ground. It is high tribute to Mark that Paul now couples his name with that of Timothy as one who will stick to the work, who will even dare the wrath of Nero to do so. The aged preacher appeals to two young preachers to come and stand by his side. That was a call to stir their blood.

Another element entered into Paul's loneliness. He had left most of his books and parchments at Troas. He was busy travelling and so left them with Carpus. He is in prison without friends (save Luke) and without books. That is a pathetic condition, indeed, and throws a keen light into Paul's nature, his love of books. He not merely exhorted Timothy to read. He had been a student himself as well as the writer of what

have proved to be the greatest letters of history. Busy
as Paul's life had been, as missionary and leader, he
had not forgotten his books. Life is dreary without
his books. Pity the old man who does not love books.
Other friends may desert you. Good books stay with
you. These "parchments" were probably portions
of the Old Testament much used by Paul and precious
to him. He may have made notes upon them.

7. *A Last Message to Timothy.*—Paul has not lost
his hold upon the workers nor his interest in the work.
He has sent messengers to various parts of the world.
By one of these, probably, this message to Timothy
is conveyed. Greatly as Paul is concerned about his
own problems, he is alert and eager to help Timothy.
He hungers for sympathy, but he bravely puts heart
into Timothy's plans. He reminds his "beloved child"
of his pious ancestry and urges him to be worthy of
such a heritage of faith (1 : 5). From a babe he has
known the Holy Scriptures. The love of these devoted
teachers should inspire Timothy (3 : 14 f.) to loyalty
to the Word of God. Paul begs Timothy to kindle
into a blaze the gift of God which he has (1 : 6). God
gave a spirit of courage and power (1 : 7). It is a
noble appeal that Paul here makes for bravery on the
part of the young preacher. Hardship is the lot to
which Paul calls him in ch. 2. Remember Jesus,
remember Paul and forget hardship.

Paul is ambitious that Timothy may be an expert
teacher of the Word of God (2 : 15). That is the best

way to meet heresy. Give people the truth. Dislodge error by the "expulsive power" of truth. Timothy will have trouble after Paul is gone, but let him be true to Paul's teaching and example (3 : 10 f.). "Out of them all the Lord delivered me." But how can Paul talk so now? God has kept him to a good old age and established the work of his hands. He must go some time. Nothing that can now happen can undo what God has done. Paul is not a pessimist as he warns Timothy against heresy and heretics. "The firm foundation of God standeth" (2 : 19). Let Timothy preach the word and fulfil his ministry (4 : 2, 5). That is his part. It is a bugle note from the old warrior.

8. *Paul's Estimate of His Own Career.*—He is the battle-scarred veteran of many conflicts and may be allowed to say a word about himself. It is a brief word and is sometimes called his Swan-song just before his death. Paul's fight is over. That is plain to him and he is not unwilling for Timothy to know it. True, he may linger on some months or a year or so. But he never expects to have his freedom again. He remembers the five years of his former imprisonment and knows the changed conditions of his present state. He has run his course. He had longed to do this though ready to die if need be years before (Acts 20 : 24). God has been good to him. His work is done. He has no regrets. He made no mistake that day when he turned to Jesus on the road to Damascus.

He stands by his guns as he falls at his post, and urges those that remain to carry on the fight. Let us to-day hear his call. There is no sign of surrender, no note of defeat. He is calm as he beholds the end. He indulges in no self-praise. He has simply carried his load to the end of the journey. That is all. He has been preacher, Apostle, teacher, and he is not ashamed (1 : 11 f.). He does not boast. He is humble at the feet of the Master. He exults in knowing that he has kept the faith. Of this he is proud. He has stood against Judaizer and Gnostic to preserve the truth of the gospel. This fact is a solace to the old preacher whose last sermon has been preached. He has never been disloyal to Christ.

9. *He Longs for Jesus.*—Paul does not doubt Jesus, for he has brought life and immortality to light through the gospel (II Tim. 1 : 10). If there is one thing in the world about which Paul can speak with authority it is fellowship with Jesus. "I know him whom I have believed" (1 : 12). In the last analysis this is the fundamental apologetic, knowledge of Jesus. Nothing can rob Paul of this. He knows Christ by a blessed experience of thirty years or more. He has the full persuasion that Jesus is able to guard that which he has committed unto him against that day (1 : 12).

Paul's face is now turned toward "that day." Indeed, he is "already being offered" and the time of his departure has come (4 : 6). He had long been ready for that consummation (Phil. 1 : 23). At last he is released from the harness like the faithful horse at the end of the day's journey. It will be sweet to rest from the toil and strife, but he is glad that he has had his share of the work.

It is futile for his enemies to attack him. "The Lord will deliver me from every evil work" (4:18). He does not mean that he will be set free from the charges against him. Not that, but something better. Jesus "will save me unto his heavenly Kingdom." There his enemies will not come and cannot harm him. Paul still has interest in earthly affairs, but his heart is in the hills on high. He looks away to the mountains. His feet are growing restless and the sun is setting in the west. Jesus is beckoning to him and he will go.

He has a "crown of righteousness" laid up for him which the Lord Jesus, "the righteous judge," will give him at that day (4:8). It matters little to Paul what the decision of Nero or his minions may be. He will appeal this time to the Supreme Judge, to the Highest Court, whose decision cannot be reversed. This "righteous judge" will give him his crown. That will be glory for Paul. He can pass by with indifference the whim of Nero. Let him do his worst. Paul is not now caring for Cæsar's judgment-seat. Once Paul had said that his aim had been to bring every thought into subjection to Christ (II Cor. 10:5). Christ is living in Paul (Gal. 2:20). With Christ he is content. He is seeking the things above where Christ is (Col. 3:1). He moves serenely in the high, clear atmosphere like the triumphant eagle. He is going soon to be at home with the Lord (II Cor. 5 : 8). He will "depart and be with Christ; for it is very far better."

10. *The Condemnation.*—The end came sooner than Paul had expected. Nero's own star suddenly set in gloom. It has never risen again. By the middle of June A.D. 68 Nero was dead in disgrace. The common tradition is that Paul was put to death before Nero's departure. Hence in May or early June we must suppose that Paul met the long-foreseen doom. If Timothy came before that time he also was made a prisoner though he escaped with his life (Heb. 13 : 23). If so, Paul had the comfort of Timothy's fellowship awhile at least. It is doubtful if Mark was able to come. But Paul may have had another look at his books.

If Paul was accused of complicity in the burning of Rome, summary judgment was rendered. As a Roman citizen, he was spared a slow, torturing death. He was not to be burned or to go to the lions. But he was to be beheaded. At last one day he heard the sentence of death pronounced upon himself. He had faced that peril many times before (II Cor. 1 : 9). It is now a reality. He is to follow in the footsteps of his Master. He had once revolted against the notion of a crucified Messiah. But the Cross had come to be Paul's glory (Gal. 6 : 14). He will bear his own cross. He already bears the brand-marks of Jesus (Gal. 6 : 17).

11. *Paul's Death.*—The details are all wanting. Tradition supplies only a few, which may be true or not. The story is that Paul was beheaded on the Ostian Road. It was customary for criminals of prominence to be executed several miles out of the city so as to avoid the crowds.

We may picture the event in a possible manner. One day in late spring or early June the executioners came to Paul's dungeon and led him out of the city. One is reminded of Jesus as he bore his cross along his *Via Dolorosa.* Paul, as a condemned criminal, would be the victim of the rabble's sport. He would have no defender. We do not know if Luke was with Paul to the very last. We may at least hope so. If he could, he would surely walk along as near Paul as would be allowed. But no band of Christians followed with him now. He was going out of Rome on his way to the true Eternal City. He knew Rome well, but his eyes were fixed on other things. Outside the city the busy, merry life of the time went on. The crowds flowed into town. Some were going out. Paul was only a criminal going to be beheaded. Few, if any, of the crowds about would know or care anything about him. At a good place on the road some miles out the executioners stopped. The block was laid down. Paul laid his head upon it. The sword (or axe) was raised. The head of the greatest preacher of the ages rolled upon the ground. Tradition says that a Roman "matron named Lucina buried the body of St. Paul

on ner own land, beside the Ostian Road." [1] Be that
as it may, no Christian can come to Rome, especially
by the Ostian Road, without tender thoughts of Paul,
the matchless servant of Jesus.

It is hard to leave Paul without a thought of Peter,
whose martyrdom was probably at Rome and may have
been not far from the same time. Legend has been
busy with that event. The story goes that Peter was
running away from Rome to escape death and was
met on the Appian Way by Jesus. He fell at the feet
of Jesus and asked, "Domine, quo vadis?" The
Master answered, "Venio iterum crucifigi." Stricken
with shame, Peter went back to Rome and to death.
There is no proof for that story. It may be just an
echo of Peter's real denial of Jesus and of Paul's martyrdom. But the time was full of change. Paul is
dead. Peter is dead. Soon Jerusalem will be in ruins.
The Temple of Jehovah will be no more. But the
Kingdom of Jesus has girt the Mediterranean Sea
and has taken root all over the Roman Empire. Paul
lived to see his dream of a world empire for Christ
largely realized. He, not Peter, is the spiritual leader
of apostolic Christianity. Peter fell into line with
Paul's masterful aggressiveness and rejoiced in the
hand of God that was laid upon the great interpreter
of Jesus.

12. *A Backward Look.*—One hesitates to add a
word more about Paul. He has gone to be with his

[1] Conybeare and Howson, Scribner's ed., Vol. II, p. 490.

Lord. But nearly nineteen centuries have rolled by since Paul planted the gospel in the Empire of Nero. His name to-day is the great name in Christian history after that of Jesus. It is not enough to say that he stood at the source of Christianity and put his impress upon it in the formative period. That is quite true, but a great deal more is true. Real Christianity has never gotten away from Paul. I do not believe that it ever will. He was the great thinker in this important era. He blazed the way in doctrine and in life. He caught the spirit of Jesus and breathed that spirit into Gentile Christianity. The uneasiness of Paul, expressed in his Epistles to Timothy, about the future of Christianity had ample justification. The time did come when that very Romanism which he had so admired in some of its phases seized upon Christianity, mixed it with the Judaism which he fought and radically perverted the gospel of Christ. The Gnostic heresies which had arisen grew in power, and Mithraism came to give battle to Christianity in the Roman Empire.

But however far men have at times wandered away from Christ, the Epistles of Paul stand as beacon lights to call them back to Christ. We can find Christ more easily because Paul saw him so clearly. He will help the modern world to find Jesus. He did not wish men to think of him. His highest hope is realized when men turn to Jesus with heart and hope because of what Paul was and is.

The theme of Paul is not exhausted in this present volume. Books about Paul will continue to come from the press. His stature grows greater with the years. He is foremost as theologian, as practical missionary, as constructive statesman, as man of boundless resource and energy. No one in Christian history approaches him in these respects.[1]

No word about Paul is complete that does not lay stress upon his mysticism. John gives us the supreme picture of the mystical side of Jesus. Paul reveals his own mystical relation to Christ. John writes in a calmer tone, while Paul loses himself in the abandon of passionate devotion to Christ and identification with him. Masterful in intellect, mighty in endeavor, high in spirit, rich in heart was Paul, whose winged words to-day challenge the world's attention and call men "to know the love of Christ that passeth knowledge" and to "be filled unto all the fulness of God."

[1] Denney ("Jesus and the Gospel," 1908, p. 20) justly considers Paul "the most important figure in Christian history." Cf. Deissmann, *The Expositor*, March, 1909, p. 215: "Jesus the One, Paul the first after the One, the first *in* the One."

A BRIEF BIBLIOGRAPHY

Commentaries on Paul's Epistles are not here given. The general works on the apostolic period are likewise omitted. Articles in the cyclopædias are passed by also. Only the most important books and articles on Paul are mentioned. Various aspects of the subject are kept in mind.

Addis, "Christianity and the Roman Empire" (1902).
Albrecht, "Paulus der Apostel Jesu Christi" (1903).
Alexander, "The Christianity of St. Paul."
Anonymous, "The Fifth Gospel. The Pauline Interpretation of Christ" (1906).
Aquelhon, "L'homme psychique d'après Saint Paul" (1898).
Arnold, "St. Paul and Protestantism" (1897).
Askwith, "Destination and Date of Galatians."
Bacon, "The Story of Paul" (1904).
Baethge, "Die paulinischen Reden."
Baldensperger, "Die messianisch-apokalyptischen Hoffnungen des Judenthums" (1903).
Ball, "St. Paul and the Roman Law" (1901).
Baring-Gould, "A Study of St. Paul" (1897).
Baur, "The Apostle Paul" (1875).
Beyschlag, "Die paulinische Theodicee."
Bird, "Paul of Tarsus."
Blair, "The Apostolic Gospel" (1896).
Bousset, "Der Apostel Paulus."
Breitenstein, "Jesus et Paul " (1908).
Bruce, "St. Paul's Conception of Christianity" (1898).
Brückner, "Die Entstehung der paulinischen Christologie" (1903).
Brückner, "Der Apostel als Zeuge wider das Christusbild der Evangelien " (Prot. Monatsch., 1906, S. 352–364).
Brückner, "Zum Thema Jesus und Paulus" (Neut. Wiss., 1906, S. 112 ff.).
Burton, "Chronology of St. Paul's Epistles."
Burton, "Records and Letters of the Apostolic Age" (1900).
Buss, "Roman Law and History in the New Testament" (1901).

Campbell, "Paul the Mystic" (1907).
Chadwick, "The Social Teaching of St. Paul" (1906).
Chadwick, "The Pastoral Teaching of St. Paul" (1907).
Chase, "Credibility of Acts" (1902).
Chrysostom, "Homiliæ in laudem S. Pauli," Opera, Vol. II, ed. Montf.
Clarke, "The Ideas of the Apostle Paul" (1884).
Clemen, "Die Chronologie der paulinischen Briefe" (1893).
Clemen, "Einheitlichkeit der paulinischen Briefe" (1894).
Clemen, "Paulus" (1904).
Cone, "Paul the Man, the Missionary" (1898).
Conybeare and Howson, "Life and Epistles of Paul" (1894). Scribner's edition.
Corbitt, "St. Paul" (1903).
Curtius, "Paulus in Athen."
Dähne, "Entwicklung des paulinischen Lehrbegriffs" (1851).
Dalmer, "Die Erwählung Israels nach Paulus."
Davidson, "The Stoic Creed" (1907).
Deissmann, "Bible Studies" (1901).
Deissmann, "New Light on the New Testament" (1907).
Deissmann, "Licht vom Osten" (1908).
Deissmann, "Die neutestamentliche Formel in Christo" (1892).
Dess, "Ein Beitrag zur Frage nach dem Hellenismus bei Paulus 2 Cor. 5 : 1-10" (1904).
Dickie, "The Culture of the Spiritual Life. Studies in the Teaching of Paul" (1905).
Dick, "Der schriftstellerische Plural bei Paulus" (1900).
Dickson, "St. Paul's Use of the Terms Flesh and Spirit" (1883).
Dill, "Roman Society from Nero to M. Aurelius" (1904).
Dobschütz, "Probleme des apostolischen Zeitalters" (1904).
Doellinger, "The Gentile and the Jew in the Courts of the Temple of Christ" (1862).
Drescher, "Das Leben Jesu bei Paulus" (1900).
Drummond, "Relation of the Apostolic Age to the Teaching of Christ" (1900).
Du Bose, "The Gospel According to St. Paul" (1907).
Dykes, "The Gospel According to St. Paul."
Eadie, "Paul the Preacher."
Erbes, "Die Todestage der Apostel Paulus und Petrus" (1899).
Ernesti, "Ethik des Apostels Paulus."
Everett, "The Gospel of Paul" (1893).
Everling, "Die paulinsche Angelologie und Dämonologie" (1888).
Fairbairn, "Philosophy of the Christian Religion" (1904).
Farrar, "Darkness and Dawn" (1893).
Farrar, "Early Days of Christianity" (1882).

Farrar, "Life and Work of St. Paul" (1879).
Feine, "Das gesetzesfreie Evangelium des Paulus" (1899).
Feine, "Jesus Christus und Paulus" (1902).
Feine, "Paulus als Theologe" (1906). Tr. 1908.
Ferrero, "Greatness and Decline of Rome" (1908).
Findlay, "Epistles of the Apostle Paul."
Forbes, "Footsteps of St. Paul in Rome" (1899).
Fouard, "St. Paul and His Mission."
Fouard, "Last Years of St. Paul."
Fraedlaender, "Der Antichrist in den vorchristlichen jüdischen Quellen" (1901).
Fraedlaender, "Synagoge und Kirche in ihren Anfängen" (1908).
Garvie, Articles in *Expositor* (March, 1908-) on Teaching of Paul.
Gibson, "Sources of St. Paul's Teaching" (*Expositor*, 1882, pp. 33-45).
Gilbert, "First Interpreters of Jesus" (1901).
Gilbert, "Student's Life of Paul" (1899).
Gloag, "Introduction to the Pauline Epistles."
Gloatz, "Zur Vergleichung der Lehre des Paul mit der Jesu" (*Theol. Stud. und Krit.*, 1895, S. 777-800).
Gloel, "Der heilige Geist in d. Heilsverk. des Paulus."
Godet, "Studies in the Epistles."
Goguel, "L'Apôtre Paul et Jésus Christ" (1904).
Goodwin, "A Harmony of the Life of the Apostle Paul" (1895).
Grafe, "Die paulinischen Lehre von Gesetz" (1893).
Greene, "The Manysided Paul."
Gunkel, "Zum religionsgeschichtlichen Verst. des N. T." (1903).
Hanson, "St. Paul and the Primitive Church."
Harnack, "Luke the Physician" (1907).
Harnack, "Die Apostelgeschichte" (1908).
Hausrath, "Der Apostel Paulus."
Heim, "Paulus" (1905).
Heinrici, "Jesus und Paulus" (*Neues sächsisches Kirchenblatt*, 1895, No. 47-51).
Heitmüller, "Im Namen Jesu."
Heitmüller, "Taufe und Abendmahl bei Paulus" (1903).
Hicks, "St. Paul and Hellenism."
Hilgenfeld, "Jesus und Paulus" (*Zeitschrift für wiss. Theol.*, 1894, S. 481-541).
Hollmann, "Urchristenthum in Korinth" (1903).
Holsten, "Zum Evangelium des Paulus und des Petrus" (1868).
Holsten, "Das Evangelium des Paulus" (1898).
H. Holtzmann, "Jesus und Paulus" (*Protest. Monatsch.*, 1900, S. 463-468).
Hönnicke, "Chronologie des Lebens Pauli" (1904).

Hort, "Judaistic Christianity" (1892).

Howson, "Character of St. Paul."

Howson, "Companions of St. Paul."

Howson, "Metaphors of St. Paul."

Hurant, "Paul, a-t-il connu le Christ historique?"

Irons, "Christianity as Taught by St. Paul."

Iverach, "St. Paul; His Life and Times."

James, "Genuineness and Authorship of the Pastoral Epistles" (1906).

Jevons, "Hellenism and Christianity" (*Harvard Theol. Review,* April, 1908).

Johnson, "Was Paul the Founder of Christianity?" (*Princeton Theol. Rev.,* 1907).

Jülicher, "Paulus und Jesus" (1907).

Jülicher, "Neue Linien in der Kritik der evangelischen Ueberlieferung" (1906).

Juncker, "Das Christusbild des Paulus" (1906).

Juncker, "Die Ethik des Apostels Paulus" (1904).

Kabisch, "Die Eschatologie des Paulus."

Kaftan, "Jesus und Paulus" (1906).

Kellermann, "Kritische Beiträge zur Entstehungsgeschichte des Christentums" (1906).

Kennedy, "St. Paul's Conceptions of Last Things" (1904).

Knowling, "Witness of the Epistles" (1892).

Knowling, "Testimony of St. Paul to Christ" (1905).

Köhler, "Zum Verständnis des Apostels Paulus" (1908).

Kölbing, "Die geistige Einwirkung der Person auf Paulus" (1906).

Krenkel, "Beiträge zur Aufhellung der Geschichte und der Briefe des Apostels Paulus."

Krenkel, "Paulus der Apostel der Heiden."

Kühl, "Zur paulinischen Theodicee."

Lewin, "Life and Epistles of St. Paul" (1875).

Lichtenbahn, "Die Offenbarung in Gnosticismus" (1907).

Lightfoot, "Biblical Essays" (1893).

Lipsius, "Die paulinische Rechtfertigungslehre."

Lock, "St. Paul the Master Builder" (1905).

Lüdemann, "Die Anthropologie des Apostels Paulus."

Luthardt, "Der Apostel Paulus, ein Lebensbild."

Lyttleton, "Observations on Saul's Conversion" (1774).

Maggs, "The Spiritual Experience of St. Paul."

Mahaffy, "The Silver Age of the Greek World" (1906).

Mansel, "The Gnostic Heresies" (1875).

Marshall, "Did Paul Use a Semitic Gospel?" (*Expositor,* July 1890).

Matheson, "The Spiritual Development of Paul" (1891).

Matheson, "The Historical Christ of Paul" (*Expositor*, Series II, Vols. I and II, 1881).

Means, "St. Paul and the Ante-Nicene Church" (1903).

Menegoz, "La peché et a rédemption d'après St. Paul" (1903).

Menken, "Blicke in das Leben des Apostels Paulus."

A. Meyer, "Wer hat das Christentum begründet, Jesus oder Paulus?" (1907).

Meyer, "Paul."

M. Meyer, "Der Apostel Paulus als armer Sünder" (1903).

Moffatt, "The Historical New Testament" (1901).

Moffatt, "Recent Literature on Jesus and Paul" (*Review of Theology and Philosophy*, July, 1908).

Moffatt, "Jesus and Paul" (*The Biblical World*, Sept., 1908).

Monod, "Five Sermons on the Apostle Paul."

Monteil, "Essai sur la Christologie de Saint Paul" (1906).

Moske, "Die Bekehrung des heiligen Paulus" (1907).

Müller, "Das persönliche Christenthum der paulinischen Gemeinden."

Nägeli, "Der Wortschatz des Apostels Paulus" (1905).

Noesgen, "Die apostolische Verkündigung und die Geschichte Jesu" (*Neue Jahrb. f. Deutsche Theol.*, 1895, S. 46–94).

Noesgen, "Paulus der Apostel der Heiden" (1908).

Nonnemann, "Jesus der Christus. Jesus und Paulus" (1907).

Oehler, "Paulus und Jesus, der Erlöste und der Erlöser" (1908).

Oertel, "Paulus in der Apostelgeschichte."

Opitz, "Das System des Paulus."

Paley, "Horæ Paulinæ" (1851).

Paret, "Paulus et Jesus" (*Jahrbücher f. d. Theol.*, 1858).

Paret, "Das Zeugnis des Apostels Paulus über die ihm gewordene Christuserscheinung" (*Jahrb. f. Deutsche Theol.*, 1859, S. 239 ff.).

Paterson, "The Pauline Theology" (1903).

Pfleiderer, "Paulinismus" (1873).

Pfleiderer, "Influence of the Apostle Paul on the Development of Christianity" (1885).

Pratt, "Life of Paul in Scripture Language."

Ramsay, "The Church in the Roman Empire" (1893).

Ramsay, "Cities and Bishoprics of Phrygia" (1895).

Ramsay, "St. Paul the Traveller," (1896).

Ramsay, "Pauline and Other Studies" (1906).

Ramsay, "Cities of Paul" (1908).

Ramsay, "Luke the Physician and Other Studies" (1908).

Renan, "St. Paul" (1869).

Resch, "Paulinismus und die Logia Jesu" (1904).

Resch, "Die Verwandtschaft zwischen den paulinischen Schriften und den syn. Evangelien" (*Zeitschr. f. k. Wiss.*, 1888, S. 279–295).

Resch, "Paulinische-lucanische Evangelienparallelen" (1893).

Resker, "St. Paul's Illustrations" (1908).

Ritschl, "Justification and Reconciliation."

Robertson, "Student's Chronological N. T." (1904).

Röhricht, "Das menschliche Personenleben und der christliche Glaube nach Paulus" (1902).

Roos, "Die Briefe des Apostels Paulus und die Reden des Herrn Jesu" (1887).

Round, "Date of St. Paul's Epistle to the Galatians" (1907).

Ruegg, "Der Apostel Paulus und sein Zeugnis von Jesus Christus" (1906).

Sabatier, "The Apostle Paul" (1891).

Schaeder, "Das Evangelium Jesu und das Evangelium von Jesus" (1906).

Schenkel, "Christus-bild der Apostel."

Schettler, "Die paulinische Formel 'Durch Christus'" (1907).

H. Schmidt, "Der paulinische Christus" (1867).

Schmidt, "Die paulinische Christologie" (1870).

Schmoller, "Die geschichtliche Person Jesu nach den paulinischen Schriften" (*Theol. Stud. n. Krit.*, 1894, S. 656–705).

Schrader, "Der Apostel Paulus."

Scott, "The Gospel According to St. Paul" (*Expositor*, 1900, II, pp. 202–210).

Seeböck, "S. Paulus der Heidenmissionar."

Selden, "In the Time of Paul" (1900).

Selwyn, "St. Luke the Prophet" (1901).

Shakespeare, "St. Paul in Athens" (1878).

Shaw, "The Pauline Epistles" (1903).

Simon, "Die Psychologie des Apostels Paulus" (1897).

J. Smith, "Voyage and Shipwreck of St. Paul."

Sokolowski, "Geist und Leben bei Paulus" (1903).

Somerville, "St. Paul's Conception of Christ" (1897).

Speer, "The Man Paul" (1900).

Spitta, "Die zweimalige römische Gefangenschaft des Paulus" (*Urchristenthum*, Bd. I.).

Stalker, "Life of St. Paul" (1889).

Steinmetz, "Die 2te römische Gefangenschaft des Apostels Paulus" (1897).

Steubing, "Die paulinischen Begriff 'Christusleiden'" (1905).

Stevens, "The Pauline Theology" (1894).

Straatmann, "Paulus de Ap. van Jezus Christus."

Sturm, "Der Apostel Paulus und die evangelische Ueberlieferung" (Programme No. 117 in 1897 and Programme No. 118 in 1900).

Taylor, "Paul the Missionary" (1882).

Thackeray, "Relation of St. Paul to Contemporary Jewish Thought" (1900).

Tholuck, "Life and Writings of St. Paul" (tr.).

Tigert, "Christianity of Christ and of the Apostles" (1905).

Titius, "Die Abhängigkeit des Paulus von der Verkündigung Jesu" (S. 8–18 in "Der Paulinismus unter dem Gesichtspunkt der Seligkeit," 1900).

Uhlhorn, "Conflict of Christianity with Judaism."

Underhill, "Divine Legation of St. Paul" (1889).

Usteri, "Entwicklung des paulinischen Lehrbegriffs" (1851).

Van Manen, "Paulus."

Voelter, "Paulus und seine Briefe" (1905).

Volkmar, "Paulus von Damascus bis zum Galaterbr."

Vollmer, "Die alttestamentliche Citate bei Paulus."

Von Soden, "Das Interesse des apostolischen Zeitalters an der evangelischen Geschichte" (*Theol. Abhandl.*, 1892, S. 111–169).

Walker, "The Gift of Tongues" (1906).

Walther, "Pauli Evangelium Jesu Evangelium (1908).

Weinel, "Paulus" (1904, tr. 1906).

J. Weiss, "Beiträge zur paulinischen Rhetorik."

J. Weiss, "Die christliche Freiheit nach der Verkündigung des Apostels Paulus" (1902).

Wendt, "Die Lehre des Paulus verglichen mit der Lehre Jesu" (*Zeitschr. f. Theol. und Kirche*, 1894, S. 1–78).

Wernle, "Paulus als Heidenmissionär."

Wernle, "Der Christus und die Sünde bei Paulus" (1897).

Whateley, "Difficulties in the Epistles of Paul."

Whyte, "The Apostle Paul" (1903).

Wilkinson, "Epic of Saul" (1891).

Wilkinson, "Epic of Paul" (1897).

Wrede, "Paulus" (1905).

Wright, "Cities of Paul" (1907).

Wustmann, "Jesus und Paulus" (1907).

Wynne, "Fragmentary Records of Jesus of Nazareth" (1887).

Zahn, "Das Gesetz Gottes nach der Lehre des Apostels Paulus."

INDEX TO SUBJECTS

INDEX TO NEW TESTAMENT PASSAGES